SECRET
LONDON
AN UNUSUAL GUIDE

Rachel Howard and Bill Nash
Photographs: Stéphanie Rivoal and Jorge Monedero

JONGLEZ

We have taken great pleasure in compiling *Secret London – an unusual guide* and hope that through its guidance you will, like us, continue to discover unusual, hidden or little-known aspects of the city. Some entries are accompanied by historical asides or anecdotes as an aid to understanding the city in all its complexity.

Secret London - an unusual guide also draws attention to the multitude of details found in places that we may pass every day without noticing. We invite you to look more closely at the urban landscape and to see your own city with the curiosity and attention that we often display while travelling elsewhere…

Comments on this guidebook and its contents, as well as information on places we may not have mentioned, are more than welcome and will enrich future editions.

Don't hesitate to contact us:
• E-mail: info@jonglezpublishing.com
• Jonglez publishing, 17, boulevard du Roi,
  78000 Versailles, France

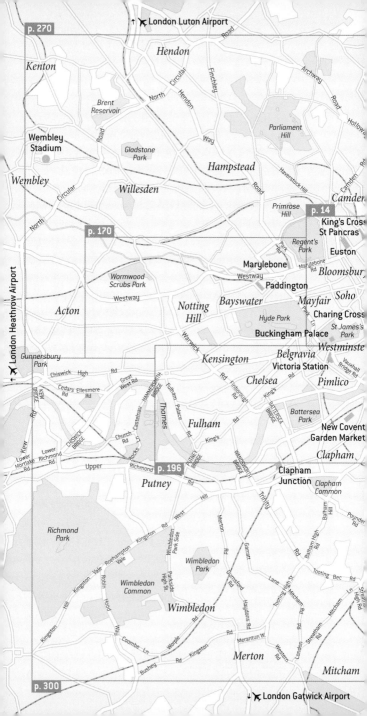

p. 66
p. 124
p. 238
p. 212

CONTENTS

TOWER BRIDGE TO SHOREDITCH

CONTENTS

CONTENTS

UNUSUAL BARS, CAFES AND RESTAURANTS

WESTMINSTER TO CAMDEN

CAMLEY STREET NATURAL PARK ❶

12 Camley Street, NW1
0207833 2311
Open Thurs–Sun 10am-5pm.
Admission free.
Transport Kings Cross tube/rail.

> *Minibeast Hotel in the urban jungle*

The redevelopment of Kings Cross, site of the new Channel Tunnel train link, has sparked a frenzied clean-up of what was recently one of the most squalid patches of central London. The crack-heads and kerb-crawlers have been driven out as developers snap up prime real estate.

Surprisingly, among the cranes and construction workers, the twitter of birds and flutter of butterfly wings have survived at Camley Street Natural Park. Tucked away behind a clogged traffic intersection, this two-acre wildlife refuge created from derelict land in 1983 is wedged between the railway tracks and Regent's Canal. Once used to store coal transported along the canal, the spot was earmarked by local authorities as a coach park, but luckily campaigners won out and created a nature reserve.

As soon as you enter, serenity engulfs you. You can hear the rush of water from the nearby lock and watch colourful house-boats coast by from the grassy verge. Everything is made from recycled and natural materials – wooden fences and bird boxes, rough-hewn benches, a log pile for creepy-crawlies, even a 'Minibeast Hotel'. Assorted insects buzz around as you wander the overgrown pathways and discover how various creatures hatch thanks to signs dotted among the foliage. There's a blackboard where you can record bird sightings at the little information and volunteer centre run by the London Wildlife Trust. Support their cause by taking home a potted plant for just £1. Rushes taller than people surround the pond, where kids are encouraged to go 'pond dipping' to see what creatures reside in the muddy depths. Beyond the pond, the path peters out and the outside world encroaches: roaring traffic, a looming gasometer, and the elegant silhouette of St Pancras clock tower. Hopefully, the post-industrial development of King's Cross won't swamp this worthy enterprise.

SIGHTS NEARBY

THE LAMP POSTS OF ST NICHOLAS ❷

Built in the 1930s, St Nicholas Flats on Aldenham Street are part of the Sidney Estate, one of the more attractive corners of Somers Town, a grim stretch of council estates behind Euston station. St Nicholas is the patron saint of sailors, which explains this small fleet of ships marooned atop the lamp posts in the courtyard of the estate.

THE COADE STONE CARYATIDS ❸

St Pancras Church, Euston Road, NW1
www.stpancraschurch.org
Transport Euston tube/rail

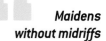

Maidens without midriffs

When it was built in 1819 for a whopping £89,296, St Pancras Church was the most expensive house of worship since the reconstruction of St Paul's Cathedral. Modelled on the Erechtheum of the Acropolis, the church's exterior has lost much of its lustre thanks to the traffic hurtling down Euston Road, one of London's least lovely thoroughfares.

On closer inspection, however, these maidens are stumpier than their Greek counterparts (one of whom is on display in the British Museum, courtesy of Lord Elgin). Sculptor Charles Rossi (1762-1839) spent almost three years crafting the caryatids out of Coade stone, an artificial material much favoured for the neoclassical monuments so popular in the 18th and early 19th centuries. The figures were built up in sections around cast-iron columns. But when Rossi transported them from his studio to the church, he discovered to his horror that the statues were too tall. Under the gaze of a bemused crowd of onlookers, Rossi took drastic action: he cut out their midriffs. Thankfully, their draped Grecian gowns help to conceal their stunted torsos.

WHAT IS COADE STONE ?

Founded by Mrs Eleanor Coade in 1769, Coade's Artificial Stone Manufactory dominated London's trade in statues, busts, tombstones, architectural and garden ornaments for almost 65 years. Cheap, easy to mould and weather-resistant, Coade stone was made to a secret formula that is no longer a mystery. According to an anonymous account from 1806: "The preparation is cast in moulds and burnt, and is intended to answer every purpose of carved stone. It is possessed of the peculiar property of resisting frost, and consequently it retains its sharpness in which it excels every species of stone, and even equals marble". This quality is evident in the many Coade stone monuments scattered around London, notably Captain Bligh's tomb in St Mary's Lambeth (see page 215), Nelson's pediment at the Royal Naval College Chapel in Greenwich, and the 13-ton lion on Westminster Bridge, one of a pair of that once crowned the Red Lion brewery on the South Bank. The other lion guards the All-England Rugby Club at Twickenham, near the Rowland Hill Memorial Gate.

Despite this success, the company went bankrupt not long after Eleanor Coade's death in 1796 at the grand old age of 88. She is buried in Bunhill Fields (see page 127).

BLEIGIESSEN ❹

Gibbs Building, Wellcome Trust, 215 Euston Street NW1
0207 611 8888
www.wellcome.ac.uk
Open Public tours on the last Friday of every month at 2pm.
Email Elayne Hodgson e.hodgson@wellcome.ac.uk
to book a place. **Admission** free
Transport Euston Square tube

*Art that
predicts the future*

When the Wellcome Trust, the UK's largest biomedical research charity, redesigned its headquarters on Euston Road, several art works were commissioned to embellish its glossy new premises. The Trust chose Thomas Heatherwick to design the centrepiece: an installation for the nine-storey atrium of the Gibbs Building. The designer faced a serious challenge: while the sculpture had to fill the 30-metre vertical space, its components also had to fit through a regular sized door.

Instead, Heatherwick resolved to design something 'that could fit through the letterbox.' Inspired by the pool of water at the bottom of the atrium, Heatherwick based his design on flowing liquid. By pouring molten metal into cold water, he created over 400 prototypes before a five-centimetre shape was selected as the outline for the sculpture. Clearly, Heatherwick had also drawn inspiration from his mother, who founded the Bead Society of Great Britain. This form was laser-scanned and replicated to scale using 142,000 glass spheres, produced in a Polish spectacle lens factory. Reflective film was sandwiched inside the beads to create a rainbow effect.

All the spheres were numbered and assembled on site – a painstaking process which involved threading the beads onto 27,000 steel wires just under a million metres long. The wires were rolled onto a giant drum then stretched between frames. A team of 18 people worked for five months, day and night, to complete the sculpture, which weighs in at 14 tons. The result is like a glowing cloud of particles suspended in mid-air. Shapes fade in and out of focus depending on how the light strikes.

Heatherwick's German grandmother christened the work Bliegiessen, or 'lead guessing.' This New Year's Eve ritual is still practiced in Eastern Europe: molten lead is poured into cold water, and the resulting shapes are interpreted to predict a person's fortune for the coming year. Created to commemorate a new beginning for the Wellcome Trust, hopefully this particular shape has auspicious omens.

The best way to see this monumental work is to take the monthly guided tour. Visitors are whisked to the top of the building in a glass lift. Alternatively, you can get a reasonably good view of the sculpture from outside University College Hospital on Gower Street. It looks best at night when the empty building is illuminated and the baubles glimmer and shimmer behind the glass walls.

MIN'S PENIS ❺

The Petrie Museum, University College London, Malet Place, WC1
0207 679 2884
www.ucl.ac.uk/museums/petrie
Open Tues - Fri 1pm-5pm, Sat 10am-1pm
Admission free
Transport Euston Square

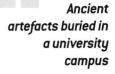

Ancient artefacts buried in a university campus

Beneath the scholarly air that hangs over this collection of Egyptian antiquities, lurk some very saucy artefacts. Set up in 1892 as a teaching resource for University College's Egyptian Archaeology and Philology department, the Petrie Museum is named after the department's first professor, William Flanders Petrie. A serial excavator, Petrie himself unearthed many of the 80,000 objects, dating from pre-history through Pharaonic, Roman, and Coptic Egypt, up to the Islamic period.

Perhaps the most striking exhibit is the marble bas relief of the Egyptian god Min. Invariably portrayed with a huge, erect penis, Min was the god of fertility and sexuality. At the beginning of the harvest, his image was taken out into the fields, where naked men would climb a huge pole in his honour. Apparently, Min used long-leaf lettuce to stimulate his sex drive. However, the results may have been negligible: lettuce was considered an aphrodisiac by the ancient Egyptians because it was tall, straight and secreted milky juices when squeezed.

Costume plays a key part in the collection– look for the world's oldest dress, worn by a dancer around 2500 BC. Besides extraordinary hieroglyphs and papyri, the plethora of everyday objects includes a 3000-year-old rat trap. There are also strangely affecting Roman funerary masks; since most Egyptian art is nearly abstract, these portraits breathe life into a culture that often feels impassive or monumental.

Although it houses one of the most important Egyptology collections in the world, the Petrie does not punch at the same weight as the Egyptian collection of the British Museum. However, this is to its advantage. The Petrie feels less dependent on plunder than the British Museum, and the collection is more thoughtfully assembled. Access to the Petrie is also easier. The Egyptian funerary rooms at the British Museum, where the most deliciously gruesome stuff is displayed, are usually packed with coach parties; even the vigorous use of knee and elbow is no guarantee of a clear view.

THE AUTO-ICON OF JEREMY BENTHAM ❻

South Cloisters, University College London, Gower Street WC1
0207 679 2825
www.ucl.ac.uk/Bentham-Project
Open Mon-Fri 7.30am – 6pm
Admission free
Transport Euston Square or Goodge Street tube

Mummified philosopher

Sitting serenely in a wooden cabinet on a landing of University College London (UCL) is the preserved skeleton of Jeremy Bentham (1748-1832), a radical philosopher and reformer. As stipulated in his will, Bentham has been seated here in the same thoughtful pose, 'wearing his usual clothes and sitting on his favourite chair', since 1850.

Bentham called this perverse monument to himself an Auto-Icon ('man in his own image'), whereby a man's actual corpse replaced the traditional memorial statue. In fact, the body beneath his fine clothes is made of nothing but straw. At a time when only the corpses of hanged criminals were available for medical research, Bentham left his organs 'to illustrate a series of lectures, to which scientific and literary men are to be invited', and then be dissected by students of anatomy.

The only part of his body that Bentham did not bequeath to science was his head, which was to be preserved by a Maori practice of desiccation and placed on his Auto-Icon. For ten years before his death, Bentham allegedly carried the glass eyes which were to adorn it in his pocket. Unfortunately, the mummified head deteriorated rapidly, so it was replaced with a less grotesque wax likeness.

For several years, the real head lay between Bentham's legs. However, in 1975, a group of students from King's College 'kidnapped' the head and demanded a ransom of £100 to be paid to the homeless charity Shelter. UCL negotiated the ransom down to £10 and the head was returned to its rightful owner. The head has since been safely stowed in the college vaults; permission to view it is granted 'only in exceptional circumstances.' Although Bentham was 80 when UCL was founded in 1826, as the first English university to welcome all students, regardless of race, creed or political belief, it embodied Bentham's conviction that education should be available to all. Marx may have called him 'a genius by way of bourgeois stupidity', but Bentham was a visionary who also believed in universal suffrage, the legalisation of homosexuality, and utilitarianism, a doctrine that aims to promote the greatest happiness of the greatest number.

According to one apocryphal tale, the Auto-Icon attends the meetings of the College Council, and its presence is recorded in the minutes with the words 'Jeremy Bentham - present but not voting.' This is, of course, absolute rubbish.

If you happen to be squeamish, afterwards you can steady your nerves with a pint in the Jeremy Bentham pub at 31 University Street.

THE GRANT MUSEUM OF ZOOLOGY ❼

Rockefeller Building, University College London, 21 University Street, Bloomsbury
0203 1082052
zoology.museum@ucl.ac.uk
www.ucl.ac.uk/museums/zoology
Open Mon–Fri 1- 5pm **Admission** free

*Old bones
and jellied eels*

O ne of the oldest – and oddest – natural history museums in Britain, this peculiar collection is buried in the labyrinthine campus of University College London. Navigate a course through the parked bicycles and security gates, and you find yourself in a bizarre shrine to animal anatomy. The cluttered gallery is like a cross between the Victorian attic of a compulsive collector and the studio of Damien Hirst. Musty cases are stuffed full of monkey skeletons, pickled toads, jars of worms, and giant elephant skulls.

The collection contains around 62,000 specimens, covering the whole animal kingdom. Some of the exhibits are truly terrifying, such as the curling skeleton of a 250-kilo anaconda, or the bisected head of a wallaby preserved in formaldehyde. Others, like the elephant heart or the hellbender – a bloated amphibian with sagging flesh – are simply gruesome. There are obscure species, like the three-toothed puffer fish, and extinct ones, like the quagga, a type of zebra. There is even a box of dodo bones. A cast of the oldest known bird, the archaeopteryx, provides evidence that birds evolved from dinosaurs.

The museum was founded in 1827 by Robert Grant, a pioneer of the theory of evolution and the first professor of Zoology and Comparative Anatomy in England. When Grant set up his department at the newly founded University of London (later University College London), he realised that he had no teaching materials. So he set about amassing these specimens, which are still used by biology students, schools, and artists. Although Grant was paid a pittance, he taught at UCL from 1828 until his death in 1874.

> Robert Edmond Grant was a Scottish zoologist and radical. While teaching at Edinburgh University in 1826, he met the young Charles Darwin, who was a squeamish and reluctant student of medicine at the time. Grant befriended Darwin and became his mentor, until the two fell out some years later. By a strange twist of fate, Darwin lived in a house on this site, at 12 Upper Gower Street, between 1839 and 1842.

SIGHTS NEARBY

WARREN STREET MAZE ❽

While you're waiting for the tube at Warren Street, look out for the red and black maze on the platform. A visual pun on the name of the station, the maze was designed by Alan Fletcher, a god among graphic designers. Since the average interval between trains is three minutes, Fletcher created a puzzle that would take longer to solve.

LOVE

Every piece of the work we do in this field...
Where we live our lives in this way the love of...
When is the sense of our ideas?

Everyone knows that the notion of love is a...
which measures the guiding we ... a notion...
lovers to grief you through us are able to...
tangible and wisdom from the great desire...
the love?

We explore some varying questions. Our task...
a philosophical. How can I learn some connection...
with my lover? How we move my a feel how can...
made to love?

We draw on ideas from philosophy, psychology...
literature and art. We discover what the idea of...
Shakespeare, Tolstoy and Freud tell us about...
compassion, empathy and self-love. And we do how...
evolutions of love, such as courtship and marriage...
have changed over the centuries – yet where the logic...
leaves us now.

LMS

EXPERTS

BIBLIOTHE...

HOLIDAYS

BROWN
BROWN

THE SCHOOL OF LIFE ❾

70 Marchmont Street, WC1
0207 833 1010
www.theschooloflife.com
Open Shop hours Mon-Fri noon-7pm, Sat 10am-6pm
Admission Shop free, course and consultation prices vary
Transport Russell Square or Euston tube

Food for thought

Billing itself as "a very small shop with very big ambitions", The School of Life is not really a shop at all. It's a cross between a literary salon, a philosophy school and an interactive self-help guide. The old-fashioned shop window is filled with a selection of aphorisms – those witty one-liners you wish you'd dreamt up yourself. Today, Mark Twain reminds passers-by: "Clothes make the man. Naked people have little or no influence on society." Inside, black crows perch among birch tree trunks and edible Scrabble sets nestle among artfully arranged books categorised by states of mind: there are volumes for "those with a god-shaped hole", or "those whose jobs are too small for their spirits".

This witty and whimsical approach to tackling life's big issues is carried through to the courses and consultations on offer - from bibliotherapy and psychotherapy sessions, to sermons on seduction and dinner parties designed to revive the art of conversation through a menu of thought-provoking ideas and mind games. Founder Sophie Howarth, who was head of public programmes at the Tate, has pulled together an impressive faculty of academics, artists, actors and authors. As well as tackling grand themes (work, play, family, love and politics), the courses address the frustrations and challenges of everyday life.

The classroom, decorated with playful murals, is tucked away in the basement. However, classes often migrate to unlikely locations across London: you might discuss romance in a Travelodge or learn about the laws of attraction in a chemistry lab. The School of Life also organises short breaks that challenge holiday clichés: a weekend at Heathrow airport or a trip up the M1 motorway.

If the prospect of interaction with strangers terrifies you, you can book a one-to-one session with an expert, whose specialist subjects range from etiquette to empathy, neuroscience to guerrilla gardening. For a £50 fee, Damian Barr will read you a bedtime story, Bompas and Parr will teach you to make jelly sculptures, Luke Dixon will share the secrets of beekeeping, and James Geary will juggle aphorisms for you. If you can't afford the real thing, you can pick up a pickled expert in a jam jar for £5.

Designed to fire the imagination, the School of Life sure beats another evening staring glumly at the TV.

THE FOUNDLING MUSEUM ⑩

40 Brunswick Square, WC1
0207 841 3600
www.foundlingmuseum.org.uk
Open Tues-Sat 10am-6pm; Sun noon-6pm
Admission £5, conc £4, under-16s free.
Transport Russell Square tube

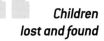

*Children
lost and found*

There is a lingering idea among tourists that London is a place of Victorian propriety, full of well-mannered, uptight ladies and gentlemen. Apart from a very brief 19th century flirtation with moral rectitude, the character of the city has always been base; drunkenness for its own sake is still very much a London pastime, as is fighting. This wildness and cruelty was at its apogee in the eighteenth century, when a man could be hanged for stealing spoons. One by-product of a society like this was hordes of unwanted children. Up to a thousand babies a year were abandoned in the streets of London in the early 18th century.

Fortunately, in 1739, after 17 years of tireless fundraising, the philanthropist Thomas Coram founded a 'Hospital for the Maintenance and Education of Exposed and Deserted Children', which cared for more than 27,000 children in a site on Lamb's Conduit Fields, before relocating to the countryside in 1953. The remarkable Foundling Museum tells the story of those children.

Thanks to William Hogarth, one of the original governors of the hospital, the museum also houses an impressive art collection, displayed in interiors restored to their original 18th century condition. Hogarth's own art is often hard-bitten and deeply cynical - his famous etching of Gin Lane is full of disgust at how the people who abandoned these children lived. But there must have been a well of compassion in him: Hogarth persuaded leading artists like Gainsborough and Reynolds to donate works to the hospital, and in doing so created the country's first public exhibition space. This eventually led to the formation of the Royal Academy of Arts in 1768. In keeping with its founding principles, most of the museum's events, including workshops and concerts, are aimed at children.

The German composer George Friedrich Handel was also a one-time governor of the hospital, which explains why the museum holds a collection of Handel material. Annual performances of his Messiah provided a source of revenue for the hospital. Today, Handel's work is occasionally performed at the atmospheric Handel House Museum, the composer's former home at 25 Brook Street, Mayfair.

PARENTAL GUIDANCE COMPULSORY
Echoes of the children's hospital resonate in nearby Coram's Fields, a seven acre park in the heart of Bloomsbury with a playground, cafe and duck pond. Adults are forbidden to enter unless accompanied by an under-16 year old.

THE HORSE HOSPITAL

Herbrand Street and Colonnade, Bloomsbury WC1
0207 833 3644
www.thehorsehospital.com
Open Exhibitions Mon-Sat 12-6pm; for special events check website
Admission Varies
Transport Russell Square tube

> *Salon of the avant garde*

Buried away down a cobbled mews off tourist-trodden Russell Square, the Horse Hospital really was a sanctuary for sick horses back in its Victorian heyday. These days, it's a haven for avant-garde artists and disciples of all things underground. From the fuchsia hall, a steep ramp with wooden slats originally intended to stop the horses slipping (beware – it's lethal in heels) leads up to a slightly spooky and faintly musty salon with a few battered seats. This is the self-styled Chamber of Pop Culture, where an audience of eccentrics enjoy the most eclectic line-up of art events in London, from cult films to performance poets, one-off musical installations and bizarre book launches. Anything goes - as long as it's defiantly anti-Establishment.

In the small bar at the back, patrons knock back shots of absinthe and other fearsome brews. It's one of those rare places in London where you can easily slip into conversation with strangers. This sense of community, along with the spirit of experimentation, is like a throwback to the Arts Labs of the '60s. Even the electric bar heaters date from another era. Often dubbed 'an alternative ICA', the Horse Hospital was founded in 1993 by stylist and costume designer Richard Burton, one of the pioneers of punk fashion along with Vivienne Westwood and Malcolm McLaren, whose boutique, World's End, was designed by Burton. The Horse Hospital opened with a splash thirteen years later with the first retrospective of Westwood's punk designs. Still run on a shoestring by a staff of three - Burton, curator James Hollands, and their vintage-clad associate Tai Shani – The Horse Hospital receives precious little public funding.

Fans can support the venue by sponsoring one of its 1384 cobblestones. Sponsors are ordained members of the 'exclusive' Grand Order of the Cobbles.

CONTEMPORARY WARDROBE COLLECTION

The building's basement is home to the Contemporary Wardrobe Collection, set up by Burton in 1978 to supply vintage clothes and accessories to the film, TV and fashion industries. His collection now exceeds 15,000 garments dating back to 1945. There's a rare selection by seminal British designers from the 1960s, such as Ossie Clark, Biba, and Seditionaries. As well as providing costumes for films like *Quadrophenia* and *Sid & Nancy*, pieces have been modelled by over 400 pop stars, from David Bowie to Kanye West. Visits are by appointment only, but twice a year, items are sold off to raise funds for the Horse Hospital. Check www.contemporarywardrobe.com for details.

THE EISENHOWER CENTRE ⓬

Chenies Street, at the junction of North Crescent, WC1
Transport Goodge Street tube

> *Ike's Underground bunker*

London's Tube system is notoriously overcrowded, but even in the 1930s congestion on the Underground was so bad that an express route was designed through central London, running below the Northern Line. During the Blitz, these eight deep-level tunnels were adapted into air raid shelters. Above ground, the shafts were protected by round 'pill box' buildings, which housed lifts and staircases, but also heavily armed guards who could fire through slits in the walls. Some were even equipped with anti-aircraft machine guns.

One of the most striking of these World War II survivors stands at the corner of Chenies Street and North Crescent, near Goodge Street station. Painted like a stick of candy in red-and-white stripes, it has been christened the Eisenhower Centre because the US President – and Supreme Commander of the Allied forces in Europe - used it as his HQ during World War II. Most of the D-Day invasion was planned right here below bustling Tottenham Court Road.

Built during 1941-2, the air-raid shelter was kitted out with 8000 bunk beds, an elaborate ventilation and gas filtration system – if you look carefully, you can see the air vents in the roof. It even had a hydraulic sewage system in case of extended incarceration. But despite the expense involved in building the tunnels, the British government quickly abandoned plans to use them as public shelters as they were so expensive to maintain. The express rail route through the centre of London was also subsequently dropped because of the cost. Instead, many of the shelters (including the Eisenhower Centre) became barracks to house troops in transit.

After a fire in May 1956, the Eisenhower Centre was closed for many years. Now owned by London Underground, it is leased out as commercial storage space. The bunk beds have been converted into shelves, stacked with documents and films from Channel 4's TV archive. Allegedly, Sir Paul McCartney also uses part of the vault to stash his gold and platinum discs.

OTHER SECRETS OF THE UNDERGROUND

Belsize Park, Camden Town, Stockwell, Clapham North, Clapham Common, and Clapham South stations all have additional underground tunnels, sadly off-limits to the public. Work on a deep shelter at St Paul's station was abandoned in 1941 due to fears that it would undermine the cathedral's foundations.

NEW LONDON ARCHITECTURE ⓭

The Building Centre, 26 Store Street, WC1
0207 6364044
www.newlondonarchitecture.org
Open 9am-6pm Mon-Fri, 9am-5pm Sat
Admission free
Transport Goodge Street or Russell Square tube

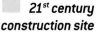

> *21st century construction site*

New London Architecture is designed to provoke awareness of design and development, as much as to display architectural innovation. Slick and spacious, the galleries are rarely busy, although situated just off Tottenham Court Road. The highlight is a monumental 1:1500 scale model of central London, which gives a real sense of the space and distance between the city's landmarks and highlights the latest developments. This is surrounded by changing displays of cutting-edge building projects around the capital, many in the outer reaches of suburbia, from a nursery cloaked in growing plants to energy-saving office blocks with wind turbines concealed on the roof.

Billing itself as 'a vital addition to the public debate about the future of London', on Tuesdays, the NLA hosts talks about the opportunities and challenges for urban regeneration, from skyscrapers and cycling routes to waste management and affordable housing. There's an excellent architectural bookshop and reference library, as well as a cute café with picture windows where you can watch the students and office workers hurrying along Store Street.

IMAGINATION GALLERY

Next door, at 25 Store Street, is the brilliantly named Imagination Building, a Victorian school converted into offices and an exhibition space. The red-brick façade conceals a soaring five-storey atrium with a wavy fabric roof and suspended steel walkways.

THE JEAN COCTEAU MURALS AT NOTRE DAME DE FRANCE

⑭

5 Leicester Place, WC2
0207 437 9363
Open Oct-March Mon-Fri 7.30am-4pm, Sat-Sun 9.30am-4pm
April-Sept Mon-Fri 7.30am-7pm, Sat-Sun 9.30am-4pm
Admission free. **Transport** Leicester Square tube.

> *Cocteau does Soho*

Notre Dame de France is the most recent incarnation of a Catholic church that has been rebuilt several times since it was first founded in 1865 to take care of the 'lower-class French' of London. Soho was, until relatively recently, a French enclave; this is one of the ghosts of that time. The original church was designed by Louis Auguste Boileau as a rotunda made entirely out of iron, and not surprisingly was quite a local talking point. This was bombed out in 1940, and the current building was inaugurated in 1955 after two years of building work.

The building itself is fairly unremarkable, although circular churches in Britain are rare. The glory of the church is the artwork within it, above all the murals by legendary French film maker, artist, and designer Jean Cocteau, which fill one chapel. Depicting themes from the Crucifixion and the Assumption of Mary, the work is vigorous, sexy and full of life in a manner quite unlike British religious art. Oddities include a black sun, and the fact that the viewer can only see the feet of Christ, as muscular soldiers in tiny skirts play dice for his robe at the base of the Cross. Cocteau included a self-portrait in the mural. Apparently, he was transported while painting it, talking to the figures as he worked.

Other notable features in the church are the tapestry above the altar by Robert De Caunac depicting Mary as the New Eve and a vast statue of the Virgin of Mercy above the entrance by Georges Saupique, who made the sculptures of the Palais du Trocadéro in Paris. The church actually seems to be still functioning, rather than a relic, like so many others in London. Light a candle, then plunge into the fleshpots of Soho and Leicester Square.

French London is fairly low-key, unlike other European groups such as the Portuguese, who have a big enclave in Stockwell. The French have been here a very long time. The first great influx was that of the Huguenots in 1675, who assimilated quickly, and built fortunes in the textile industry in the East End. Modern French London is most visible in South Kensington, especially around the Lycée Français Charles de Gaulle - a large French secondary school opposite the Natural History Museum - and the French Institute, home to a Francophone cinema. There are numerous French bookshops and cafes in the area.

GHOST STATIONS ON THE UNDERGROUND

Mystery lurks in the London Underground – and not just the Robot Yeti that terrified a generation of children on the 1970s TV show, Doctor Who. There are 267 Tube stations in operation. However, several stations do not appear on any maps: 21 have been taken off-line since 1900. Most of them were closed when London Transport was created in 1933, merging several independent transit operators who had built stations very close to each other to compete for passengers. Some are a real loss for commuters – British Museum, Aldwych (see also p115) and Lord's were all deemed economically unviable. Others were just badly designed: such as King William Street, northbound terminus of the City & South London railway - the world's first electric underground railway. The station was opened by the Prince of Wales (later Edward VII), but the inaugural train broke down on its return journey. A commemorative plaque marks the site of the old station near the Monument (see page 151). Brompton Road was so rarely used that train drivers didn't bother to stop there during rush hour. The cry "Passing Brompton Road" became the title of a 1928 stage play.

Most of these ghost stations have been abandoned or walled up. Some were used as air raid shelters during the Second World War. Down Street was the underground operation centre for Churchill, before he moved to the Cabinet War Rooms in Whitehall. Churchill's bath is still down there. The brick and concrete drum above the old entrance to the Northern Line branch of Stockwell station was the entrance to the bomb shelters, now used for document and film storage. The drum is covered in a mural depicting French Resistance heroine Violette Szabo, who lived nearby.

Visiting the stations is largely impossible. However, keen eyes will see remains of platforms as they pass through deserted stations. Bull and Bush – a station that never actually opened – can be glimpsed between Hampstead and Golders Green on the Northern Line. Wood Lane is visible when travelling east between White City and Shepherd's Bush. The white walls of British Museum station can be seen through the right-hand windows of the Central Line train between Holborn and Tottenham Court Road. This station was the setting for Death Line, a 1970s horror movie in which trapped construction workers morph into commuter-eating zombies.

Above ground, look out for the ox-blood tiles that line the former entrances to Down Street and South Kentish Town station on Kentish Town Road, now a shop. The station was closed during a power cut – and never opened again. However, a passenger once alighted at the closed station by mistake – the inspiration for John Betjeman's short story, South Kentish Town.

See http://underground-history.co.uk/ and www.abandonedstations.org.uk for more tales of the hidden Underground.

BORIS ANREP'S MOSAICS ⑮

National Gallery, Trafalgar Square, WC2
Open daily 10am-6pm Wed 10am-9pm
Admission free
Transport Charing Cross tube

*Art
underfoot*

The throng of visitors who traipse through the grand foyer of the National Gallery each day barely spare a glance for the intricate mosaics that decorate the three vestibules and halfway landing. Created between 1928 and 1952 by Russian artist Boris Anrep (1885-1969), the mosaics were sponsored by Samuel Courtauld and other private patrons. Although Anrep used Byzantine techniques and colours, the four mosaics are a celebration of everyday life, peppered with famous personalities and inside jokes.

Anrep liked the idea of visitors walking on his works of art, so it could be viewed from different angles and approached with less reverence than a framed, hanging painting. This irreverent attitude is plain in Anrep's choice of subject matter. In The Awakening of the Muses, he casts his contemporaries from the Bloomsbury Group as modern heroes: Virginia Woolf as Clio, muse of history, and art critic Clive Bell as Bacchus. There's even a cameo from Greta Garbo as Melpomene, muse of tragedy. Only Calliope, muse of poetry, is an unknown sitter – perhaps one of Anrep's secret crushes.

The Modern Virtues continues the theme of 'eminent people in fantastic situations.' Defiance is embodied by Winston Churchill on the white cliffs of Dover, fending off a fearsome beast shaped like a swastika. Look out for Margot Fonteyn as Delectation, Bertrand Russell as Lucidity, and Loretta Young as Compromise. In Leisure, TS Eliot contemplates Einstein's formula, while a naked girl frolics in Loch Ness with the fabled monster. One of Anrep's biggest patrons, Maud Russell, represents Folly – a strange gesture of gratitude! But Anrep also shows a healthy degree of self-mockery: Here I Lie depicts his own tomb, complete with a self- portrait.

The Labours of Life features – as far as we know – ordinary working folk: a Covent Garden porter, a woman washing a pig, a coal miner. The Pleasures of Life are summed up by a Christmas pudding, mud pies, cricket, football and less traditional pursuits such as 'Profane Love' – a man with two lovers.

The mosaics were not laid in situ. Cartoons were traced onto backing paper and laid in reverse, then glued into place and polished. Anrep's glorious, mischievous work was inspired by the pavement chalk artists whose successors are still at work on Trafalgar Square today.

Anrep also created the mosaic floors in the Blake Room at Tate Britain and several religious mosaics in Westminster Cathedral (see page 203).

BRITAIN'S SMALLEST POLICE STATION

Trafalgar Square, WC2
Transport Charing Cross tube

A peeping pillar

On the south-east corner of Trafalgar Square, surely London's biggest tourist trap, is Britain's smallest police station. The hordes of tourists posing before Nelson's Column and clambering on Sir Edward Lanseer's bronze lions are oblivious to this one-man sentry box fashioned from a hollowed-out granite lamp post. Allegedly, the secret police box was installed by Scotland Yard in 1926 so that the cops could keep an eye on the demonstrators and agitators who routinely gathered in Trafalgar Square (still London's most popular protest site). With its narrow slits for windows and claustrophobic proportions, this human CCTV camera must have been even more unpleasant during a riot. It was equipped with a telephone with a direct line to Scotland Yard in case things got out of hand.

Today, the look-out post is used to store street cleaning equipment. The only clue that it has links to the police is a faded list of bye-laws hanging outside. For the record, offences in Trafalgar Square include feeding birds, camping, parking a caravan, public speaking, playing music, washing or drying clothes, exercising, or using any 'foot-propelled device' – unless you have written permission from the Mayor.

> Originally installed in 1826, the ornamental light on the top may or may not be from Nelson's HMS Victory, depending on which source you believe.

SIGHTS NEARBY

IMPERIAL STANDARDS

At the foot of the steps below the National Gallery, well worn by the boots of weary sightseers, a series of small brass plaques mark the standard imperial measures of an inch, a foot, two feet and a yard. Replicas of the standards of measurements at the Royal Observatory in Greenwich (see page 259), they were installed by the Board of Trade in 1876.

THE CENTRE OF LONDON

The centre of London is located on a traffic island on the corner of the Strand and Charing Cross Road. A plaque on the pavement marks the spot from which all mileage distances in Britain are measured. When Queen Eleanor of Castile died in 1290, Edward I erected a cross at each of the twelve stops on her funeral procession from Lincoln to Westminster. All distances from the capital are still measured from the queen's resting place. Although her cross has been replaced by a statue of King Charles I, a replica stands outside Charing Cross station.

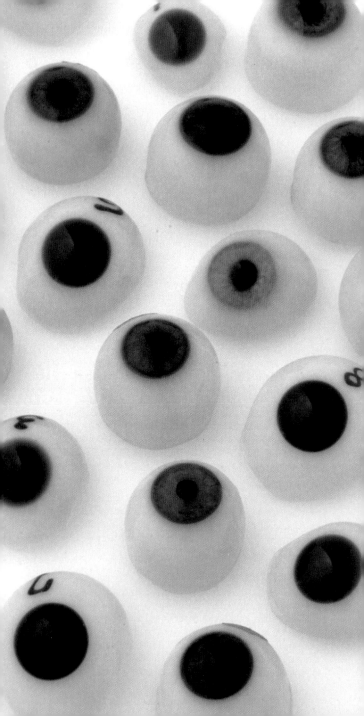

THE BRITISH OPTICAL ASSOCIATION MUSEUM ⑲

42 Craven Street, WC2
0207 766 4353
www.college-optometrists.org/museum
Open by appointment Mon-Fri 9.30am-5pm
Admission free; £5 for a tour of the meeting rooms
Transport Charing Cross tube

Eyeballs galore

In the basement of a fine Georgian terrace a stone's throw from Trafalgar Square, this obscure but delightful museum contains over 11.000 objects relating to the history of optometry. Founded in 1901, the collection includes over 2000 pairs of eyeglasses. There are pince-nez, lorgnettes, magnifiers, quizzing glasses, goggles and monocles, opera glasses with secret snuff compartments, 'jealousy glasses' with lenses concealed in the sides, rose-tinted sunglasses, wig spectacles that slid into your hairpiece and all manner of fancy spectacle receptacles. There are celebrity specs - including Dr Johnson, Ronnie Corbett and Dr Crippen, or you can get an eyeful of Leonardo de Caprio's contact lenses. Some models - like the windscreen wiper glasses with battery attached and a spring-loaded contraption to catapult contact lenses into the eyeball – did not take off.

Curator Neil Handley gives every visitor a personal guided tour, pointing out rare items such as an ancient Egyptian amulet of the Eye of Horus, ensuring the dead could see in the afterlife, and a sixteenth century statue of Saint Odilia, bearing two eyeballs on a bible. The optometric instruments are historical eye-openers, such as a Victorian self-testing machine with a religious text, improving users' morals as well as their vision. Visitors can test their eyesight in a 1930s optician's chair with a built-in refraction unit, try on different frames, or explore foreign cities through an early View-Master. A drawer full of artificial diseased, deformed and injured eyes, dating from 1880, is definitely not for the squeamish.

For a fee, you can also view the portraits of bespectacled sitters and optically themed prints and satirical drawings in the meeting rooms on the first floor.

SIGHTS NEARBY

BENJAMIN FRANKLIN'S HOUSE ⑳

36 Craven Street. 0207 839 2006; www.benjaminfranklinhouse.org

He may be famous as one of the founding fathers of the United States, but in 1790, the year of his death, Benjamin Franklin also invented bifocal spectacles. Franklin's only surviving home, a few doors down from the Optical Museum, is now a museum, where actors in period costumes carry on for visitors. During the restoration, a stockpile of cut and trepanned bones was unearthed in the basement – the remnants of an anatomy school run by Franklin's friend, William Hewson. Franklin probably attended Hewson's public dissections of human bodies.

YORK HOUSE WATERGATE

㉑

Embankment Gardens, WC2
Transport Embankment or Charing Cross tube

> *Last vestige of a riverside mansion*

The enclosure of the Thames within the Embankment in the second half of the 19th century is generally held to be a miracle of Victorian engineering, giving London a state-of-the-art water system as well as creating more land for building. However, it dramatically changed the city's relationship to the river, and nowhere is this more visible than this watergate in Embankment Gardens, tucked away beside Charing Cross station. At first sight, the baroque archway looks like a folly, a gate to nowhere marooned in a small park. In fact, it was once the river entrance to York House, one of a line of mansions that originally stood along the route from the City of London to the royal court at Westminster. The river now lies 150 metres from the bottom step of the watergate, giving an idea of how far into the city the tidal Thames previously extended. If you stand on the opposite embankment at high tide, especially near Blackfriars Bridge on the South Bank, the height of the water and its closeness to the lip of the wall both underline the river's power.

The watergate itself was created by Inigo Jones in 1626, as an extension to the palace built by the first Duke of Buckingham in 1620. The design looks florid in comparison to its surroundings, and still bears the Buckingham family coat of arms. Alongside Banqueting House and the Temple Bar Arch next to St Paul's, it is one of the few surviving reminders in London of the Italianate tastes of King Charles I. The second Duke of Buckingham was the King's favourite, and one of London's wealthiest landowners. Like the King, the Duke was an art lover. The 1635 inventory of his collection shows 22 paintings and 59 pieces of Roman sculpture in the Great Chamber alone. Gentileschi and Rubens both lodged at the house during their visits to London.

GEORGE VILLIERS, DUKE OF BUCKINGHAM'S CRYPTIC NAMESAKE

On the wall of York Place, next to the McDonalds on the Strand, is a grimy little plaque commemorating the strange street's original name, Of Alley. The second Duke of Buckingham sold York House to developers in 1672, but made it a condition of the sale that his name and title should be commemorated by George Street, Villiers Street, Duke Street, Of Alley, and Buckingham Street (thus spelling out George Villiers, Duke of Buckingham). The streets are still there, though Of Alley was renamed York Place and George Street is now York Buildings.

HENRY VIII'S WINE CELLAR   ㉒

Ministry of Defence, Whitehall, SW1
020 7218 9000
Open by appointment. Visits with guided tour available to groups only
(min ten, max twenty persons; children under 12 are not permitted).
Admission free
Transport Embankment or Charing Cross tube

Subter-
ranean state
secret

T he main residence of English monarchs from 1530 until 1698, Whitehall Palace was once the largest palace in Europe. A sprawling warren of buildings with over 2,000 rooms and 23 acres of grounds, Whitehall was like a small town where courtiers could suck up to royalty. All this went up in flames when a fire ravaged the palace in 1698; most of the buildings were wooden, apart from a brick wine cellar which survives to this day – though buried deep within the bowels of the Ministry of Defence. Although known as Henry VIII's cellar, it was actually built by Cardinal Wolsey, Lord Chancellor and Archbishop of York, between 1514 and 1529. When Wolsey fell out of favour, Henry VIII land-grabbed his estate and incorporated the cardinal's well-stocked cellar into Whitehall Palace.

Access to the cellar is complicated by the security surrounding the hulking Ministry of Defence headquarters overlooking Whitehall. This only adds to the frisson as you are led along drab corridors and downstairs into a murky chamber lined rather incongruously with heating pipes. At the centre is the subterranean cellar, its Tudor vaulting, pillars and brickwork preserved exactly as they were four centuries ago (with the addition of some trestle tables and olde-worlde lights, a coat of lime-wash, and some decorative barrels, which the authoritative guide insists are empty). Originally, the cellar was at street level and the doorway led to a riverside ramp, so that barrels of booze could be rolled right in. Shortly after World War II, news that the cellar would be destroyed to accommodate Emmanuel Vincent Harris' new Ministry of Defence building caused a public stink. So the ingenious engineers resolved to shift it 9 ft north-west and 19 ft down. Encased in a steel frame and propped onto metal rollers, the 70x30 ft room was carefully sunk into position a quarter inch at a time. Today, this Gothic time warp is a backdrop to parties for defence officials.

The extensive military bunkers beneath the ministry are strictly off-limits.

Other elements of Whitehall Palace that have survived are Inigo Jones' Banqueting House, with its superb ceiling paintings by Rubens (Whitehall and Horse Guards Avenue; 0844 482 7777. Open Mon-Sat 10am-5pm £4.50), Cockpit Passage, and the gable wall of Henry VIII's tennis court at 70 Whitehall (now the Cabinet Office, closed to the public).

Whitehall is the widest street in London.

GIRO'S GRAVE   ㉓
Next to 9 Carlton House Terrace, SW1

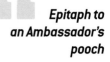

*Epitaph to
an Ambassador's
pooch*

Between St James Park and Piccadilly Circus, Waterloo Place was designed by the 19th century architect John Nash as an overblown testament to the splendour of the British Empire. Countless statues of heroic commanders and louche aristocrats vie to outdo each other in size and stature. Buried among these grand memorials, a tiny tombstone lies at the foot of an enormous tree between the Duke of York Steps and an underground garage. Shielded by what appears to be a miniature kennel, the German epitaph on the gravestone reads: "Giro, ein treuer Begleiter! London, im Februar 1934, Hoesch". This 'true companion,' Giro, was the beloved Alsatian of the German Ambassador, Leopold von Hoesch, who served in London from 1932 to 1936. Now fenced off by railings, his grave lies on a patch of land that was once the garden of the Ambassador's residence at No 9 Carlton House Terrace. The hapless Giro met his maker after colliding with an electricity cable while scampering about in what is now the Institute of Contemporary Arts. Apocryphal reports suggest that Giro received a full Nazi burial, though this seems highly unlikely since Hoesch was openly opposed to the rise of the Third Reich. The strain proved too much for Hoesch, who died of a stroke in 1936.

THE MARBLE STAIRCASE OF MUSSOLINI

After Hoesch's replacement – and Hitler's close associate - Joachim von Ribbentrop moved into Carlton House Terrace, the Führer's favourite architect, Albert Speer, was dispatched to London to give the embassy a flashy revamp. The British government did not deport Hitler's diplomats until 1939, when the building was taken over by the Foreign Office and stripped of its Nazi trappings - although a staircase of Italian marble, donated by Mussolini, is apparently still intact.

SIGHTS NEARBY

THE DUKE OF WELLINGTON'S MOUNTING STEPS   ㉔

The British Empire may be defunct, but Gentlemen's Clubs still reign supreme in this upper crust corner of London. Both the Athenaeum Club and the Institute of Directors preside over Waterloo Place, their lavish interiors off limits to the hoi polloi. Outside each is a pair of kerb stones, bearing a rusty plaque: 'This horseblock was erected by desire of the Duke of Wellington 1830'. Possibly recycled from materials from Carlton House or the Duke of York Steps, they allowed the Duke to mount and dismount from his horse with ease while visiting the Athenaeum. Whether the shorter members of the club were also permitted to take advantage of the Duke's steps is unknown.

THE LONDON LIBRARY ㉕

14 St James's Square, SW1
0207 766 4716
www.londonlibrary.co.uk
Open Mon-Wed 9.30am-7.30pm, Thurs-Sat 9.30am-5.30pm
Admission Day membership £15; weekly membership £50
annual membership £435
Transport Green Park or Piccadilly Circus tube

A historic haven for literary luminaries

Founded by the curmudgeonly Thomas Carlyle in 1841, the London Library is a little-known gem. Carlyle's desperate – and fruitless - quest for a 'Silent Study' (he loathed the British Library, then housed in the British Museum, because it was full of 'snorers, snufflers, wheezers, [and] spitters') inspired him to create a subscription library.

Despite a prestigious roll call of past and present readers (Charles Dickens, Charles Darwin, Arthur Conan Doyle, Henry James, Winston Churchill and Agatha Christie), membership is open to all – and at a reasonable price: in this spirit of democratic independence, rules are set by the readers themselves.

The London Library is located in a purpose-built town house on one of the most exclusive – and gorgeous – squares in London. The deceptively narrow entrance leads into a warren of floor-upon-floor of row-upon-row of bookshelves, which is delightfully disorienting. With its cracked leather armchairs and aged portraits, the interior has retained all its original charm, as well as a quirky Edwardian cataloguing system. Books are stored alphabetically by subject matter; so you might stumble upon a book on bullfighting while looking for a treatise on celibacy. The collection contains over one million books and periodicals, dating to the 16th century. One room contains a full run of The Times newspaper from 1820 until 2000. All but the most fragile editions can be browsed on open-access shelves, taken home, or dispatched to members anywhere in Europe, so like Carlyle, you can peruse them in private. Better still, there is no due date: you can hold onto a book until another reader requests it. However, many writers use the reading rooms as their study; there is even free wireless internet. As author John McNally eloquently puts it: 'It is the stuff of fiction, the gentleperson's Google.'

To accommodate 8,000 new titles a year, the library has bought an adjoining building, which opens onto Mason's Yard, home to the achingly hip White Cube gallery. With £25 million required for the extension and essential restoration, the library needs generous support from London's intellectual heavyweights to ensure its survival. As former President TS Eliot said in 1952: 'I am convinced that if this library disappeared, it would be a disaster to the world of letters, and would leave a vacancy that no other form of library could fill.'

On your way out, flip through the Readers' Suggestions book and marvel at the meticulous responses to even the most eccentric requests handwritten by the dedicated team of librarians.

QUEEN ALEXANDRA MEMORIAL ㉖

Marlborough Road, SW1
Transport Green Park tube

> *Ghoulish tribute to a long-suffering queen*

Tucked away on Marlborough Gate, beside St James' Palace, is this dreamy (but not necessarily in a pleasant way) Art Nouveau memorial to Queen Alexandra, long-suffering wife of King Edward VII. Commissioned in 1926, the memorial was sculpted by Alfred Gilbert, who created the famous statue of Eros on Piccadilly Circus.

The memorial is set into the garden wall of Marlborough House, once Queen Alexandra's London home. Cast in bronze and finished in blackened enamel, the statue has a ghostly, neo-Gothic appearance. The Queen is seated behind allegorical figures representing faith, hope and charity.

The Alexandra Memorial was a great boon to Alfred Gilbert, exiled in Belgium at the time, after declaring bankruptcy. The terms of the commission, which included a permanent residence in Kensington Palace, relieved Gilbert of his financial worries. The day after King George V unveiled the memorial on June 8th 1932, Gilbert was knighted. He was subsequently given to swanning around St James' wearing a giant fedora hat.

Gilbert also created a spectacular memorial to Edward and Alexandra's son, Albert Victor, in Windsor Castle. A very odd character, Victor was implicated in a gay brothel scandal and subsequently earmarked as a suspect for the Ripper murders by the lurid conspiracy theorists that case has attracted.

EDWARD VII, A SPECTACULARLY ROTTEN HUSBAND

An active commissioner of good deeds, Queen Alexandra was a universally loved member of the royal family. However, Edward VII was a spectacularly rotten husband. Although doubtless colourful and famously charming, he was noted throughout Europe for his gluttony and kept a string of very public mistresses, including the actress Lily Langtry, Jennie Jerome (mother of Winston Churchill) and Alice Keppel, great-grandmother of the current Prince of Wales' latest wife, Camila Parker Bowles. Edward was twice a witness in law court — unheard of for a royal. He appeared in a divorce case where he perjured himself about an affair with a young woman. He also testified in a case concerning a friend accused of cheating at baccarat, an illegal card game that Edward played heavily. Edward spent years waiting to become King, which may explain his excesses. On the other hand, he was unusually tolerant for his time and deplored the casual racism that characterised the British Empire.

PISTOLS DRAWN AT PICKERING PLACE   ㉗

Behind 7 St James' Street, SW1
Transport Green Park tube

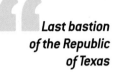

> *Last bastion
> of the Republic
> of Texas*

Pay close attention when looking for this tiny courtyard tucked away behind swanky St James Street. If the gate is closed, the only indication you are at Pickering Place is the number 3 on it. The narrow, arched alleyway leading to the courtyard retains its 18th century timber wainscoting.

A relatively unspoilt Georgian cul-de-sac still lit by original gaslights, Pickering Place is named after William Pickering, the founder of a coffee business in the premises now occupied by the famous wine merchants Berry Bros and Rudd.

In the 18th century, Pickering Place was notorious for its gambling dens. Its seclusion also made it a favourite spot for duels, although the limited space suggests that fooling around with any kind of weapon - let alone pistols - would have been instantly fatal. It is claimed that the last duel in England was fought here, although an episode with pistols between two Frenchmen at Windsor in 1852 is the more likely contender.

Graham Greene, who lived in a flat in Pickering Place, housed his fictional character Colonel Daintry from *The Human Factor* in a two-roomed flat looking out over the paved courtyard with its sundial. In real life, Pickering Place was the base of the diplomatic office of the independent Republic of Texas, before it joined the United States in 1845.

DUELLING DANDIES

Beau Brummel, a notorious dandy and friend of King George IV, is said to have fought here. But it is hard to imagine the man who invented the cravat, took five hours to dress, and recommended that boots be polished with champagne, having anything to do with bloodshed. Indeed, Brummel embarked upon a military career as a young man, but promptly resigned his commission when he learned that his regiment was to be sent to Manchester.

SIGHTS NEARBY

A SECRET CELLAR   ㉘

Located at 3 St James Street since 1698, Berry Brothers. & Rudd is Britain's oldest wine merchant. The shop has the quality of a (very expensive) museum. Its underground cellars, previously part of Henry VIII's royal residence and later a hideout for the exiled Napoleon III (the famous Napoleon's nephew) have been converted into meeting rooms. However, a secret tunnel, now blocked by wine bottles, leads to St James' Palace. It was used by philandering royals to pay clandestine visits to the ladies of the night who hung out at the shop in the 18th century. Or perhaps they just wanted a nightcap.

K2 TELEPHONE BOXES

Burlington House, Piccadilly W1
Transport Green Park tube

㉙

> **The smallest listed buildings in London**

A British design classic, the tomato red telephone box has been rendered obsolete by the mobile phone. Upstaged by uninspired British Telecom booths in the 1980s and '90s, the few original kiosks that survive are plastered with explicit adverts for buxom call girls or used by lager louts to relieve themselves.

Just inside the gates of the Royal Academy, on either side of the arched entrance, two of the first kiosks designed by Sir Giles Gilbert Scott in 1926 remain intact, though sadly neglected. They are the smallest listed buildings in London. In 1923, the General Post Office launched a competition to design a new telephone kiosk to replace the first 1921 model. All the prototypes were put into public service around London, but Scott's winning design is the only one that survived.

Known as K2 (Kiosk 2), Scott's cast-iron booths had a domed roof with tiny holes to provide ventilation. At first, they were widely reviled; people particularly objected to their bright red colour. In fact, Scott had specified a silver exterior and blue interior for the K2, but the Post Office plumped for vermillion. Instantly recognisable, the red phone box is now an icon of twentieth century Britain.

After three more modifications by Scott, in 1936 the improved K6 was launched to commemorate King George V's Silver Jubilee. 70.000 booths were installed nationwide. However, vandalism and high maintenance costs led to their gradual withdrawal and substitution with utilitarian modern booths. There was even a scheme to convert the old kiosks into mobile phone masts. After a conservation campaign in the 1990s, some of the old telephone boxes have been renovated and re-installed. The rest have been sold off for scrap or as souvenirs.

> Sir Giles Gilbert Scott (1880-1960) was the architect of many other London icons, including Waterloo Bridge, Battersea Power Station and Bankside Power Station (now the Tate Modern).

SIGHTS NEARBY

THE FORTNUM AND MASON CLOCK

181 Piccadilly, W1.

㉚

Above the entrance to London's finest food emporium is a clock flanked by two miniature sentry boxes. Every fifteen minutes, an 18th century jingle tinkles on the clock's eighteen bells. On the hour, four-foot replicas of the original Mr. Fortnum and Mr. Mason pop out and bow to each other as the clock chimes. According to the store's website, 'Messrs F&M themselves appear to check that standards are being upkept.'

JOHN SNOW'S CHOLERA PUMP

Broadwick Street, W1

㉛

*A tribute
to Soho's
seedy past*

At the corner of Broadwick and Poland Street is a black iron pump on an octagonal plinth. A small plaque informs the passer-by that this replica pump was installed in 1992. The original pump was probably located across the road, outside the John Snow pub, whose namesake discovered the cause of cholera.

As Judith Summers writes in *A History of London's Most Colourful Neighborhood*: 'By the middle of the 19th century, Soho had become an unsantary place of cow-sheds, animal droppings, slaughterhouses, grease-boiling dens and primitive, decaying sewers. And underneath the floorboards of the overcrowded cellars lurked something even worse - a fetid sea of cesspits as old as the houses, and many of which had never been drained. It was only a matter of time before this hidden festering time-bomb exploded. It finally did so in the summer of 1854.'

In September 1854 alone, 500 Soho residents died of cholera. Dr John Snow (1813-1858), an anaesthetist who lived in Soho Square, concluded that the polluted water pump on Broad Street (as it was called then) had caused the epidemic. Initially, the establishment scoffed at Snow's theory. The Reverend Henry Whitehead, vicar of St Luke's church on nearby Berwick Street, claimed the deceased were the victims of divine intervention. But soon after Snow forcibly removed the handle of the water pump, the outbreak ended.

In his research into the causes of the disease, Dr Snow had to look no further than the Broad Street brewery. One of the perks of employees was an allowance of free beer, so they all abstained from drinking water. None of the 70 workers caught cholera.

Ironically, Snow himself was teetotal. At the tender age of 23, Snow gave an impassioned speech on the evils of alcohol which began thus: 'I feel it my duty to endeavour to convince you of the physical evils sustained to your health by using intoxicating liquors even in the greatest moderation; and I leave to my colleagues the task of painting drunkenness in all its hideousness, of describing the manifold miseries and crimes it produces.'

John Snow was already famous for an earlier discovery in 1853: chloroform. This primitive anaesthetic was used to help Queen Victoria overcome the agonies of labour during the birth of her son, Prince Leopold. But Snow's tireless medical research and abstemious lifestyle did not help his own health; he died of a stroke in 1858, aged 45.

is a safe and easy operation; but, if attempted by the unskilful, may occasion the most frightful and dangerous consequences"

The Dental Art, A Practical Treatise on Dental Surgery, C.A. Harris, 1839.

John Tomes designed a refinement to the forcep in which the beaks were shaped to fit the crowns of the teeth. This helped to reduce slippage of the instrument on the teeth and to stop the damage to the surrounding gums.

THE BRITISH DENTAL ASSOCIATION MUSEUM ㉜

64 Wimpole Street, W1
0207 935 0875
www.bda.org/museum
Open Tues and Thurs 1-4pm
Admission free
Transport Oxford Circus tube

*A visit
to the dentist ...*

This tiny little museum is an adjunct to the library of the British Dental Association, and as such is set up as an educational display. But it's still a museum of dentistry. Although the glass cases might be bright and clean, the room warmly lit, and every effort made to avoid any Chamber of Horrors or overly clinical undertones, the collection of tools, teeth and other odontological artefacts is still unsettling.

What is immediately striking is how lucky we are to have the dental service we do today. Dentists were only fully regulated in 1921; before this, anyone could have a go. Dental drills were adapted from carpenters' drills and had a similarly robust mechanical air, as the advertisement for "Shaw's Dental Engine, Complete with Oil Can and Spanner" attests. Replacement teeth were usually made from hippo or walrus ivory. Dr Edward H. Angle's Head Gear, a fearsome brace attached to sieve-like headgear, is a testament to how far orthodontics has come. Possibly the most alarming exhibit is the extraction display case containing various dental keys - bolt-on handles that were used to twist teeth out of the mouth, and often resulted in the tooth breaking or jaw fractures.

Beautifully made dental tools with carved mother-of-pearl handles in custom-made cases are the centrepiece of the exhibition – but they are impossible to admire without a grimace as you imagine the pain they could inflict. There is also a computer loaded with dental health films that are terrifying and hilarious by turns: "Oral Surgery Part 2 1948" is like a short film made by Francis Bacon; "No Toothache for Eskimos" looks like a spoof; and "Came The Dawn", from 1912, includes a mystifying sequence in which a fat soldier in a kilt and his friend laugh at a man with no front teeth for five minutes.

LONDON'S MEDICAL MUSEUMS

There is a wide variety of medical museums dotted around London, including the Old Operating Theatre (p229); the Alexander Fleming Laboratory Museum (p181), and the British Optical Association Museum (p45). See www.medicalmuseums.org for a full list. Further afield is the Bethlem Royal Hospital Museum (www.bethlemheritage.org.uk). The descendant of London's infamous mental hospital, "Bedlam" moved from its original site, which is now the Imperial War Museum, to suburban Beckenham. As well as extensive archives, the museum has a fascinating collection of art relating to mental illness.

In this church
was solemnised
the marriage of
Robert Browning
and
Elizabeth Barrett
12th September
1846

THE BROWNING ROOM 33

St Marylebone Church, Marylebone Road NW1
0207 935 7315
www.stmarylebone.org
Open Sunday afternoons or by appointment
Admission free
Transport Baker Street or Regent's Park tube

*A shrine
to forbidden love*

The Victorian poets Elizabeth Barrett and Robert Browning enjoyed one of literature's most chronicled courtships: they exchanged 574 love letters over a twenty-month period. They wrote mutually appreciative – and increasingly passionate – letters for five months before they even set eyes on each other. It was an unlikely union. She was an opium-addicted invalid confined to her bed at the family home on Wimpole Street, watched over by her puritanical father. He was an erudite and handsome poet from a humble family in Camberwell. She was a spinster of almost 40 – positively ancient by Victorian standards; he was already an over-ripe 36.

But when they finally met in 1845, love blossomed. Mr Barrett knew of Browning's visits to his daughter's bedroom, but believed they were exchanging literary pleasantries. On September 12, 1846, Elizabeth crept out of the house and headed for nearby St Marylebone Parish Church, where she and Robert were married in secret. A week later, the couple eloped to Italy, never to return. When Elizabeth's sister Henrietta broke the news to their father, he allegedly flew into such a rage that he flung Henrietta down the stairs and never spoke of his daughter Elizabeth again.

But these illicit lovers are commemorated today at St Marylebone church, which still holds the couple's original wedding certificate. As you enter, The Browning Room is on the left. It is now only open when in use for church functions – primarily after Sunday services. Since some of Browning's original furniture was stolen, it stands fairly empty, but does contain two small reliefs of Barrett and Browning and a pretty stained glass window commemorating them. The room is usually locked, so call the verger or parish office to arrange a visit.

SIGHTS NEARBY

MARYLEBONE CONDUIT 34

St Marylebone was originally called St Mary-by-the-Tybourne, after the Tybourne stream which ran close by. The last remaining trace of this river - once the main source of water for the City of London - is a tiny white plaque inset into the wall at 50 Marylebone Lane, which reads: 'Conduit belonging to the City of London 1776.' Hidden beneath the gaudy photographs advertising the Depilex hair removal clinic, this little fragment of forgotten history is overlooked by most passers-by.

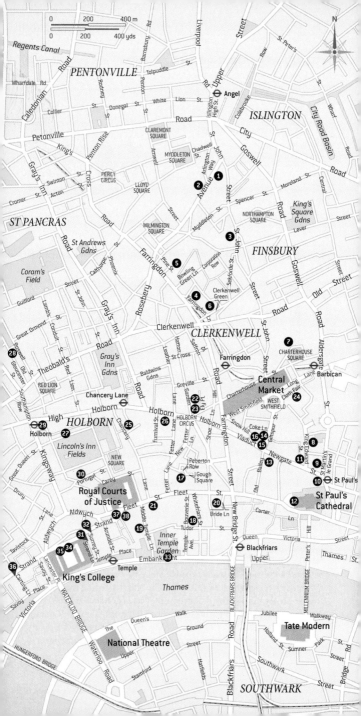

TEMPLE TO ANGEL

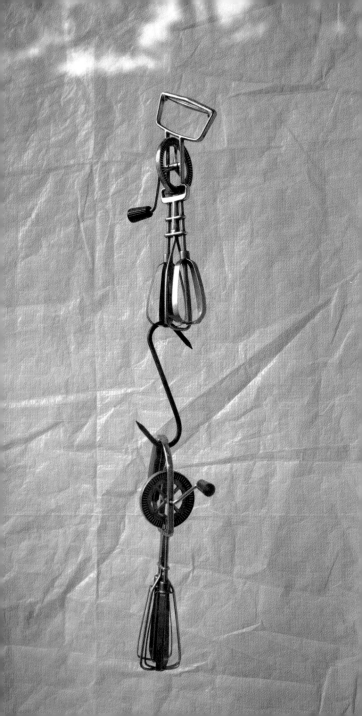

WINDOWS 108

①

108 Rosebery Avenue, Islington EC1
0207 278 7368
www.windowsoneoeight.com
Open 24 hours
Admission free
Transport Angel tube

*Window into
an artist's world*

With retail space and rents at such a premium in central London, it might seem strange to see a vacant shop as you wander down Islington's affluent Rosebery Avenue. But number 108 is no ordinary shop window. Artist Maggie Ellenby, has used this blank canvas as an ingenious installation space since 1993.

Ellenby often uses mundane objects in unusual guises to create her artworks: like 'Marigolds,' a mass of yellow and red rubber gloves twisted into floral patterns, or 'No' spelled out by hundreds of marshmallows suspended in the window. Simple slogans like 'Wet Paint' or 'Reserved' are guaranteed to catch the eye of passers-by.

According to Ellenby, the installations are 'deliberately simple.' 'Designed to be seen from the bus, car or by passing pedestrians, each one leaves you slightly dissatisfied, wondering what comes next.' The fact that the works are not labelled heightens the mystique.

Light, another recurring feature of Ellenby's work, creates a startling effect if you are driving by after dark. You might spot a backlit climber scaling the window pane, or an illuminated 'Speed Kills, Jesus Saves.' And whenever Ellenby is contemplating her next project, she puts up a 'Pause' sign.

SIGHTS NEARBY

THE OAK ROOM

②

173 Rosebery Avenue • 0207 833 9527

Finsbury, the residential area between Clerkenwell and Islington, used to be a spa which supplied London with its water via the New River (actually a canal). So it was fitting that the Metropolitan Water Board had its 17th century headquarters in this grand building next to Sadlers Wells theatre. Now renamed New Riverhead and converted into luxury flats, the building's original oak-panelled function room remains intact, with decorative details attributed to master woodcarver Grinling Gibbons. There are four public viewings a year – but if you ask nicely, the security guard at the front door might let you take a peek.

JOE ORTON'S LIBRARY BOOKS ❸

Islington Local History Centre, Finsbury Library, 245
St. John Street EC1
0207 527 7988
http://joeorton.org
Open Mon 9.30am-8pm, Tues 9.30am-5pm, Thurs 9.30am-8pm,
Fri 9.30am-1pm, Sat 9.30am-5pm, Closed Wed, Sun
Admission free. **Transport** Angel tube

'Have a good shit while you're reading!'

"Libraries might as well not exist; they've got endless shelves for rubbish and hardly any space for good books,' Joe Orton bemoaned in 1967. Orton, a playwright and provocateur, achieved notoriety in the 1960s for his black comedies, and even more so for his premature death at the age of 34 – bludgeoned to death by his jealous boyfriend Kenneth Halliwell, who then committed suicide. Halliwell and Orton had been lovers since they met at drama school. They shared a cramped bed-sit at 25 Noel Road in Islington, which they decorated with images torn out of local library books. In addition to stealing volumes that took their fancy, the pair developed a taste for defacing books, by altering their covers and writing new, crude blurbs in their dust jackets. Orton enjoyed loitering in the library, watching the bemused or outraged reactions of readers to his handiwork.

Islington Library was not amused. Extra staff failed to nail the culprits. It was Sydney Porrett, a clerk at Islington Council, who caught them out. He sent a letter to Halliwell asking him to remove an illegally parked car. The typed reply matched typeface irregularities in the defaced books. On April 28 1962, police raided Orton and Halliwell's flat and retrieved 72 stolen books and 1,653 plates from art books. They were sentenced to six months in prison and fined £262. Later, Orton claimed this unreasonably harsh sentence was 'because we were queers.'

Today, the 44 vandalised volumes are the pride of Islington's Local History Centre. Colour copies are kept in two ordinary looking photo albums, which you would expect to contain wedding or family photos. Instead there are curious collages of subversive images. John Betjeman is replaced by an elderly man in his underpants, covered in tattoos. *The Collected Plays of Emlyn Williams* is covered with crude slogans like 'KNICKERS MUST FALL' and 'OLIVIA PRUDE FUCKED BY MONTY'. *Queen's Favourite* shows two half-naked men wrestling. The yellow rose on the cover of Collins Guide to *Roses* has a gorilla face. The pair had a penchant for reworking Shakespeare covers with rather elegant collages. Other books received less reverential treatment: the blurb of *Clouds of Witness* has been re-imagined as a tale of a child-molesting policewoman, which concludes: 'Have a good shit while you're reading!'

If you want to see the originals, you must apply in writing, although a few of them are on permanent display in the Islington Museum downstairs.

A·D 1800
WILL. ROUND/CHURCH
JOSEPH BIRD/WARDENS

For the better accommodation
of the Neighbourhood,
this Pump was removed to
the Spot where it now
stands.
The Spring by which it is
supplied is situated four
Feet eastward, and round
it, as History informs us,
the Parish Clerks of London
In remote Ages annually
performed sacred Plays.
That Custom caused it to be
denominated Clerks-Well,
and from which this Parish
derived its Name.
The Water was greatly
esteemed by the Prior and
Brethren of the Order of
S. John of Jerusalem, and
the Benedictine Nuns
in the Neighbourhood.

THIS   TABLET
WHICH WAS FORMERLY
FIXED ON THE SITE OF
THE ANCIENT CLERKS' WELL
VIZ THE PUMPHOUSE
Nº 2 RAY STREET
118 YARDS WESTWARD WAS
FIXED HERE AS A MEMENTO
OF THE PAST IN 1878.
W.J. HARRISON/ CHURCH
GEO. BLACKIE / WARDENS

THE CLERK'S WELL

④

14–16 Farringdon Lane EC1
Open Call Islington Local History Centre on
0207 5277988 to arrange a visit
Transport Farringdon tube

*Medieval
water source*

ondon's first suburb, medieval Clerkenwell was a leafy neighbourhood north of
the City walls, peppered with farms,
spas, and 'excellent springs, the water of which
is sweet, clear and salubrious,' according to
William Fitzstephen, who compiled the first topographical history of London in
the 12th century.

The area takes its name from the Clerk's Well, or Fons Clericorum, which has
remarkably survived from the Middle Ages to this day. Although the well is now
locked inside the basement of the Well Court office building, with limited public
access, you can peer through the glass walls and read about the history of the
well and the surrounding area.

The well was originally located in the boundary wall of St Mary's, an Augustinian
nunnery founded in 1140. It was nicknamed the 'Clerks' Well' because parish
clerks performed Mystery Plays based on biblical themes close to this spot, one
of the cultural highlights of the medieval calendar. After the dissolution of the
nunnery during the Reformation, the boundary wall was destroyed and the well
was covered over by new buildings. In 1800, a pump was placed at street level to
facilitate public use, but it was closed in 1857 because of pollution. The well was
rediscovered by accident in 1924 during building work in Farringdon Lane.

Now a world famous dance theatre, Sadler's Wells has housed performances
ever since Dick Sadler opened his 'musick house' here in the 1680s. When an
ancient well was discovered in the grounds, the enterprising Mr. Sadler was
quick to promote the water's medicinal properties. Although the spa fell out of
fashion, the theatre is still known as Sadler's Wells.

SIGHTS NEARBY

FINSBURY HEALTH CENTRE

⑤

17 Pine Street EC1 • 0207 530 4200

Designed by Berthold Lubetkin in 1936-8, this modernist landmark behind
Exmouth Market is still used as a medical centre. With its glass walls, red and
blue interior, and colourful murals exhorting locals to enjoy 'fresh air night
and day,' the building embodied Lubetkin's belief in modern architecture as a
tool for social progress. Finsbury was one of London's poorest boroughs and
this health centre was the pièce de resistance of its socialist health and
housing policy. As Lubetkin famously commented, 'Nothing is too good for
ordinary people.' Besides doctors' surgeries, the clinic contained a delousing
station, a TB clinic, and a solarium – symbols of how times have changed.

MARX MEMORIAL LIBRARY ❻

37a Clerkenwell Green, EC1
0207 253 1485
www.marx-memorial-library.org
Open 1-2pm daily
Admission free
Transport Farringdon tube

*Lenin's
London office*

The bright red door is the only clue to what lies inside this pretty Georgian town-house that sits inconspicuously beside the snazzy jewellery and architecture studios of Clerkenwell Green. A brass plaque by the doorbell proclaims that this is the Marx Memorial Library, home to over 150.000 volumes of leftist literature.

From the Peasants' Revolt in 1381 to the Poll Tax demonstrations of the 1980s, this quaint corner of London has long been a breeding ground for rebels, rioters, and political refugees. Among them was Vladimir Ilyich Ulyanov who in 1902-3 shared space in this building with Harry Quelch, editor of the left-wing Twentieth Century Press. Lenin's poky office is intact, with its blue cupboards, leather-bound socialist tracts, a Braille edition of the Communist Manifesto, and countless busts of the man himself donated by admirers. This is where Lenin edited issues 22-38 of his Russian newspaper *Iskra (The Spark)*, printed on extra thin paper so it was easier to smuggle into Tsarist Russia.

Built in 1737 as a charitable school for Welsh boys, the building acquired its first radical residents when the London Patriotic Society arrived in 1872. The Marx Memorial Library and Workers' School was established 1933, on the 50th anniversary of Marx's death, as an angry response to the public burning of books in Nazi Germany. In 1935, Viscount Jack Hastings, an aristocratic Communist and pupil of the Mexican radical artist Diego Riviera, painted a giant mural grandly titled 'Worker of the future clearing away the chaos of capitalism;' the figures of Marx, Engels, and Lenin loom larger than life behind the reception desk. Downstairs, the archive of the International Brigade has pride of place in a meeting room decked with revolutionary posters.

The library's red shelves and blue linoleum floors are scuffed, old-fashioned, slightly down at heel – exactly as they should be. In keeping with its socialist principles, membership costs just £10 a year (£5 for pensioners).

In 1986, some 14th century tunnels were discovered in the basement, which can be viewed on Open House weekend.

MARX IN LONDON
Karl Marx wrote much of Das Kapital seated in Chair G7 at the British Museum Reading Room. In 1850-55, Marx lived in a squalid apartment above what is now the Quo Vadis restaurant in Soho. But the restaurant's original owner, Peppino Leoni, was loath to have a blue plaque commemorating a Communist outside his fancy establishment at 28 Dean Street.

CHARTERHOUSE

❼

Charterhouse Square, EC1
0207 251 5002
Open Guided tours every Wed pm April-Aug. **Admission** £10
Pre-booking essential on or by sending a cheque and SAE
to the address above
Transport Farringdon tube/rail.

> *Cloistered home for retired gentlemen*

Wandering beneath the plane trees of sleepy Charterhouse Square, it's hard to believe this was once a plague pit, where 50,000 victims of the Black Death were buried in the 14th century. A Carthusian monastery was founded here in 1371, but the monks' cloistered existence was brutally interrupted by the Reformation: the Prior was hung, drawn, and quartered, with one of his arms being nailed to the gate. After the monastery was shut down in 1537, it became a playground for the aristocracy. Lord North turned it into a sumptuous mansion, where he treated Queen Elizabeth I to such extravagant hospitality that he went broke and fled to the country. Charterhouse (the name is an anglicised corruption of Carthusian) was eventually purchased by Sir Thomas Sutton, a philanthropist, who endowed a school for 40 poor boys and an almshouse for 80 male pensioners ('gentlemen by descent and in poverty, soldiers that have borne arms by sea or land, merchants decayed by piracy or shipwreck, or servants in household to the King or Queen's Majesty').

The only surviving Tudor town house in London, Charterhouse is still home to around 40 'retired gentlemen'. The criteria for entry are less rigorous these days – even Catholics are acceptable – but there's still a strict pecking order among residents, not unlike the eponymous boarding school, which moved to Surrey in 1872. Once a week, from April to August, one of the 'Brothers' guides visitors around the cobbled compound they call home. The oldest resident is 102.

Behind the 15th century gateway, there's no trace of the place's sinister past and little evidence of modernity - although visitors are required to watch a dated 15-minute video seated on antique leather chairs. Despite damage during the Blitz, the buildings are marvellously preserved, with quaint names like Master's Court, Preacher's Court (air raid shelters under the mulberry trees), and Washhouse Court.

Tables are laid for afternoon tea in the Great Hall, where 80 knights were once dubbed by King James I, overlooked by portraits of dashing aristocrats with Bee Gees hairdos. The chapel is open to the public on Sundays – if you can get past the guard at the front gate. Look out for Sutton's tomb and the carved dog heads that decorate the pews. 'They've optimistically provided a font for baptisms,' laughs our guide, Peter. 'Presumably it's for grandchildren!'

Charterhouse makes a handsome income by renting flats and offices in a separate building. But the waiting list for the affordable accommodation is very long indeed.

WILLIAM·DRAKE
OST HIS LIFE IN AVERTING A
ERIOUS ACCIDENT TO A LADY
IN HYDE·PARK
APRIL·2·1869
HOSE HORSES WERE UNMANAGE-
ABLE THROUGH THE BREAKING
OF THE CARRIAGE POLE

DWARD BLAKE·
OWNED WHILE SKATING
THE WELSH HARP
WATERS·HENDON
THE ATTEMPT TO
CUE TWO UNKNOWN
LS FEB·5·1895

WATTS' MEMORIAL

❽

Postman's Park, King Edward Street, EC1
Open during daylight hours
Transport St Paul's or Chancery Lane tube

*Memorials
to everyday
heroes*

Thrillingly gruesome or wistfully sad depending on your point of view, this strange series of memorials lines one side of Postman's Park, named after the General Post Office on its southern boundary. Set up by G.F. Watts in 1900 to mark Queen Victoria's Jubilee, the plaques memorialise acts of fatal heroism by anonymous Londoners. In an era characterised by public euphemism - a common epitaph of the time was 'fell asleep' – the description of the fates of those commemorated are surprisingly forthright. Most of these tragic tales involve children, fires, drowning, or train accidents. Touchingly, most of those remembered died trying to save the lives of complete strangers.

Watts erected 13 tablets; his wife Mary added a further 34 after his death. The first local hero immortalised was Alice Ayres: *'Daughter of a bricklayer's labourer, who by intrepid conduct saved three children from a burning house in Union Street, Borough, at the cost of her own young life. April 24, 1885.'*

Then there is Frederick Alfred Croft, who *'saved a lunatic woman from suicide at Woolwich Station, but was himself run over by a train.'*

And Sarah Smith: *'Pantomime artiste. At Prince's Theatre died of terrible injuries received when attempting in her inflammable dress to extinguish the flames which had enveloped her companion. January 24 1863.'*

The thought, or hope, of the kindness of strangers is deeply romantic, and to see it rendered on the homely ceramic tiles of Watts' Memorial is pleasing. Watts hoped to see similar memorials erected in every town in England. Ever the optimist, he left lots of space on the walls of the park so people could continue to put up tablets. But the spaces remain unfilled.

'ENGLAND'S MICHELANGELO'

Watts, a noted Victorian painter dubbed 'England's Michelangelo,' was outspokenly socialist. He declared in a letter to *The Times* of London that 'the national prosperity of a Nation is not an abiding possession, the deeds of its people are.' This progressive ideology was the inspiration for his memorial.

The glazed tiles, bearing decorative motifs reminiscent of William Morris, were made at the famous Doulton factory, still in operation today.

POLICE CALL BOX
St Martin Le Grand, EC1

❾

> **Kiosks for coppers**

The BBC's perennially popular hero, Doctor Who, journeys through space and time in his TARDIS, a time machine that looks like a blue telephone box. The Tardis has now entered British parlance as a synonym for something that appears deceptively small, but contains hidden depths. A few of these mysterious blue boxes have survived on the streets of London, like this disused signal post outside Postman's Park (see page 79).

Before the advent of the walkie-talkie and the mobile phone, British 'bobbies' on the beat relied on these police boxes to report crimes, request back-up, or even to lock up a suspect until a patrol car arrived. If the blue light on the roof was flashing, passing officers would pop in to call the nearest station then hotfoot it to the crime scene. The phones also served as emergency hotlines for the public. The first wooden police boxes appeared in Britain in 1888. They cost a trifling £13 to build and were equipped with a desk, log book, first aid kit, fire extinguisher and electric heater. No doubt they also contained a kettle in case coppers wanted a cuppa. In 1929, Gilbert Mackenzie Trench devised a sturdier concrete design. With sirens replacing the flashing lights, they doubled as air raid warning signals during World War II. By 1953, there were 685 police boxes in London; but technology soon rendered them obsolete and in 1969 the Home Secretary ordered their removal.

Very few police posts have survived in London, most of them in the City. You can locate them on Victoria Embankment (opposite Middle Temple Lane), at the corner of Queen Victoria and Friday Street, on Walbrook (opposite Bucklersbury), in Guildhall Yard, outside St Botolph Church in Aldgate, outside Liverpool Street station, and on Aldersgate Street near Little Britain. Look out for other survivors on Piccadilly Circus and outside the US Embassy on Grosvenor Square. Ironically, the latter is not locked and is still in working order, despite the heavy 24-hour police presence.

In 1996, a brand new police box appeared on Earl's Court Road, outside the tube station. In keeping with the Metropolitan Police's obsession with surveillance, it was fitted with a CCTV camera, allegedly to scare off prank callers. Plans to distribute similar boxes throughout London were abandoned. Perhaps it was no coincidence that this box materialised soon after the BBC attempted to copyright the Tardis for merchandising purposes.

WHEN Y HAVE SOVGHT
THE CITTY ROVND
YET STILL THIS IS
THE HIGHE GROVND
AVGVST THE 27
1688

THE BREAD BASKET BOY ❿

Panyer Alley, EC4

An enigmatic statue

Smokers huddled outside Café Nero and commuters dashing in and out of St Paul's tube station are oblivious to the naked boy perched on a bread basket who watches over them, proffering what appears to be a bunch of grapes. Beneath this little stone relief is a weathered inscription: 'When ye have sought the citty round yet still this is the highest ground. August the 27, 1688.' This couplet does not make much sense in reference to its current location, a decidedly flat passage running between the tube station and St Paul's churchyard; however, the statue originally stood in Paternoster Row. When the building on which he sat was demolished in 1892, the boy was moved to Farrows Bank on Cheapside as its mascot. The baker boy's luck must have run out, because the bank folded in 1930. In 1964, the statue was moved to this innocuous alley, which was once the centre of London's baking business. Panyer Alley was named after the boys who sold their wares from baskets, or panniers, after a law was passed in the 14th century forbidding the sale of bread in bakers' houses; it could only be sold in the king's markets. Bakers bypassed the law by selling loaves in baskets on the streets. As commuters rush past, croissants in hand, they should spare a thought for the bread peddlers of bygone years.

SIGHTS NEARBY

CHRISTCHURCH GREYFRIARS GARDEN ⓫

Built on a Wren church
Newgate Street & King Edward Street, EC1

A stone's throw from St Paul's cathedral, this peculiar little rose garden is contained within the bombed-out walls of a derelict church. This was the site of a Franciscan monastery in the Middle Ages, whose monks were so devout that folk believed that anyone buried in their grey robes would go straight to heaven. Perhaps that is why four queens chose to be buried in the church, before it burned down in the Great Fire. Christopher Wren soon set to work on a new church, which was completed in 1704. But German bombs destroyed Wren's handiwork in 1940, leaving only the west tower standing. This small rose garden matches the floor plan of Wren's church. On either side of the central aisle are hedges and flowerbeds where the pews once stood; the ten wooden towers covered with climbing roses and clematis represent the pillars which held up the roof.

The garden is said to be haunted by the ghost of Queen Isabella, the ruthless French princess who allegedly murdered her bisexual husband, King Edward II, by sticking a red hot poker up his bum. Avoid visiting after dark.

ST PAUL'S TRIFORIUM   🕛

St Paul's Cathedral, Ludgate Hill, EC4
0207 246 8357
www.stpauls.co.uk
Open Mon, Tues 11.30am and 2pm, Fri 2pm
Other times by prior arrangement; Booking essential
Admission £14 including entry to the church and crypt
Transport St Paul's tube

> *Secret
> history of a
> London landmark*

St Paul's is hardly a London secret; however, the triforium of the cathedral is relatively unknown to the public. A triforium is a shallow gallery of arches between the inner and outer wall of a church, which stands above the nave. Effectively, it is a secret passage running the length of a wall, high above the congregation, although in English churches triforia are traditionally visible through galleries. The effect is like being backstage in a theatre. Some old furnishings and props from the cathedral are stored in the triforium, including two old pulpits, one a Victorian monstrosity of coloured marble that looks like it was looted from an Italian church. The galleries are linked by a passageway across the western entrance to the cathedral, which affords incredible views down the length of the nave. There's also a row of electric trumpets, installed for Royal visits. However, this one apparently sounds like the opening of the gates of hell, so when the Queen visits a more discreet fanfare of live trumpeters herald her arrival from the balcony.

The glory of the triforium lies in two rooms on either side of the church. One is the library, a real bibliophile's fantasy – wood-lined, comfortable, quiet, and with a gallery carved by master woodcarver Grinling Gibbons. The other is known as the Trophy Room: Nelson's prizes were displayed here after his death. Now it houses an extraordinary collection relating to the cathedral's construction, including Wren's Great Model, an earlier design based on a Greek cross with an extra dome.

Other treasures are plentiful: parts of the old cathedral that was destroyed by fire in 1666, and a bust of Dean Inge, a melancholy clergyman apparently given to reading detective novels during service. The Geometric Staircase inside the great clock tower that leads up to the triforium is also astonishing. Each step is supported only by its predecessor and a four-inch join with the wall, which accounts for its nickname - the Flying Staircase.

Influenced by the Baroque, Wren's original plan for St Paul's was far more European. However, it looked a little too Papal to London's puritanical Church Commissioners, and Wren was forced to redraw the cathedral along more conventional lines. Several drafts and models line the Trophy Room, including the 'Pineapple', which would have given London a very early version of the Swiss Re building, better known as Norman Foster's 'gherkin'.

NEWGATE CELLS ⓭

Beneath the *Viaduct Tavern*, 126 Newgate Street, EC1
www.pubs.com/viadec1.htm
Open during the week at pub hours
Admission free
Transport St Paul's tube or City Thameslink rail

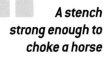

A stench strong enough to choke a horse

In the 19th century, London society was obsessed with imprisonment and punishment. Capital crimes included impersonating an Egyptian (a gypsy), stealing an heiress, or poaching a rabbit. As a result, punishment centres flourished. Tate Britain is built on the site of Millbank prison, which was eventually closed because the inmates tiresomely persisted in dying.

Little remains of the infamous Newgate prison, the city's main jail for almost five centuries. Originally located by a medieval gate in the Roman London Wall, it was extended over the years, remaining in use between 1188 and 1902. The Central Criminal Courts now stand on the site. However, if you go into the *Viaduct Tavern* and ask nicely, the staff will show you some of the cells that survived the prison's closure, and are now used in part as beer cellars.

The underground cells still look like the real deal. Although the pub owners have hung prints in the passage down to the cells, there is no suggestion of a tourist recreation. One of the cells is a magnet for ghost hunters, but visitors don't need to be psychic to sniff out the misery. The cells are genuinely horrible: bitterly cold, damp and dark, with walls of imposing thickness. Up to twenty criminals - usually debtors - were crammed into each one. There was no toilet; one jailer described the stench as being bad enough to choke a horse. The only daylight comes from a tube leading to street level, used by relatives or sympathetic passers-by to drop down scraps of food. Because prisons were privately run, prisoners had to pay for the privilege of being locked up – or starve to death. Wealthy prisoners could opt for private cells, complete with regular visits from prostitutes.

Even more grisly is the old cell for the condemned across the road at the Old Bailey. This was larger than normal cells, as those waiting to be hanged received more visitors. The corridor leading from the cell to the scaffold is increasingly narrow so the victim couldn't turn around and flee in terror – a frighteningly well-thought-out architectural detail.

> By contrast, the *Viaduct Tavern* is a beautiful Victorian pub, with a wrought copper ceiling and a triptych of oils representing the four statues of Commerce, Agriculture, Science and Fine Arts on nearby Holborn Viaduct. The floor above allegedly housed an opium den in the 19th century.

This Boy is
in Memmory Put up
for the late FIRE of
LONDON
Occasion'd by the
Sin of Gluttony
1666

THE GOLDEN BOY OF PYE CORNER **⑭**
Cock Lane and Giltspur Street, EC1
Transport Chancery Lane or St Paul's tube

> **Glutton who got the rap for the Great Fire**

Igh above the corner of Cock Lane and Giltspur Street is a gilded statue of a fat little boy that marks the limits of the Great Fire of London.

The Golden Boy was erected to put an end to the conflicting theories surrounding the cause of the Great Fire. At first, the Fire was blamed on a deranged French silversmith called Robert Hubert after he made a confession. He was promptly executed, but it was later discovered that he had arrived in the country two days after the fire started. William Lilly, a famous astrologer who predicted a fire the year before, almost went to the scaffold with the unfortunate Hubert, but talked his way out of it in front of a special committee at the House of Commons. The Catholics were the next to get the rap. Eventually, the City elders decided to blame the fire on the sin of gluttony. To make their point, they inscribed their pudgy effigy thus:
'The Boy at Pye Corner was erected to commemorate the staying of the Great Fire which beginning at Pudding Lane was ascribed to the sin of gluttony when not attributed to the Papists as on the Monument, and the Boy was made prodigiously fat to enforce the moral.'

A PUB THAT SELLS CORPSES...
The site of the Golden Boy used to be home to *The Fortunes of War*, a pub favoured by 'resurrection men' who sold corpses to the anatomists at St Bartholomew's hospital over the road. The corpses - fresh from the road, the river, or occasionally the grave - were exhibited in an upstairs room by the landlord, labelled with the finder's name.

EAT SQUIRREL
In February and March, the famously carnivorous St. John restaurant serves a rare and delicate dish: squirrel. Not to be missed, unless you are fond of these furry creatures that populate London's parks.
26 St. John Street EC1, 0207 2510848, www.stjohnrestaurant.co.uk

---

A BUTCHER'S BREAKFAST
Meat on slabs is also displayed in Smithfield, the central butchers' market, 100 metres away. *The Cock Tavern* under the market is ideal for a last drink after a night on the town or indeed a full Butcher's Breakfast (bacon, sausage, black pudding, liver, kidney, steak, with eggs, tomato and chips). But always beware of drunk butchers.

THE ONLY PUBLIC STATUE OF HENRY VIII IN LONDON
Further down the street, another prodigiously fat boy is immortalised in stone. Henry VIII, at his most whale-like, glowers above the Henry Gate entrance to St Bartholomew's Hospital. Topped with a strange little crown and wearing a codpiece that draws the eye, this is the only public statue of Henry VIII in London.

THE FIRST
METROPOLITAN
PUBLIC DRINKING
FOUNTAIN
ERECTED ON
HOLBORN HILL
IN 1859 AND
REMOVED WHEN THE
VIADUCT WAS
CONSTRUCTED IN
1867.

ACE THE

⓯

LONDON'S FIRST DRINKING FOUNTAIN

Corner of Giltspur Street and Holborn Viaduct, EC1
Transport Barbican or Farringdon tube

*"Replace
the cup"*

As well as an execution site for heretics and dissidents, Smithfield Meat Market was once a slaughterhouse. The anxious herds awaiting the butcher's blade were at least granted a drink of water at the cattle trough on West Smithfield. The trough bears the logo of the Metropolitan Drinking Fountain and Cattle Trough Association, "the only agency for providing free supplies of water for man and beast in the streets of London", according to early advertisements. The association was established in 1859 by Samuel Gurney, an M.P. alarmed by the insalubrious quality of London's drinking water after Dr. John Snow (see page 61) had identified it as the source of a cholera outbreak.

Down the road from Smithfield, on the corner of Giltspur Street and Holborn Viaduct, is London's first drinking fountain. It's an inconspicuous red granite memorial to Gurney's philanthropy, set into the railings of St Sepulchre Church. The church was keen to be seen as a patron of the poor – and to provide an antidote to beer. Huge crowds gathered for the fountain's inauguration on 21 April, 1859. Mrs Wilson, daughter of the Archbishop of Canterbury, was the first to taste the water from a silver cup. The filtered water came from the New River (see page 289). The inscription urges thirsty passers-by to "REPLACE THE CUP". Today, in less trusting times, the two original (somewhat mildewed) metal mugs are fastened to the railings with chains. By 1870, the Drinking Fountain Association had installed 140 fountains in London. Many of them have also survived.

The Geffrye Museum (see page 133) contains an impression of the original fountain, which was more elaborate, painted by W.A. Atkinson in 1860.

MINIATURE BLUECOATS

On the corner of Hatton Garden and St Cross Street, embedded into the façade of an office building, stand the twee statuettes of a boy holding a cap and Bible and a girl who seems to be clutching a shopping list.

These figurines, which are found across London, signal that this was once a charitable "blewcoat" school for underprivileged girls and boys. In Tudor and Stuart times, blue clothes were the mark of the lower classes as blue was the cheapest dye available.

This school, dating from 1690, was probably designed by Christopher Wren. The 18th century figurines were stowed away in Berkshire for safe-keeping during the Blitz – a wise move, as the building was damaged by bombs.

THE EXECUTIONER'S BELL
OF ST SEPULCHRE-WITHOUT-NEWGATE

⓰

Holborn Viaduct, opposite the Old Bailey.
Open Tues & Thurs 12pm-2pm, Wed 11am-3pm
Transport Farringdon or Blackfriars tube

*For whom
the death bell tolls*

S t Sepulchre church is one of the 'Cockney bells' of London, named in the nursery rhyme Oranges and Lemons as the 'bells of Old Bailey' because it stands across from the Central Criminal Court, better known as the Old Bailey. The latter was formerly the site of the infamous Newgate prison, thankfully demolished in 1902.

This rather plain church was rebuilt after the Great Fire, but subsequently butchered by the Victorians. The odd name refers to the church's position outside the former city walls, specifically at Newgate, which was the north-western entrance to the City.

The area between the prison and church was used as London's execution ground after public executions diminished in the late 19th century. In the 18th century, London law was exceptionally bloody - over 350 crimes were punishable by death, including minor theft, but by 1861 only treason, piracy, mutiny and murder were capital offences. Charles Dickens witnessed an execution at St Sepulchre, though what he seems to have remembered best was the sight of his great rival William Thackeray looking green as the criminal was hanged. The tenor bell at St Sepulchre-without-Newgate was rung whenever there was an impending execution. The hand-held 'execution bell,' still in the church, was also rung at midnight by a clerk who would repeat the following verse three times as he paced outside the condemned cells:

All you that in the condemned hold do lie / Prepare you, for tomorrow you will die. / Watch all, and pray, the hour is drawing near / That you before th' Almighty must appear. / Examine well yourselves, in time repent, / That you may not t' eternal flames be sent; / And when St Sepulchre's bell tomorrow tolls, / The Lord have mercy on your souls!

A revoltingly pious cloth merchant named Robert Dove gave £40 to the parish in 1604 to ensure that this gruesome ritual was performed in perpetuity.

OLD BAILEY FLOWER RITUAL

Trials at the Old Bailey are open to the public, but you cannot reserve a seat. Queuing for the public gallery starts at about 9.30 am. A list of trials is published outside the main gate; Court One is generally where the most notorious trials are set. One tradition that has survived since the Old Bailey was located in the grounds of Newgate prison is that the judges carry a bunch of flowers at the start of each session, a practice initiated as a feeble attempt to mask the stench from the cells.

DR JOHNSON'S HOUSE ⑰

17 Gough Square, EC4
0207 353 3745
www.drjohnsonshouse.org
Open Mon-Sat 11am-5.30pm (5pm in winter) **Admission** Adults £4.50,
senior citizens & students £3.50, children £1.50, family ticket £10.00
Transport Blackfriars, Temple, Holborn or Chancery Lane tube

> *"You find no man, at all intellectual, who is willing to leave London"*

London loves Dr Johnson – it's hard not to be seduced by a man who said: 'You find no man, at all intellectual, who is willing to leave London. No, Sir, when a man is tired of London, he is tired of life; for there is in London all that life can afford'. This confirmation of their superiority makes Londoners simper.

Like most people living in London, 'Dictionary' Johnson wasn't a native; he was from the Midlands city of Lichfield and arrived in London in 1737 aged 28, after a disastrous career as a schoolteacher. He scraped a living for the next thirty years writing biographies, poetry, essays, pamphlets and parliamentary reports, and most famously his dictionary. So he lived at a number of addresses until finally moving into this house in Gough Square in 1748, where he remained until 1759.

Johnson's house is a little hard to find among the surrounding maze of courtyards and passages. The house itself is remarkable as one of the few remnants of Georgian London left in the City. Built in 1700, it fell into disarray and was used variously as a hotel, a print shop, and a storehouse, until it was eventually acquired in 1911 by MP Cecil Harmsworth, who restored and opened it to the public. The lovely, delicate interior is characteristic of the era, with panelled rooms and a collection of period furniture, prints and portraits. Children can try on the replica Georgian costumes in the garret to see how they would have looked as 18th century Londoners.

As well as occasional temporary exhibitions and lectures, the museum stages events (www.drjohnsonshouse.org/events.htm) that highlight the house's associations with other parts of London, and may include walking tours or the opportunity to explore buildings generally closed to the public.

JOHN WILKES STATUE

Johnson didn't choose this house by accident. It lies very close to Fetter Lane and Fleet Street, historically a hotbed of scurrilous and pithy journalism. On Fetter Lane, look out for the statue of Johnson's friend John Wilkes, an incendiary journalist who was famously hideous. (The statue flatters him greatly.) Wilkes' writing made him many enemies in the monarchy and government, yet thanks to popular support he was largely able to resist imprisonment. His statue, like Cromwell's outside Parliament, is something of a totem for the area.

MAGPIE ALLEY CRYPT 🔞

Between Bouverie Street and Whitefriars Street, EC4
Transport Blackfriars tube

> *Relics of a medieval monastery*

Back in the 13th century, the Carmelite order of the White Friars – so called because they wore white cloaks over their drab brown habits on special occasions – owned a swathe of land that contained cloisters, a church, and cemetery and stretched all the way from Fleet Street to the Thames. All that remains is this crumbling crypt from the late 14th century, now trapped behind glass and hemmed in by the dark granite fortress of a multinational law firm.

Whitefriars Monastery was one of the few buildings that survived the 1381 Peasants Revolt unscathed. However, Henry VIII pulled the plug on the priory in the mid 16th century and appropriated most of the monks' property for his doctor, William Butte. The Great Hall was converted into the Whitefriars Playhouse, a theatre for child actors, and the crypt was used a coal cellar. The area soon degenerated into a seedy slum, nicknamed 'Alsatia' after Alsace, the territory disputed by France and Germany. Outlaws on the run sought refuge in the monastic crypt, exploiting the legal immunity once enjoyed by the friars.

The crypt lay buried for centuries until it was unearthed in 1895, but it was not restored until the 1920s when The *News of the World* moved in. The *Daily News, Punch, News Chronicle, Daily Mirror,* and *The Sun* all once had their offices in Bouverie Street. Just as little trace of the publishing industry remains, there is no sign to alert visitors to the crypt's existence. Walk down Bouverie Street and turn into Magpie Alley (where the monks' dormitories once stood). At the end of the alley is a courtyard; go down two flights of stairs on the left to the basement where you will find the crypt. A fake lantern burns in the doorway day and night.

MAGPIE ALLEY MURALS

Printed onto the white tiles of Magpie Alley, a series of black and white photographs, illustrations, and captions tell the potted history of Fleet Street's publishers. From Wynkyn de Worde's first primitive printing press, set up around 1500, to the grubby tabloid newsrooms of the 1960s, Fleet Street was synonymous with the newspaper industry until the acrimonious exodus to Wapping in 1986. Beaming paper boys on bicycles, bearing posters of the day's headlines – 'Burglars with dynamite in Holborn!' – seem far more sophisticated than the hawkers thrusting free trash at today's harried commuters.

'Brilliantly the Temple Fountain sparkled in the sun, and laughingly its liquid music played and merrily the idle drops of water danced and danced, and peeping out in sport among the trees, plunged lightly down to hide themselves'

Martin Chuzzlewit
Charles Dickens

FOUNTAIN COURT ⑲
Middle Temple, EC4
Transport Chancery Lane or Temple tube

> *Literary oasis in a legal maze*

Fountain Court is a beautiful tree-shaded spot to rest after exploring the City. This hidden square is in the Middle Temple, part of the labyrinthine legal district known as the Inns of Court, which were set up on the remains of properties belonging to the Knights Templar in the 14th century. There has been a small fountain here for around three hundred years. Once surrounded by railings, the fountain now stands free. A single jet of water rises some ten feet, dropping into a basin full of goldfish. The courtyard's name may also derive from one Sir Edward de la Fontaigne, who owned a house in the Temple.

The large Gothic building at the edge of the court is Middle Temple Hall, where Shakespeare's acting troupe, the Chamberlain's Men, gave the first recorded performance of *Twelfth Night* in 1602, with Shakespeare himself in the cast.

LITERARY LANDMARK
Fountain Court turns up regularly in connection with literary London. Charles Dickens uses it in *Martin Chuzzlewit* as the meeting-place between Ruth Pinch and her lover. Irish playwright Oliver Goldsmith lived close by, at No. 2 Garden Court, in a house that has long since disappeared. And Paul Verlaine stayed here while he was giving lectures in England after his release from prison in Belgium.

SIGHTS NEARBY
ST BRIDES' CHURCH ⑳

St Brides' church has historically served as the journalists' church, thanks to its proximity to Fleet Street. Its multi-tiered steeple is also said to be the inspiration for the modern wedding cake, after a local cake-maker, Thomas Rich, created a replica in icing. Literary parishioners of St Brides include John Milton, Dr. Johnson and Samuel Pepys, London's most famous diarist.

PRINCE HENRY'S ROOM ㉑
Pepys was born in Fleet Street in 1633. A small but fascinating collection of manuscripts, prints, and paintings dedicated to Pepys is on display at No. 17 Fleet Street. This half-timbered house is one of the few buildings in London that survived the Great Fire. It looks like an ordinary office building, but the collection is housed in a wood-panelled room with stained glass windows and a wonderful Jacobean ceiling on the first floor. Confusingly called Prince Henry's Room, because the design features his initials and coat of arms, it may have been used by the Prince as a Council Chamber.

THE RELIC OF ST ETHELDREDA ㉒

St Etheldreda's Church, 14 Ely Place, EC1
0207 405 1061
www.stetheldreda.com
Open Mon-Fri 7.45am-7pm **Admission** free
Transport Chancery Lane or Farringdon tube

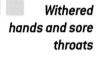

Withered hands and sore throats

“To the public it is one of those unsatisfactory streets which lead nowhere; to the inhabitants it is quiet and pleasant; to the student of Old London it is possessed of all the charms which can be given by five centuries of change and the long residence of the great and noble." Thus wrote George Walter Thornbury of Ely Place in 1878.

Today, Ely Place remains a fascinating little cul-de-sac, guarded by a formidable gate and miniature lodge for the beadles who once patrolled the street. Every hour, beadles in top hats and greatcoats would cry out the time and a weather report to the fortunate inhabitants of the grand Georgian townhouses.

Tucked between them is St Etheldreda's, the oldest Roman Catholic church in England. Built in 1250, this is the last vestige of the palace of the bishops of Ely, whose 58 acres of orchards, vineyards and lawns stretched down to the Thames. Administered by the See of Ely, 100 miles away in Cambridgeshire, the estate was beyond the jurisdiction of the City of London – and thus much favoured by criminals on the run.

Inside the small, Gothic, and rather gloomy church, among the martyrs of the Reformation, is a creepy relic of its patron, St Etheldreda. A fragment of her pale white hand, donated to the church in the 19th century, is kept in a bejewelled chest to the right of the altar. Removed in Norman times, her hand was hidden during the persecution of Catholics on the Duke of Norfolk's estate. Requests to view this peculiar relic are welcome.

The tasty strawberries from St Etheldreda's garden are mentioned in Shakespeare's Richard III.

THE BLESSING OF SORE THROATS

As well as patron saint of chastity (she died a virgin, despite being married twice), Etheldreda is believed to cure sore throats. She died of the plague in 679, blaming the tumour on her neck on her sinful fondness for fancy necklaces. In February, on the day of St Blaise (apparently, he was sainted for saving a child from choking to death on a fishbone), people with throat and neck infections flock to St Etheldreda to be anointed with two lit candles that are tied together.

Henry VIII and his first wife Catherine of Aragon binged at a five-day feast in the crypt of St Etheldreda in 1531.

THE CHERRY TREE AT THE MITRE TAVERN ㉓

Ye Olde Mitre, Ely Court (between Hatton Garden and Ely Place), EC1
Open Mon-Fri 11am-11pm
Transport Chancery Lane or Farringdon tube

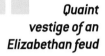

> *Quaint
> vestige of an
> Elizabethan feud*

J ust off Hatton Garden, London's gemstone centre, is Ely Court, where *Ye Olde Mitre* is hidden. The pub's largely intact 18th century interior is split into three small rooms downstairs, one of which, known as Ye Closet, is large enough to hold a table surrounded by benches and nothing more. Best of all, there is no piped music or fruit machines, a far rarer thing in London pubs than might be imagined.

Inside a glass case in the front bar is the preserved remains of a cherry tree trunk – the land on which the pub was built was originally part of the garden of Ely Palace, property of the Bishop of Ely (see page 101 St Etheldreda). In 1576, Elizabeth I's favourite, Christopher Hatton, finagled his way into possession of the site, with the connivance of the queen and against the wishes of the bishop. The cherry tree marked the dividing line where, like two teenagers sharing a bedroom, the two men split the garden. Legend has it that the queen danced the maypole around the tree, but this smells of Merrie England wishful thinking.

Other notable pub interiors nearby include the *Jerusalem Tavern* on Britton Street, a former watchmaker's shop dating from 1720 that looks like a Georgian coffee house, and *The Black Friar* on Queen Victoria Street. The latter's marble and copper interior is decorated with bas-reliefs of jolly monks, and there's a barrel-vaulted snug lined with mottoes such as "Finery is Foolery" and "Wisdom is Rare", presumably there for the pleasure of more lugubrious drinkers.

LONDON'S WORST STATUES?

Ely Place faces Holborn Viaduct, a Victorian bridge whose parapets are adorned with statues representing Commerce, Agriculture, Science and Fine Arts. At the north-west corner, above the steps down to Farringdon Street, is one of London's least flattering statues of public figures: Sir William Walworth, killer of Wat Tyler, depicted with teeny-weeny legs.

Competition in the ugly statue stakes includes the British Library's bust of Anne Frank, rendered rather like an arthritic gnome; the library, to its credit, displays it in a dark corner near the cloakroom.

A recent addition to this ignominious list is Paul Day's *The Meeting Place* at St Pancras station, one of London's most beautiful public spaces. Featuring two reunited lovers embracing, this 30 foot bronze looks like an aesthetic hybrid of Stalin and Barbara Cartland.

SECRETS OF ST BARTHOLOMEW'S THE GREATER

㉔

Cloth Fair, EC1
Tel 0207 606 5171
www.greatstbarts.com
Open Tues-Fri 8.30am-5pm (4pm mid-Nov-mid-Feb); 10.30am-1.30pm Sat
8.30am-1pm and 2.30pm- 8pm Sun
Transport Farringdon or St Paul's tube

*Bad puns,
briny floods*

Very little of early medieval London remains intact today, because Londoners, like the unwise Little Pig, built houses of wood, and the city burned down in 1077, 1087, 1132, 1136, 1203, 1212, 1220 and 1227. Almost anything left intact from these was destroyed in the Great Fire of 1666. This church is a rare survivor, despite having suffered from Zeppelin bombing in World War I and the Blitz in World War II. It was also occupied by squatters in the 18th century. The Lady Chapel was used as a commercial property; Benjamin Franklin served a year there as a journeyman printer.

Inside, the crossing and choir are mostly Norman, with round arching and massive decorated pillars; these muffle sound and light, creating a grey, crepuscular atmosphere. Notable features include the tomb of Rahere, founder of the church. Opposite this is an oriel window into an oratory, or semi-private chapel, for a wealthy Prior named Bolton. The window is decorated with Bolton's rebus, a visual pun depicting the symbol of a barrel pierced by an arrow (a bolt plus a tun, meaning barrel). There's also the bust of Edward Cooke made of 'weeping marble'. This used to cry if the weather was wet enough; nowadays, unfortunately, central heating has dried out the stone. The inscription beneath the statue still exhorts visitors to *'unsluice your briny floods'*.

Bart's remains connected to the hospital across the street that was founded at the same time; within the hospital is a smaller church, called (naturally) Bartholomew the Lesser. There is also a small museum open Tuesday to Friday, 10am-4pm (call in advance 0207 601 8152) whose crowning glory is a very unusual pair of large murals by William Hogarth depicting the Good Samaritan and the Christ at the pool of Bethesda. Hogarth allegedly painted them for free in order to prevent an Italian getting his hands on the job.

The church has historic links with the 'Worshipful Companies' of London. These include traditional professions such as The Haberdashers' Company, The Butchers' Company (the church serves nearby Smithfield, London's meat market) and The Fletchers' Company, a guild for arrow makers, as well as modern ones like the Information Technologists' Company, the Tax Advisors' Company, and the Guild of Public Relations Practitioners.

LONDON SILVER VAULTS ㉕

53–64 Chancery Lane, WC2
0207 242 3844
www.thesilvervaults.com
Open Mon- Fri 9am - 5.30pm Sat 9am - 1pm
Admission free
Transport Chancery lane tube

> *Subterranean shrine to silverware*

Containing the world's largest retail collection of antique silver, London's silver vaults are located three floors underground, below a non-descript office block. It's an improbable setting for a glittering arcade of over 40 shops, their dazzling wares crammed into converted safety deposit boxes. Originally known as the Chancery Lane Safe Deposit, this subterranean store-house opened in 1876 as a place where wealthy Londoners could safeguard their valuables. Impressed by the tight security, the silver dealers and jewellers of nearby Hatton Garden, the centre of London's diamond trade, began using the strong rooms to stash their precious goods overnight. Before long, it evolved into a kind of discount outlet, where bargain hunters could buy direct from dealers at wholesale prices.

Today, it's more like a museum than a shopping mall. The shops still have the original walls reinforced with steel. Dealers trade in all manner of silverware from candlesticks to cutlery, pepper pots to place-card holders, watches to wine goblets. Many a royal banquet has been served on a silver service purchased from these vaults. Don't worry about buying a fake. According to a 14th century law, all silver items over 7.78 g must be hallmarked before sale to verify their purity. In those days, forgers were hanged; today, they face a spell in jail.

Although the building upstairs was bombed during World War II, there was no damage below ground. The original front door also remains intact; almost a metre thick, it's a heavy-duty deterrent for thieves. So far, no heist has even been attempted.

SIGHTS NEARBY

FREE LECTURES AT GRESHAM COLLEGE ㉖

Barnard's Inn Hall, Holborn EC1
0207 831 0575
www.gresham.ac.uk

Founded in 1597, Gresham College moved to these Tudor premises, featured in Dickens' *Great Expectations*, in 1991. Tucked away down an alleyway in the Inns of Court, the college provides free public lectures on eight subjects: Commerce, Astronomy, Divinity, Geometry, Law, Music, Physics, and Rhetoric. Topics range from the search for extra-terrestrial intelligence to sustainable business models, computer viruses to classical composers. There are occasional free chamber music recitals in a medieval hall overlooking a secret courtyard.

CANDLELIT TOURS OF SIR JOHN SOANE'S MUSEUM

㉗

12-13 Lincoln's Inn Fields, WC2
0207 405 2107
www.soane.org
Open Tues—Sat 10am—5pm. Candlelit tours 6-9pm
on the first Tuesday of every month
Admission free • **Transport** Holborn tube

> *Candlelit tours of an eccentric art collection*

Over a twenty-two year period, from 1792 to 1824, Sir John Soane demolished and rebuilt three houses on the north side of Lincoln's Inn Fields to house his enormous collection of classical art and architectural artefacts.

After the death of his wife in 1815, Soane lived alone amidst the collection, constantly adding to and rearranging it. Disappointed by his two sons, who failed to follow in his professional footsteps, Soane established a museum to which 'amateurs and students' should have access. In 1833, he negotiated an Act of Parliament to preserve his house and its contents for the nation.

Soane's vast and varied collection reflects a magpie or hoarder's mentality; but the overall effect is intensely personal and visually rich. Highlights include the sarcophagus of Seti I, one of the finest Egyptian pieces outside Egypt, three Canalettos, and two series of brilliant, cartoonish paintings (*A Rake's Progress* and *An Election*) by Hogarth, the great, unregarded genius of British art. There are collections of watches and clocks, furniture, stained glass, architectural drawings, models of antique monuments and Soane's own buildings, as well as a large stockpile of gems. The museum also mounts exhibitions, usually related to Soane or his contemporaries.

Although certainly less of a tourist attraction than the British Museum and the crowded museums in South Kensington, the museum is hardly a secret to Londoners. But few people know that on the first Tuesday of every month, the house stays open until 9pm and is entirely lit by candles. The over-populated collection retreats into shadow, creating a fantastically gothic atmosphere.

> A bricklayer's son, Soane (1753-1837) rose to become one of the foremost architects of his day. His more notable buildings include the Dulwich Picture Gallery and the Bank of England. Some of his designs remained unbuilt - a great pity as they were often wildly eccentric, such as the proposed piazza across the Thames, supported by hundreds of columns, which would have blocked most river traffic.

SIGHTS NEARBY

THE OCTOBER GALLERY

㉘

(www.octobergallery.co.uk) at 24 Old Gloucester Street showcases an equally eclectic mix of contemporary art from every continent. Much more than a gallery, this intimate arts space also hosts readings, screenings, lectures, and dance. The secret courtyard café is a great spot for lunch.

KINGSWAY TRAM SUBWAY
Southampton Row WC2

29

*Tracks
from the past*

If you are brave enough to dodge the traffic roaring down Kingsway, in the middle of Southampton Row, just beyond Holborn tube station, is a ramp leading to a disused tunnel. This is one of the last vestiges of London's tram network, which criss-crossed the city until the early 1950s.

The gates to the tunnel are now permanently locked, but if you peek through the railings you can see the old tram tracks running along the cobblestones. Between the tracks, you can just make out the underground electricity cable that powered the trams along this route from Angel to Aldwych. It took just ten minutes to make the journey from Islington to Waterloo Bridge – an enviable record by today's standards.

Built in 1906, the two-way tunnel originally passed though a subterranean station at Holborn, and then down the length of Kingsway to another tram stop at Aldwych, before surfacing by Waterloo Bridge. The subway was part of a grand urban regeneration scheme, intended to clean up the slums to the east of the Strand and to create a commercial hub on Kingsway, London's widest boulevard at the time. Named in honour of King Edward VII, Kingsway embodied the modern face of London. In the early 1930s, the tunnel was extended to accommodate the new double-decker trams, which proved to be a huge hit with the public. But the advent of the automobile soon put paid to the popularity of the tram. In the early 1950s, the tram network was dismantled. The last tram clattered through Kingsway on July 5, 1952.

In 1964, part of the tunnel was converted into the Strand underpass to ease traffic congestion. The rest of the tunnel was used as a flood control centre in the 1970s, but this was closed down in 1984 when the Thames Barrier opened (see page 255). The derelict Kingsway subway is now used to store old street signs and traffic cones. Although attempts to convert it into a film studio were rejected on safety grounds, the tunnel has featured in several movies, including *Bhowani Junction* (1955) and *The Avengers* (1998). It was put to most imaginative use in 2004 by a group of art students from Central St Martin's, who staged an exhibition called 'Thought-Crime,' inspired by George Orwell's 1984, in this spooky subterranean setting. Ironically, London's authorities are now planning to reinstate a tram network in the capital to relieve its chronic congestion problem. Whether the Kingsway subway will be revived remains to be seen.

P1521

HUNTERIAN MUSEUM ③⓪

Royal College of Surgeons, 35-43 Lincoln's Inn Fields, WC2
0207 405 3474
www.rcseng.ac.uk/museums
Open Tues-Sat 10am-5pm
Admission free
Transport Holborn or Temple tube

> *Frankenstein's torture chamber*

O riginally part of the medieval Guild of Barber-Surgeons, the Royal College of Surgeons houses two museums: the Wellcome Museum (only open to medical practitioners and students), and the Hunterian, based on the eminent 18th century surgeon John Hunter's gruesome collection of comparative anatomy and pathology specimens.

Hunter started out as an assistant in the anatomy school of his elder brother, William. A fast learner with a knack for the dissection of the dead, John Hunter developed new treatments for common ailments such as gunshot wounds and venereal disease. An avid collector, he moved to a large house in Leicester Square in 1783, where he organised his collection into a museum. (There is still a statue of him in the square). A notorious curmudgeon, Hunter became the leading teacher of surgery of his time. Success did not mellow him: he died in 1793 after suffering a fit during an argument.

His collection was then bought by the government in 1799, and became part of the Museum of the Royal College of Surgeons when it opened in 1813. By the end of the 19th century, the museum comprised some 65,000 specimens covering anatomy and pathology, zoology, palaeontology, archaeology and anthropology. Today, the museum contains skeletons, bones, skulls and teeth; alarming wax teaching models; historic surgical and dental instruments; paintings, drawings, and sculpture. Rows of random 'things' in glass jars lend the place the atmosphere of a Frankenstein movie.

THE SKELETON OF A 7'7" GIANT

In the 18th century, surgeons were widely regarded as butchers and the museum still has one foot in the seamier past of the anatomy trade. One of the centrepieces of Hunter's collection is the skeleton of Charles O'Brien, an Irish giant who stood at 7'7" and caused a sensation at fairs and fetes nationwide. When O'Brien fell ill in 1782, Hunter haunted his sickbed. Knowing his body would be a great prize for the anatomist, O'Brien gave strict instructions that his corpse should be sealed in a lead coffin and paid some fishermen to bury him at sea. Hunter was not to be thwarted. After O'Brien's death, he paid the fishermen £500 for the corpse, which was then boiled in a copper vat so that only the bones remained. They are on display in the museum.

ROMAN BATH　㉛

5 Strand Lane, WC2
To arrange a visit of the interior, call 0208 232 5050
or email romanbath@nationaltrust.org.uk
Admission free
Transport Temple tube

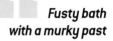

*Fusty bath
with a murky past*

Strand Lane allegedly follows a stream that once ran from Drury Lane to the Thames. Today, it is a dingy cul-de-sac littered with rubbish bins, wedged among the grand old buildings of Victoria Embankment. (Alternative access from Surrey Steps is closed for construction works.) Ignore the notice that warns 'Private Property Keep Off'; half way up the alley you will find a street sign confirming that this is, indeed, Strand Lane. At the end, on your right, is a so-called 'Roman' bath that may in fact date from the 18th century. A National Trust plaque describes it as 'one of the archaeological puzzles of London.' Flick on the light switch – indicated by a bulb crudely drawn on the wall – and peer through the window. You can't see much: just a musty plunge pool in a vaulted room although it's possible to arrange a visit of the interior (see above). The bath's history is equally obscure. In 1854, author Charles Knight wrote of an 'Old Roman spring bath' and suggested its healing waters came from the Holy Well of St Clement. In the late 19th century, the current proprietor boasted that it 'is known to be the most pure and healthy bath in London, ensuring every comfort and convenience to those availing themselves of this luxury.' At the time, a spring fed the bath with ten tons of fresh water a day. Charles Dickens subjected David Copperfield to several icy plunges here.

SIGHTS NEARBY

AN ABANDONED UNDERGROUND STATION　㉜

Closed since 1994, the red brick façade of Aldwych Underground on the corner of the Strand and Surrey Street has been turned into a passport photo booth. During the Second World War, the station was used as an air-raid shelter, while the Elgin Marbles and other treasures from the British Museum were stashed away in its tunnels. Today, the abandoned station is often featured in film shoots, from *Patriot Games* to *V for Vendetta*. One platform allegedly serves as a rifle range for the King's College shooting club. Access to the public is denied, but visits can sometimes be arranged through the London Transport Museum (www.ltmuseum.co.uk).

CAMEL BENCHES　㉝

Along Victoria Embankment are benches with front row views of the River Thames that are worth a closer look: each end is decorated with a sculpted camel, complete with a golden tassel around its neck. The decoration probably refers to the short-lived Imperial Camel Corps, formed in 1916 to serve in the Middle East.

MATERIALS LIBRARY

Division of Engineering, King's College London, The Strand, WC2
www.instituteofmaking.org.uk
Open By appointment only. Join the mailing list for details of open
days, events and exhibitions at various venues around London
Admission Free, material donations welcome
Transport Temple or Charing Cross tube

> *Hold the
> world's lightest
> solid*

hat is flesh? If someone were to ask you that question, would you imagine a pork chop or a ripe fig? A bodybuilder or a plastic surgeon? Rubens' nudes or the circumference of your thighs? Investigating the substance of stuff like flesh is the raison d'être of Materials Library, an archive of matter from the abstract (silicon nitride ball bearings, which can smash concrete without a scratch) to the familiar (a colossal slab of silly putty).

This ongoing collection of over 800 remarkable materials is stored in a ramshackle science lab in the basement of King's College London. Zoe Laughlin, one of a curatorial team of three, describes it as "a workshop for the curious that blurs the boundaries between art and science". Designed as much to fire the imagination of artists and designers as to facilitate new production methods for emerging materials, this unique resource encourages tactile interaction. You can weigh up the difference between a set of cubes made from wood, foam, sugar, wax, and metals, whose atomic mass and density determines how heavy they are. You can listen to the music of matter by pinging a collection of tuning forks and hand-bells made from different materials, or examine broken wineglasses, casualties of an experiment to test the sound frequencies at which glass shatters. There are glass cases with hand-holes where would-be dentists and serial killers can practice drilling teeth or sawing bones.

Materials Library also has an amazing selection of prototype materials collected from research labs, such as glass that cleans itself, transparent concrete, and a sliver of aluminium nitride that conducts the heat from your hand to slice through ice as if it were butter. You can hold the world's lightest solid - a translucent blob of Aerogel, designed by NASA to catch stardust, which consists of 99.8% air. Laughlin blasts a small twist of wire with a blow torch and it miraculously morphs into a paper clip; it's made of shape memory alloy, an ingenious material used mainly for keyhole surgery, which returns to its original shape when heated.

From the wonder of modern science to the alchemy of the everyday, Materials Library offers a fresh perspective on the stuff that surrounds us.

THE DEAD HOUSE

35

Strand, WC2
0207 845 4600
www.somersethouse.org.uk
Open guided tours first and third Saturday of the month at 12.15, 13.15, 14.15
and 15.15. On the day from the information desk in the Seamen's Waiting Hall.
Admission free **Transport** Temple, Covent Garden or Embankment tube

*The riddle
of the tombstones*

With its skating rink in winter and jet fountains in summer, the magnificent courtyard of Somerset House throngs with visitors all year round. It's hard to believe it was closed to the public until 2000 and used as a car park for tax inspectors from the Inland Revenue (who still rent offices here). Besides the elegant Courtauld Institute galleries and Admiralty Restaurant, this former palace contains layers of history that are revealed on fortnightly tours of Somerset House's Hidden Spaces.

Little remains of the original Somerset House, built in 1547 by Edward Seymour, Duke of Somerset and self-proclaimed protector of his nephew Edward VI, the under-age heir to Henry VIII. "Uncle Eddy's big job gave him a big head, so now he needed a big house," our American guide informed us. Seymour's ambition led to a sticky end. After his execution in 1552, Somerset House was used by a succession of queens as a venue for glitzy pageants until George III commissioned William Chambers to raze the riverside plot and put up a Palladian office block for government offices and learned societies.

The first tenant was the Navy Board, which stayed for ninety years, leaving a rich collection of nautical art and architectural flourishes such as Nelson's staircase, a cantilevered design that resembles the prow of a ship. Before Joseph Bazalgette built the Thames Embankment (see page 47 York House Watergate), naval officers could access their HQ through an archway on the river and moor in what is now the courtyard. One of their gold and scarlet barges is parked in the basement. Walking along the light well that surrounds Somerset House like a moat, you can see why it's popular for Jack the Ripper shoots. Spookiest of all is the Dead House, a damp, disused vault where five tombstones are inlaid in the walls. One of the deceased appears to be a Portuguese surgeon; another commemorates Father Hyacinth "who died 169½" (presumably this refers to the date, not his age). How and why they ended up there is a mystery. The theory goes that these were Roman Catholics employed by Queen Henrietta Maria, French wife of Charles I. She commissioned Inigo Jones to build her a Catholic chapel on this site in 1630 – the only one in England at the time. The queen also created a small Catholic cemetery in the grounds of Somerset House, where members of her household could be buried. These five tombs are, apparently, all that remain.

Above the arched entrance, Chambers built statues representing the four continents – the fifth had yet to be "discovered" by the British.

PATENT SEWER VENTILATING LAMP   ⊛

Carting Lane, WC2
Transport Charing Cross tube

*The odyssey
of 'Iron Lily'*

N ow powered by conventional household gas, the ornate lamp post opposite the stage door of the Savoy Theatre was originally designed to burn methane waste from the sewage system.

The Patent Sewer Ventilating Lamp was invented by J.E. Webb, an eco-pioneer from Birmingham, who realised that firedamp from London's new-fangled sewage system could be recycled as a cheap source of energy. Equipped with a hollow post to allow slurry from the sewers running beneath the Thames Embankment to shoot up to the flame, the sewage lamp thus fulfilled two important functions: illuminating this scruffy back alley and masking unpleasant odours for residents at the nearby Savoy Hotel. Little did these glamorous guests realise their effluents were being used to cast light on Carting Lane.

Webb patented his sewage lamp in 1895. He sold around 2500 of his lamps worldwide, but their success was tempered by the risk of stinky leaks and dangerous explosions from the highly combustible gasses. In 1950, a careless lorry driver backed into the light, thus destroying one of the last vestiges of Victorian ingenuity. 'Iron Lily' was restored and operates as the standard gas lamp that you see today.

LONDON RECORDS

London's first gaslit street: Pall Mall (1807)
London's longest road: Western Avenue (11.3 miles)
London's smallest square: Pickering Place (see page 57)
London's longest bridge: Waterloo (381 metres)
London's narrowest street: Brydges Place (15 inches wide)

SAVOY STREET:
THE ONLY STREET IN BRITAIN WHERE TRAFFIC DRIVES ON THE RIGHT

This tiny street, running from the Strand to the entrance of the Savoy Hotel, is the only street in Britain where traffic drives on the right. This quirk dates back to the time when hansom cabs delivered guests to the hotel, but is just as useful today when most of the moneyed guests arrive in stretch limousines or black cabs, which are too big to turn around in such tight space. Drivers have to perform a U-turn to exit the street, staying on the right-hand side.

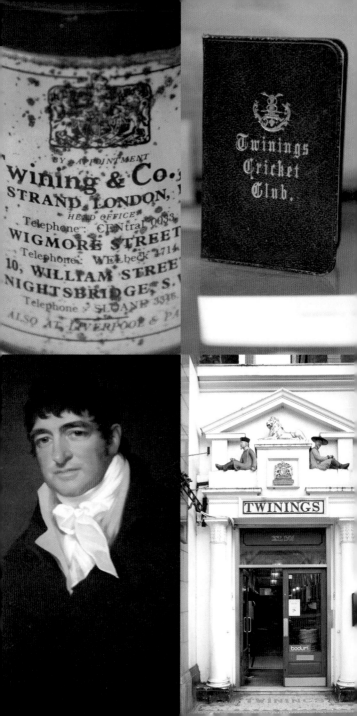

TWININGS TEA MUSEUM

🕗

216 Strand, WC2
0207 353 3511
www.twinings.com
Open Mon-Fri 9am-5pm, Sat 10am-4pm
Admission free
Transport Temple tube

*Teapots
and tips*

Drinking tea may be as quintessentially British as sinking pints on a Friday night, but the tradition of taking tea originated in China back in 2737 BC. This heritage is hinted at in the exotic façade of Twinings tea shop on the Strand, with two Chinamen draped over the doorway. One of the first importers of tea to Britain in 1706, Thomas Twining's flagship store has been located here since 1717.

Twining's first business, Tom's Coffee House, was just behind the existing shop. Ironically, tea was first introduced to London society at the city's disreputable coffee houses; Twinings still stocks various blends of filter coffee among the packets of Earl Grey and English Breakfast. Thankfully, prices have dropped since the early 18th century, when tea cost the equivalent of £160 for 100g. In those days, tea was the beverage of the wealthy elite. At the back of the fragrant little shop, fetchingly decorated with portraits of the Twinings dynasty through the ages, is a small museum that sends American tourists into paroxysms of delight. The collection includes a copy of Queen Victoria's Royal Warrant from 1837, several antique tea caddies, random invoices and old advertisements. "The giant teapot is currently on a nationwide tour," the shop assistant explains apologetically. The most remarkable exhibit is a plain wooden box bearing the initials T.I.P. – short for "To Insure Promptness". Patrons of coffee-houses would drop a few pennies into these boxes to encourage swifter service - the origins of the modern-day "tip".

> If you'd like to peruse more antique teapots, head to the *Bramah Tea and Coffee Museum*, which also serves afternoon tea in a fittingly chintzy tea-room. (40 Southwark Street, SE1; www.teaandcoffeemuseum.co.uk Open 10am-6pm daily)

SIGHTS NEARBY

LLOYDS BANK LAW COURTS BRANCH

🕘

In 1825, the Twining family branched out into banking. Twinings Bank merged with Lloyds Bank in 1892; their joint venture at 215 the Strand (now Lloyds Bank, Law Courts Branch) is surely the most flamboyant bank in London. The ceramic beehive above the intricate wrought-iron entrance is the first clue that this is no ordinary depository. The foyer is clad in a kaleidoscope of green, white and gold Doulton tiles, punctuated with fluted columns, gilded fish and gleaming marble basins. Built in 1883, this was originally The Royal Courts of Justice Restaurant; the gaudy décor must have made diners vaguely nauseous, as the restaurant closed shortly afterwards.

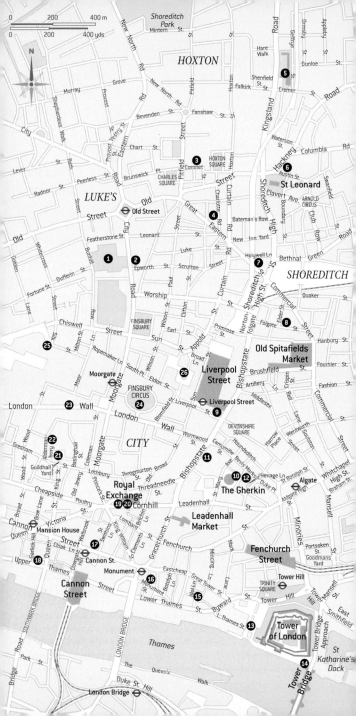

TOWER BRIDGE TO SHOREDITCH

BUNHILL FIELDS ❶

38 City Road, EC1
0208 4723584
Open Oct-March Mon-Fri 7.30am–4pm, Sat-Sun 9.30am-4pm,
April-Sept Mon-Fri 7.30am-7pm, Sat-Sun 9.30am-4pm
Admission free
Transport Old Street tube/rail

Deliverance for Dissenters

Bunhill Fields is the site of a small graveyard to the north of the old City Wall. Bunhill supposedly derives from Bone Hill: around the year 1549, the charnel house (or bone deposit) of St Paul's was cleared for new burials, and over a thousand cartloads of bones were dumped here, on what was damp, marshy ground – enough to provide foundations for three new windmills. In 1665, the City of London Corporation decided to use the land as a burial ground for those who could not be buried in conventional churchyards, primarily plague victims. Enclosing walls for the cemetery were built, but it seems to have never been consecrated and as a result became popular with Nonconformist Protestants who practiced outside the orthodoxy of the Church of England. Catholic and Jewish Londoners who could afford the fees were also buried there. The list of burials in this small yard reads like a who's who of dissenters in London intellectual life – the visionary poet and painter William Blake, *Robinson Crusoe* author Daniel Defoe, anti-slavery philanthropist Thomas Fowell Buxton, and poet and hymn-writer Isaac Watts are the most noted examples. The London poet Robert Southey called it the 'Campo Santo of the Dissenters.'

The Fields were filled with 120,000 graves before being closed in 1853. Most of the graves are fenced off, but an on-site curator will happily escort you around any of them.

ABNEY PARK CEMETERY

In 1840, Nonconformist burials were moved to Abney Park in Stoke Newington, another graveyard well worth a visit – one of the original seven cemeteries circling London that include Nunhead and Kensal Green (see pages 321 and 173). The entrance to Abney Park is built in the Egyptian Revival style – a conscious decision, as it was the first cemetery in Europe explicitly designated as nondenominational, or with 'no invidious dividing lines,' according to the group of Nonconformists led by George Collison who founded it. The most famous internees are Catherine & William Booth, founders of the Salvation Army, but large numbers of abolitionists and 19th century missionaries are typical residents. The overgrown park is full of mature woods now. It also contains one of the two UXBs (unexploded bombs) known in Stoke Newington, so don't go digging no holes!

JOHN WESLEY'S HOUSE

49 City Road, EC1
0207 253 2262;
www.wesleyschapel.org.uk
Open 10am-4pm Mon-Sat, noon-1.45pm Sun
Admission free, donations welcome
Transport Old Street tube/rail

The
Venerable Crapper

"The world is my parish" pronounces the statue of John Wesley, founder of Methodism, in the courtyard of Wesley Chapel, a welcome refuge from the thrum of City Road. During his 88 years, Wesley lived up to his word, travelling a quarter of a million miles on horseback to deliver some 40,000 sermons.

From 1779 until his death in 1791, Wesley spent his winters in the compact Georgian townhouse beside the chapel. Though simple to the point of severity by today's standards, Wesley's three-storey home was fitted with all mod cons – wallpaper, built-in cupboards, and a fireplace in every room. New-fangled furniture included a "cock fighting chair", to be straddled like a modern massage chair, with an adjustable easel for reading and writing. The bureau has secret compartments where Wesley hid correspondence from his jealous wife, Mary Vazielle. Wesley was fond of his Chamber Horse, precursor of the exercise bike, a tall wooden chair with a springy seat that simulates riding a horse. Apparently, "the vigorous bouncing would stimulate the liver". Another example of Wesley's fascination with "Primitive Physick" is the Electrical Machine, which administered electric shocks to cure depression, migraine, and all manner of ailments. Wesley did not try this out himself until he had experimented with his flock for a good three years.

Downstairs are a few of Wesley's personal possessions including a pair of "straights", buckled shoes that could be worn on either foot, and his "laptop" – a wooden writing case with quills and ink, which he would balance on his saddle, composing sermons as he trotted through the countryside.

In Wesley's day, the house had no running water. His chamber pot was concealed in a wooden box in his bedroom. But in 1899, Methodist ministers installed a fine set of gentlemen's toilets to serve the congregation at the chapel, which are miraculously intact. With its red-mottled marble urinals and a dressing room with frosted-glass partitions, these public conveniences must have been the height of Victorian hygiene. The mahogany cubicles contain original Thomas Crapper toilets, their rims imprinted with "The Venerable" in red letters. The porcelain handle on the chain instructs users to: "Pull and let go".

A MUSEUM OF METHODISM

In the crypt of John Wesley's Chapel next door is a small Museum of Methodism, which tells the history of this faction of the Anglican church, aimed at social outcasts and taught mainly by itinerant preachers.

CIRCUS SPACE   ❸

Coronet Street, N1
0207 729 9522
www.thecircusspace.co.uk
Open For classes and performances only
Admission varies
Transport Old Street tube

*Electric
acrobatics*

Unbeknown to the poseurs pressed into Hoxton Square's style bars and galleries, a block away a bunch of less self-conscious Londoners tumble around in a huge, red brick building, whose scrubbed-up façade masks an unconventional agenda. In a former power station, the Circus Space, which offers the only university degree in circus skills in Britain, is where aspiring acrobats and trapeze artists from all over Europe hone their skills. But plucky amateurs can also sign up for evening and weekend classes in tight-wire walking, trampoline, stilt-walking or clowning.

The building had been derelict since the 1950s until a troupe of circus performers took it over as a rehearsal space in 1994. Thanks to a £1.2 million redevelopment, students now rehearse in post-industrial style in the vast, vaulted Generating Chamber and Combustion Chamber.

Look out for occasional big top performances by graduates and Circus Space Cabarets, usually held in August or September.

SIGHTS NEARBY

STUDIO 23   ❹
23 Charlotte Road, EC2 • 0207 729 2323 • www.mouththatroars.com
Open 11am-late daily • **Admission** free.

Affordable films for troublesome teens

With cinemas brazenly charging a tenner for cramped seats and small screens, Studio 23 is a treat for cineastes strapped for cash. In an intimate scarlet and black space are a handful of cosy booths with plasma screens and two to four proper, padded cinema seats. For £2 per person, you can choose from a DVD selection of art-house and classic films by the likes of Pedro Almodovar, Mike Leigh, and Alfred Hitchcock. An old fashioned popcorn machine churns out fresh stuff for £1 per cup. Coffee, cake, and Turkish tea are just as cheap.

Studio 23 opened in April 2005, but the organisation behind it, the Mouth That Roars, has been around since 1998. A community project that runs free film-making workshops for 13-19 year olds who live in Hackney, the enterprise encourages cultural diversity and creativity through an approach that is practical rather than pretentious. Most evenings, you'll find teenagers cutting their films in the professional editing suite at the back of the café/cinema. You might even catch a free screening of the finished product.

THE GEFFRYE MUSEUM

136 Kingsland Road, E2
2007 739 9893 • www.geffrye-museum.org.uk
Open Tues-Sat 10am-5pm; Sun, national holidays 12-5pm. Herb garden open
1 April-31 Oct during museum hours. Almshouse open 11am-4pm first Sat of
month and occasional Weds. **Admission** museum free; almshouse £2,
under-16s free. **Transport** Old Street tube, then Bus 149, 242, or Bus 394, 67.

> *'Through the Keyhole' down through the ages*

Amid the Vietnamese cafés and Turkish corner shops of Kingsland Road is a patch of London that will forever be quintessentially British. The Geffrye Museum stands back from the road, buffered by neat lawns where acrobatic squirrels abound. This 18th century almshouse has been converted into an homage to the British living room through the ages.

If you are one of those people who cannot resist peering through the half-open curtains of strangers' front rooms you will take curious pleasure in peeping at the parlours of the British middle classes from 1600 to the 1990s. It's 'Through the Keyhole' with a historical spin.

The odd layout is determined by the building's elongated structure. Off a long corridor is a chronological series of period rooms recreated in meticulous detail, from the oak-panelled austerity of the Elizabethans to the ornate flourishes of the Victorians. Period music and audio snippets from contemporary literature and letters bring these stage sets to life.

A sunny, flag-stoned café with exposed brick walls and picture windows overlooks the pretty walled gardens at the back. The café serves honest British food – home-made pâté on toast, afternoon tea, or crumble with custard - at very reasonable prices.

Opposite the museum, on the side wall of 199 Kingsland Road, are the remains of the Gardener's Mural, a paint and mosaic landscape of vegetable plots and gardens. This seems incongruous now, but in the 18th and 19th century this patch of urban sprawl was devoted to market gardens and plant nurseries. Inspired by this horticultural history, the Geffrye Museum's gardens are planted according to the fashions of the interiors. For example, the knot garden was inspired by a parquetry motif on the oak cupboard in the Elizabethan room. There's also an herb garden with over 170 different herbs.

Support this free, user-friendly museum by stocking up on British seeds and unusual books about London in the gift shop. Visitors can also browse through interiors magazines in the reading room, which doubles as a small gallery of paintings of British interiors.

Sir Robert Geffrye, whose statue presides over the museum entrance, was an ironmonger who founded the almshouse to provide care for the poor. One of the original almshouses, decorated as it would have been in the 18th century, can be visited on the first Saturday of each month.

WHITE CUBICLE ❻

George & Dragon Pub, 2 Hackney Road, E2
www.whitecubicle.org
Open daily 6-11pm
Admission Free
Transport Old Street tube

*Bog
Standard Art Space*

Just a couple of blocks away from Jay Jopling's pristine (and slightly pretentious) White Cube, the contemporary art gallery that put Hoxton Square on the global art map, is White Cubicle, an irreverent art space housed in the ladies toilet of the George and Dragon pub. Billed as a gallery with 'no budget, staff or boundaries,' White Cubicle was dreamed up by Pablo Leon De La Barra, a maverick Mexican curator, gallery owner, and magazine publisher, and a champion of London's queer art scene.

Measuring just 1.4 square metres, the White Cubicle may be claustrophobic but its grotty confines offer a refreshing antidote to the po-faced sterility of the traditional gallery space. The art is anything goes - but the more camp, kitsch and erotically charged the better. Photographer Wolfgang Tillmans stuck a portrait of Richard Branson in the toilet. Carl Hopgood's 'Hustler Freeze' featured a collage of photographs of men offering sexual favours, snipped from gay magazines. For his 'Temple of the Golden Piss,' Terence Koh plastered the cubicle in gold leaf, with artfully placed golden sculptures of erect cocks. Exhibition openings are a riot, often accompanied with performances by drag queen DJs, go-go boys, or guacamole chefs. There's the usual collection of ridiculous haircuts that are an essential accessory if you hang out in Hoxton. Eighties classics spin on the turntables. Dancing on tables is not uncommon.

On the edge of St Leonard's graveyard and London's first council estate (the Boundary Street estate, built in the early 1890s), the *George and Dragon* has a cult following. When it closed in the mid-1980s, after 95 years of service to East End boozers, it was squatted by a bunch of Italian anarchists. Performance artist Richard Battye bought the place in 2002, on the cusp of Shoreditch's reinvention as a magnet for trendy bars and avant-garde art galleries. From the outside, it looks like any other semi-derelict, late-Victorian corner pub. Inside is an old-fashioned, old-man's boozer cluttered with a curious jumble of stuffed animals, plastic flowers, china figurines, tasselled lampshades, antiques inherited from Battye's grandmother, and random junk shop finds. It is like London's answer to Kumpelnest 3000, the legendary Berlin gay bar housed in a former brothel.

VILGE UNDERGROUND ❼

54 Holywell Lane EC2
07886 751 205
www.villageunderground.co.uk
Open occasionally for special events
Admission varies
Transport Old Street tube

*Mind
the gap*

Avoid the tube at all costs? Some Londoners pay good money to spend eight
hours a day in a tube carriage. Mainly
designers, architects, and film-makers, they
share four Jubilee Line carriages salvaged from
the scrap heap and recycled as affordable offices for creative start-ups.

"I needed a studio space but couldn't afford one, so I figured I'd build my own,"
shrugs furniture designer Auro Foxcroft, who spent four years realising his
ambition. After persuading London Undergound to sell him four obsolete
carriages for £500 each, Foxcroft spent two years searching for somewhere to
park them. Eventually, the local council granted permission for the carriages to
be hoisted onto a viaduct in Shoreditch, as long as Foxcroft renovated the
derelict warehouse below it.

Now this cavernous space - all brick vaults and skylights - has evolved into
Village Underground, a unique showcase for emerging artists. Exhibitions and
performances are subsidised by film shoots and fashion shows. The four tube
carriages are accessed via a vertiginous spiral staircase on the side of the building.
The offices are private, but if you ask nicely, someone will show you around. They
might even grill you a hot dog on the 'roof garden,' a haven of creative energy
high above the traffic roaring down Great Eastern Street.

Foxcroft and architect Nicholas Laurent remodelled the carriages using
eco-friendly features like biodegradable paint, reclaimed materials, and solar
panels. They spent months dismantling the "mad amount" of electronic wiring
hidden under the seats. Otherwise, all the original fittings from 1983 are intact,
including retro handles and No Smoking signs. And the doors still open at the
press of a button. Like all tube trains, they are a magnet for graffiti artists; one
carriage is covered in around 50 layers of paint.

Now Foxcroft plans to open similar arts centres with affordable offices attached
in Berlin and Toronto. Social entrepreneurship is harder to sustain in London,
with property at a premium and high-rise buildings cropping up at an ever-
increasing rate. Ironically, this once derelict site will be even more valuable when
the construction site next door is complete: a bridge to the new Shoreditch High
Street train station.

Great Ormond Street children's hospital is home to another defunct tube
carriage, converted into a studio for Radio Lollipop. The 26-ton carriage was
chopped in half and rejoined at a right angle so it could be squeezed into the
hospital courtyard.

DENNIS SEVERS' HOUSE ❽

18 Folgate Street, Spitalfields
www.dennissevershouse.co.uk
0207 247 4013
Open 2-5pm first and third Sunday of each month, and 12-2pm
on the following Monday. Candlelit tours every Mon eve; booking essential
Admission Mon £5; Sun £8; £12 for candlelit tours
Transport Liverpool Street tube/rail

*Spooky
still life drama*

O ne house stands out among the spruce Georgian terraces of Folgate Street. With its flaming lantern and cutout silhouettes framed by crimson shutters, Number 18 seems strangely detached from the commercial throb of nearby Bishopsgate, where City traders scurry about their business.

When Dennis Severs, a Canadian artist, bought this ten-room house in the late 1970s, Spitalfields was a slum. He filled his dilapidated home with chipped antiques and anonymous portraits picked up from flea markets, determined to recreate an authentic 18th century household. Armed with a candle and bedpan, Severs slept in every room, soaking up the energy and imagining the lives of its previous inhabitants. Gradually, these imaginary companions took shape as the Jervis family, Huguenot silk-weavers whose make-believe lives became an elaborate 'still life drama' for visitors to explore.

Although Severs died in 1999, visitors can still immerse themselves in his decaying fantasy world. Each room is designed to evoke a moment in time as experienced by successive generations of the Jervises from 1724 to 1914. The experience is an assault on the senses where every object is apparently charged with hidden meaning – not just a visual overload, but also the smells of ginger biscuits and mulled wine, the sounds of horse hooves, church bells, and whispered snatches of conversation. The effect is deliberately theatrical as you follow a trail of clues that suggest the ghostly presence of the Jervis clan - a half-eaten boiled egg and soldiers, a black cat asleep on an unmade bed, and what appears to be a chamber pot full of pee.

There is social commentary, too. Try not to look out the window at the office blocks under construction as you climb up to the gloomy servants' quarters. Soiled white undergarments are strung between cobwebs, a blackened pot of mouldy cabbage sits beside a filthy hearth, and gunshots sound a death knell. It all conjures up a deeply bleak existence.

Sadly, the compelling atmosphere is punctured by patronising notes telling patrons to shut up and use their imagination. For example: "A visit requires the same style of concentration as does an old masters exhibition, and a most absurd but commonly made error is to assume that it might be either amusing or appropriate for children."

A young man still lives in the attic. Well, someone has to feed the cat and canaries.

THE MASONIC TEMPLE AT ANDAZ HOTEL ❾

40 Liverpool Street, EC2
0207 961 1234;
www.andaz.com
Open by appointment or for special events
Transport Liverpool Street tube/rail

*Occult
lodge in a
boutique hotel*

With its distinctive red-brick facade, the former Great Eastern Hotel is an impressive Victorian landmark beside Liverpool Street station. Built for the Great Eastern Railway Company, the hotel was designed by Charles and Edward Barry, whose father, another Charles Barry, built the Houses of Parliament.

When it opened in 1884, the Great Eastern Hotel had its own tracks into the station for the delivery of provisions, including sea water for the hotel's salt-water baths. Despite this swanky heritage, the hotel gradually fell into disrepair until restaurateur Terence Conran snapped it up in the late 1990s and embarked on an extravagant makeover. During the renovation, concealed behind a false wall, the builders were surprised to discover a wood-panelled antechamber leading to an intact Masonic temple. Decked in twelve types of Italian marble, with a blue and gold ceiling decorated with the signs of the zodiac and a mahogany throne at either end, this Gothic showstopper was built in 1912 for £50,000, the equivalent of around £4 million today. The Freemasons, who helped to build the Great Eastern Hotel, held clandestine meetings here for decades.

A second temple, decorated with Egyptian motifs with seating around a chequer-board floor, was discovered in the basement. Evidently not intimidated by the occult, Conran converted it into a gym.

Now owned by the Hyatt hotel group, the building has been rebranded as the Andaz.

> To avoid tampering with the original architectural fittings, the Andaz is fitted with vacuum drainage like that used on planes. So when you flush the toilet, the waste is sucked upwards and disposed of through the hotel roof.

SIGHTS NEARBY
ROMAN GIRL'S GRAVE ❿

During construction of Norman Foster's Swiss Re building (better known as the Gherkin) at 30 St Mary Axe, builders stumbled upon another extraordinary discovery: the grave of a teenage girl who died between AD 350 and 400. A small plaque in the low slate wall to the rear of the building marks the spot where she was given a Roman reburial after the building was finished. The inscription – in Latin and English – reads: "To the spirits of the dead the unknown young girl from Roman London lies buried here".

THE TENT ⑪

St Ethelburga's Centre for Reconciliation and Peace, 78 Bishopsgate, EC2
0207 496 1610
www.stethelburgas.org
Open Fri 11am-3pm. Visits at other times by prior arrangement
Admission free
Transport Liverpool Street or Bank tube

> *A Bedouin tent in the heart of the City*

I t's easy to walk past St Ethelburga's without noticing it. The slender church sits quietly amid the hubbub of Bishopsgate, with its high-rise offices and harried bankers. When it was founded around 1400, St Ethelburga's was the largest building on Bishopsgate: today, it's the smallest.

Behind the medieval façade is a surprisingly modern interior, empty apart from a simple wooden altar and a handful of artworks. Though it survived the Great Fire and the Blitz, the church collapsed after an IRA bomb blast nearby in 1993. Fragments of the original features were salvaged to create this new space. Though consecrated, it's no longer technically a church; there's no parish and no priest. It's now a Centre for Reconciliation and Peace, focusing on the role of faith in war and conflict resolution.

The derelict land behind the church has been transformed into a peace garden (also accessible via an alleyway off Bishopsgate). With its intricate mosaic tiling and tinkling fountain, it's like stepping into a Moroccan riad. The centrepiece is The Tent, a 16-sided structure with walls of woven goats' hair, modelled on traditional Bedouin tents. Tents are also associated with the nomadic origins of Judaism, Christianity and Islam – just the thing for a sacred space dedicated to inter-faith dialogue. Take off your shoes and step into a serene cocoon, carpeted with rugs woven in conflict regions and lined with low benches. The seven stained-glass windows contain messages of peace written in Chinese, Sanskrit, Arabic, Japanese, Hebrew, English and Inuit. Even the occasional siren cannot shatter the peace.

The Tent hosts devotional gatherings, meditation, storytelling and recitals. The events held in the main building range from Sufi meditation through talks on Martin Luther King. You might catch a Tibetan sand mandala, an Afro-Cuban concert, or a discussion on civil disobedience. The unifying philosophy underlying all these eclectic events is that peace begins within.

St Ethelburga's has a long tradition as a progressive church. William Bedwell, rector from 1601 to 1632, was an Arabic scholar. In 1861, rector John Rodwell published the first reliable English translation of the Qur'an (still in print). And in the 1930s and 1940s, this was one of the few churches in London where divorced people could remarry.

BEVIS MARKS SYNAGOGUE ⓬

2 Henage Lane, EC3
0207 626 1274
www.bevismarks.org.uk
Open Sun 10.30am—12.30pm, Mon 10.30am-12.30pm,
Tues, Wed 11am—1pm, Fri 11am—1pm (summer only)
Tours Sun 11.15am, Wed, Fri 12pm (except on Jewish holidays)
Transport Aldgate or Liverpool Street tube

> *The oldest synagogue in England*

Opened in 1701, Bevis Marks is the oldest synagogue in England. It was established by Spanish and Portuguese Sephardic Jews in response to a surge in congregation numbers at the small synagogue in Creechurch Lane, when Cromwell re-admitted Jews into England after their expulsion in 1290 by Edward I (also known as the 'Hammer of the Scots', a villain familiar to fans of the film *Braveheart*).

Cromwell never formally revoked the expulsion, but made it clear that the ban was not going to be enforced. The government was badly in need of Jewish funds, and the ultra-Protestant Cromwell believed that the conversion of the Jews to Christianity was essential before Christ's return to reign on earth. Cromwell's policy exemplified the equivocal attitude of the English establishment to Jews - a kind of grudging acceptance.

The synagogue is a pretty little thing, largely unchanged in the 300 years since its construction. Its light and airy interior calls to mind a Wren church. Embedded in the roof is a beam from a royal ship presented to the congregation by Queen Anne. The Ark (which holds the scrolls of the Pentateuch) at the east end reflects the late 17th century taste for classical architecture, again in the manner of Wren. The synagogue also has a very good collection of Cromwell-era and Queen Anne furniture, which remain in regular use.

From the adjoining Bevis Marks restaurant you can see the chandeliers of the synagogue. The only kosher restaurant in the City of London, it seems to belie the stereotype of Jewish food in London as offering plenty to eat at a reasonable price.

Aldgate was the 19th century centre of London's Jewish community. There are still vestiges such as the dirt-cheap, 24-hour bagel shops at the top of Brick Lane, but mostly there are ghosts: Jewish schools, bath houses, and soup kitchens, now converted into gracious flats for City workers... Look out for the colourful mural commemorating the Jews of the East End, opposite the Brune Street Soup Kitchen, and the arch on Wentworth Street, the only survivor of the Four Percent Industrial Dwellings Company, founded in 1885 by Sir Nathaniel Rothschild to clear the area's slums and provide decent housing for Jewish residents — albeit with a 4% profit for investors. Now one of London's largest mosques, the synagogue at 59 Brick Lane used to be so busy that classrooms were built on the roof — look up and you can still see them.

TOWER SUBWAY ⑬

Tower Hill, EC3
Transport Tower Hill tube

A lost passage under the Thames

When Italian writer Edmondo de Amicis visited London in 1883, he described a "… gigantic iron tube, which seems to undulate like a great intestine in the enormous belly of the river". This river monster was in fact Tower Subway, built beneath the Thames in 1869 to shuttle passengers between the north and south banks. All that survives of this engineering feat is a small, circular brick tower beside the Tower of London ticket office. This is not actually the original entrance to the Subway - it was built by the London Hydraulic Power Company, when they took over the defunct tunnel in 1897. The other entrance on Vine Street, south of the Thames, has been demolished.

Unlike its predecessor, Marc Isambard Brunel's Thames Tunnel , which cost £60,000, two lives and took almost eighteen years to complete, Tower Subway was built in ten months for £16,000 by a 24-year-old named James Henry Greathead. The tunnel's innovative structure, clad in an iron tube, was the template for London's first tube, the City & South London Railway, built in 1890. A dozen passengers were shuttled across the Thames in an "omnibus" that ran along a single-gauge track. After a series of mechanical mishaps, this service folded after just three months and the tunnel was converted into a gas-lit walkway. Charles Dickens Jr warned: "… it is not advisable for any but the very briefest of Her Majesty's lieges to attempt the passage in high-heeled boots, or with a hat to which he attaches any particular value." Though damp and claustrophobic, this did not deter the 20,000 pedestrians who used the Subway every week, paying a halfpenny each way.

When toll-free Tower Bridge opened in 1894, Tower Subway became redundant. It was sold to the London Hydraulic Power Company for a measly £3,000. The water pipes have since been replaced by TV cables.

SIGHTS NEARBY
DEAD MAN'S HOLE ⑭

Before Tower Subway was built, Londoners relied on wherrymen to transport them across the river (see page 225, Wherryman's Seat). One popular route ran from Horselydown Steps in Bermondsey to Dead Man's Hole on the north bank. As the name suggests, not all the passengers were alive. The boatmen didn't forfeit the corpses' fares: they sold them for medical research to Barts Hospital, which paid 6d more for bodies than Guy's Hospital on the south bank. A sign marks the spot beneath Tower Bridge, where mildewed steps lead into the murky river where countless corpses were dumped.

THE GARDEN OF ST DUNSTAN-IN-THE-EAST ⓯

Idol Lane, EC3
Open dawn to dusk daily.
Admission free.
Transport Monument tube.

Secret garden in the heart of the City

One of the few little green lungs in the City, this garden hidden within the walls of a bombed-out church is popular with office workers during their lunch hours. The high walls of the ruins trap heat in the summer, and the relative secrecy of the garden makes it ideal for a liaison or a nap. In good weather, the garden encourages idleness. In bad weather, it invites melancholy.

Twisting paths lead through the garden, whose walls are covered by ivy and shrubbery. A lawn and trees have been planted and a low fountain sits in the middle of what was once the nave. The park and its ruins give the impression of being one of those artful Gothic follies "…beloved by the Victorians – its tight enclosure by office buildings on all sides heightens the effect of its secrecy. The church spire, one of the few examples of Gothic-style architecture that Wren built, was added after the building was severely damaged in the Great Fire of London in 1666." Rather than being completely rebuilt, the damaged church was patched up between 1668 and 1671 – the spire was designed to complement the medieval church that had remained largely intact since 1100.

However, the church was bombed out in 1941, leaving only the tower and steeple intact, which now house the offices of the Wren Clinic, a complementary medicine centre. Surrounding the church tower are iron railings commissioned by Wren, with putti on the gate, an unusual decoration in London.

ST DUNSTAN-IN-THE-WEST:
THE ONLY OPEN-AIR STATUE OF QUEEN ELIZABETH I IN LONDON

Dunstan, an eccentric English scholar, has another church dedicated to him: St Dunstan-in-the-West on Fleet Street.. Access is unfortunately limited to Tuesdays between 11am and 3pm, but the church is famed for its exterior clock from 1671, showing the biblical giants Gog and Magog, traditional guardians of the City. The churchyard also includes a statue of Queen Elizabeth I from 1586, the only one known to have been carved while she lived, and the only open-air statue of her that survives in London, as well as statues of King Lud, the mythical re-builder of London, and his sons. All of the statues originally stood in Ludgate, one of the historically sacred parts of London, so the church may have more than its fair share of London voodoo. The celebrated London diarist Samuel Pepys used the church as a place to pick up serving-girls, generally with little success.

ASCENT OF THE MONUMENT 🔟

Monument Street, EC3
0207 626 2717
www.themonument.info
Open 9.30am–5pm daily
Admission £2, children £1.50
Transport Monument or Bank tube

> *Climb the tallest freestanding stone column in the world*

This oddity is much seen, but rarely visited. A single Doric column of Portland stone, the Monument contains an internal staircase of 311 steps winding up to a viewing balcony. When it was built in 1677, this would have afforded long-distance views; after 300 years of continuous building, the views are less spectacular. Once visible for miles, today visitors almost stumble across the column - the effect is like discovering a sailing ship in a canyon.

Designed by London's greatest architect, Sir Christopher Wren, and Dr. Robert Hooke to commemorate the Great Fire of London, the 61 metre Monument is the tallest freestanding stone column in the world.

The Monument is topped by a flaming copper urn that symbolises the Great Fire, but looks more like a flaming pudding. Originally, the column was to be topped with a phoenix (embodying the motto of London: 'Resurgem' – 'I am reborn'), then with a colossal statue of King Charles II. But the committee responsible opted for the gilt pudding instead.

The walk up inside the column is precipitous: a thin, worn handrail is all that lies between you and oblivion. Many visitors are undone by the climb, but each receives a certificate after scaling the damn thing. The summit was a favourite place for staging suicides until the balcony was fenced in with a metal cage. This cage is strong enough to support vigorous gymnastics and pull-ups, a very effective way of terrifying your friends.

The height is supposedly equal to the distance between the column and the baker's house in Pudding Lane where the fire reputedly began.

Look closely and you will see that the base of the column is clad with a finely executed relief by Caius Gabriel Cibber, depicting a personification of London grieving before a backdrop of flaming buildings. Peace and Prosperity hover in the clouds, promising renewal, and King Charles II is on the right, all dressed up. Cibber is most famous for two statues, *Melancholy* and *Raving Madness*, made for the gates of the infamous mental hospital Bedlam, which can still be seen at the Royal Bethlem Hospital Museum. His son, Colley Cibber, a famously bad poet and actor, was the chief target of Alexander Pope's satirical poem *The Dunciad*.

THE LONDON STONE   🇭

111 Cannon Street, EC4
Transport Cannon Street tube

> **The rock from which Arthur pulled Excalibur ?**

Embedded in the wall of the Overseas Chinese Banking Corporation, behind a small, illuminated grill at knee height, is an unadorned rock with two grooves in the top. This is all that remains of the London Stone.

There is more wild speculation about this shapeless lump of limestone than seems possible. Possibly over 3,000 years old, nobody really knows what the London Stone was. Allegedly, this is just a fragment of the original, which was bigger than a man. Some claim it was brought to London by Brutus, son of Priam, who supposedly fought and killed a race of giants led by Gog and Magog (whose images are still carried in the Lord Mayor's Parade), and erected a temple to Artemis with this stone as its altar.

Alternatively, it may have been the rock from which Arthur pulled Excalibur. Or perhaps it marked the start of a Roman milestone system to facilitate navigation of the new road network around their latest colony. Although there are no written Roman references to the stone, it was certainly an important landmark after the city's foundation by the Romans. For many hundreds of years, the London Stone was recognised as the symbolic heart of the City of London, before which deals were made, oaths were taken, laws were passed, and official proclamations were made. In 1450, the rebel Jack Cade struck his sword against it to signify his seizure of sovereignty after his forces entered London.

The London Stone has always attracted mystical enthusiasts. Dr John Dee, Elizabeth I's astronomer, was fascinated by its occult powers. Many believe it was a sacrificial stone for Druids. William Blake, London's seer poet, imagined the groaning of the Druids' execution victims in his poem *To the Jews*. To this day, new-agers revere the stone, which they believe sits on a key ley line linking St Paul's and the Tower of London - making it the spiritual centre of London, or even Britain.

THE LONDON STONE LEY LINE

London's most powerful ley line - a hypothetical alignment of ancient sacred places - runs along Cannon St, connecting the churches of St Martin's Ludgate, St ThomasSt John's Walbrook with the London Stone, St Leonard's Milk church and All Hallows Barking, near the Tower of London. The hub of all ley lines in London is thought to be Ludgate Circus, where a megalithic stone circle, like Stonehenge, is believed to have stood.

THE MUMMY OF JIMMY GARLICK **⑱**

St James Garlickhythe church, Garlick Hill, EC4
0207 236 1719
www.stjamesgarlickhythe.org.uk
Open by special arrangement only
Transport Mansion House or Bank tube

> *A 300-year-old mummy with a mysterious identity*

Christopher Wren built over fifty churches in London. Many of them, like St James Garlickhythe, are relatively unknown. The tombs of six medieval mayors are not the only secrets contained within this church. Hidden high in the bell tower is the desiccated corpse of a man believed to be over 300 years old.

Discovered by workmen under the chancel floor in the mid-19th century, the cadaver was nicknamed Jimmy Garlick. It's a mystery how Jimmy was so perfectly preserved. Temporarily embalmed in pitch and spices, he had not been eviscerated. Carbon dating suggests he died around the time of the Great Fire, so he might have been "cooked" by the flames while he lay in state. His identity is also the subject of fierce debate. Some researchers have argued that this is the body of Seagrave Chamberlain, "some time Resident at Barbados", who died aged 16 in 1675 and is commemorated in the church. The verger, Ellis Pike, disputes this, because a "mummy autopsy" revealed that poor Jimmy was suffering from both osteoporosis and baldness.

At the time of his discovery, the canny beadle didn't care about Jimmy Garlick's true identity. He hid Jimmy behind the organ and charged people a few pennies to gawp at him. About a century later, Jimmy was moved to a cupboard in the vestibule "where we keep the toilet rolls and hymn books now", says Pike, throwing the door open to prove his point. Jimmy remained in the closet until the 1960s, though allegedly he was occasionally taken out for choir practice. In the 1980s, he was moved to his present resting place.

Pike leads the way up the claustrophobic staircase of the bell tower. In a dusty chamber is an oddly modern casket. He lifts the lid to reveal a blackened, emaciated body with a gleaming set of white teeth grinning in the gloom. For decency's sake, Pike has draped Jimmy in a white nightgown, which only heightens the creepy effect of his curled toes, elegant fingers, and pierced ears poking out. I am too deferential (read: terrified) to touch him; but Pike seems quite unfazed by Jimmy's shrivelled presence: "I touched his face and he felt like a man who needed a shave." A reminder of our mortality is inscribed on the casket: "Stop stranger stop as you pass by. As you are now so once was I. As I am now so shall you be / *So pray prepare to follow me.*"

St James Garlickhythe takes its name from the Saxon "hythe", meaning a landing place or wharf. Imported garlic, a vital preservative and medicine in the Middle Ages, was unloaded at the wharf below St James and traded on Garlick Hill, the narrow lane where the church stands.

THE ROYAL EXCHANGE AMBULATORY PAINTINGS

⑲

Royal Exchange, between Cornhill and Threadneedle Streets, EC3
Open Closed weekends.
Admission free
Transport Bank tube

> *A pictorial history of England*

Sandwiched between the Bank of England and Mansion House, the Royal Exchange is a grand repository of the City's history. The current building, with its sweeping atrium and arcade of luxury shops, dates from 1844.

The original Royal Exchange – twice destroyed by fire - was founded in 1566 "as a comely bourse for merchants to assemble upon" by Sir Thomas Gresham a merchant who cannily offered to build London a Bourse at his own expense, in return for a lifetime interest in its profits. The building doubled as an Elizabethan shopping mall. The apothecaries and wig makers have since been supplanted by Cartier and Tiffany, but the courtyard bar still hums with the quick pulse of commerce.

The pinstriped powerbrokers lunching in the mezzanine restaurants seem perfectly oblivious to the 24 giant murals hanging in the shadowy recesses of the ambulatory. All the tables face the courtyard, rather than these patriotic interpretations of landmarks in English history. Lords and ladies, kings and queens, admirals, cardinals and ordinary Londoners are shown feasting and fighting, trading and signing treaties. The subtext is to impress upon the viewer the financial and political might of the City. Until the 1950s, these images were used to illustrate school history books, but today they are strangely overlooked. Many precious works, commissioned from the likes of Edwin Austin Abbey, J. Seymour Lucas and Sir Frederic Leighton (see page 193: Leighton House), are concealed behind the restaurant kitchens, doomed to be splattered with bacon fat. Even though the paintings are poorly lit and the titles are barely legible, their splendour remains awesome.

SIGHTS NEARBY

GRESHAM'S GRASSHOPPER

⑳

The weathervane of the Royal Exchange is tipped with a gilded grasshopper, Gresham's crest, which survived both the Great Fire and another devastating blaze in 1838. A golden grasshopper also hovers above Gresham's former HQ in Lombard Street. Allegedly, his ancestor Roger de Gresham was abandoned in a field of long grass as a baby, but was rescued by a woman drawn to the spot by a chirping grasshopper. A more likely explanation is that the grasshopper is a rebus of Gresham, since gres meant grass in Middle English. Traditionally a symbol for the merchant, the grasshopper is also an ancient good luck charm.

THE ROMAN AMPHITHEATRE OF GUILDHALL YARD

㉑

Off Gresham Street, EC2. The amphitheatre can be visited
via the Gallery on the east side of Guildhall Yard
Open Mon–Sat 10am-5pm, Sun 12pm - 4pm
Admission £2.50, conc £1, children under 16 free. Free all day Fridays
and from 3.30pm on other days
Transport St Paul's or Moorgate tube

> *Shadowy remains of a Roman past*

In the yard of the Guildhall, the ancient administrative centre of London, is a curved line of dark stone that suggests a great loop under the surrounding buildings. This circle marks the edge of the city's Roman amphitheatre; within the line was the arena. It does not take much imagination to conjure up what the amphitheatre must have looked like.

In Roman times, London was a backwater, although Tacitus refers to the city as a mercantile hub. The existence of such an amphitheatre suggests the bloody give-and-take that often characterises rowdy markets. After the Romans abandoned London in the 4th century, the amphitheatre was dismantled. Like much of the city, the site lay derelict for hundreds of years. Perhaps the local inhabitants, descendants of the waves of barbarians from Germany that looked to colonise Western Europe, were afraid of approaching the ancient buildings, which must have looked as though they were built by giants. Most of the remains of their settlements lie on the periphery of the Roman city.

It was only in the mid-11th century that overcrowding in London led to the reoccupation of the area. The first Guildhall was built in the early 12th century just north of the arena. But the amphitheatre was not rediscovered until 1988, after Museum of London archaeologists unearthed its foundations by chance, during an exploratory dig prior to construction of the Guildhall Art Gallery next door. Several well-preserved timber and wattle buildings were uncovered. Today, the Guildhall stands above the largest medieval crypt in the city. Entry to the amphitheatre is via the Guildhall Art Gallery, and is included in the admission price.

SIGHTS NEARBY

THE CLOCKMAKER'S MUSEUM

㉒

Guildhall Library, Aldermansbury EC2 • 0207 606 3030 • www.clockmakers.org.
Mon – Sat. Admission free. Open 9.30am-4.45pm

Horologists will love this one-room collection of clocks and watches from the 16th century to the present day, including marine chronometers, sundials, gas-operated gadgets, and the first electric clock. Go at noon to hear the clocks all chime at once. Look out for Mary Queen of Scots' gruesome skull pocket watch shaped like a silver skull. You prise open the teeth and pull back the cranium to tell the time.

LONDON WALL ㉓
London Wall, Tower Hill
Transport Moorgate tube

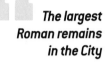

The largest Roman remains in the City

Like most great European cities, London is a palimpsest of generations of building. What we mostly see today is a very strongly built Victorian city, on top of dainty Georgian foundations that retain the medieval street pattern that was laid over the original Roman plan.

Ghosts of the Roman past litter the city, but require a certain amount of seeking out. The Temple of Mithras on Walbrook Street is one example. Battle Bridge in King's Cross is another - reputedly the site of the final battle between the Romans and Boudicca, who is buried, legend has it, under Platform 9 at King's Cross station.

However, the largest remains are those of the defensive wall built by the Romans after Boudicca sacked the city in 60 AD (the only time the city has been utterly wiped out), which remained largely intact for the next 1,000 years. London Wall is mostly built from stone shipped up the River Thames from Maidstone in Kent. Originally enclosing an area of about 1.3 km², in comparison to the monstrous 1,579 km² that Greater London has become, the wall stretched from Blackfriars in the west, via Ludgate, Moorgate and Aldgate to the Tower of London in the east. London Wall must have been an astonishing edifice in Roman times. It stood about five metres high, with a two metre deep ditch in front of it, and was lined with a number of bastions; the best preserved of these is in the Barbican estate, next to the church of St Giles-without-Cripplegate - a fragment of old London entirely surrounded by an extremely modern landscape.

What remains of London Wall today is largely the core, as much of its facing and cut stone was carted off for other building after the Romans left Britain. The biggest intact section lines the street now known, imaginatively, as London Wall. Other chunks stand at Tower Hill and within the Museum of London, but a careful walk of the streets that would have formed the wall often turns up other bits and pieces.

The oddest location for a fragment of Roman London is on display in the basement of Nicholson and Griffins (www.nicholsonandgriffin.com), a hairdresser in Leadenhall Market. This is the base of an arch in what was the city's basilica, or civic centre. At over 150 metres, it was the same length as St Paul's, and the largest building north of the Alps in 150 AD. This suggests that London was not a colonial backwater of the Roman Empire.

CITY OF LONDON BOWLING CLUB (24)

Since 2011, The City of London Bowling Club has become « nomadic »
Please check http://cityoflondonbowlingclub.webs.com/ for more information

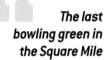

*The last
bowling green in
the Square Mile*

Until the 1980s, many of London's City workers wore bowler hats. These days, the only bowlers you are likely to see are members of the City of London Bowling Club, whose pitch sits smack in the centre of Finsbury Circus. This circular garden, lined with handsome buildings (including BP's HQ), is a glorious - if unlikely - setting for a game of bowls. Founded in 1924, the bowling club has around 40 members, including ten 'lady members'. Matches are held every Tuesday evening, and the Finals take place in early September. Until 1978 you had to either work or live in the City of London to become a member; these days, anyone is welcome.

If you don't fancy joining the players, dressed in immaculate whites or traditional blazers adorned with the club crest, you can always watch the action with a cucumber sandwich and a glass of Pimms from The Pavillion, the old wooden clubhouse now converted into a wine bar. Like so much in the Square Mile, it's a slice of Britain from a bygone era.

FINSBURY CIRCUS: THE OLDEST PARK IN LONDON

Dating back to 1606, when it was known as Moorfields, Finsbury Circus Gardens is the oldest public park in London. The name 'Finsbury' derives from 'Fensbury', a reference to the 'fens', or marshes, which had formed after the Romans left and the culverts cut into the City Wall to allow the Walbrook River to flow through were blocked. The land was dried out again in the 15th century when the wall was breached and Moorgate was built. An Iron Age burial ground and Roman remains have been discovered here, along with Britain's oldest cricket bat, a relic from Tudor times. Finsbury Circus was also the site of the first hot air balloon flight in England in 1784. During World War II, a less auspicious balloon was moored here: a barrage balloon to discourage dive bombing and low-level air raids.

A ROYAL WRITING DESK

Viscount Linley, Britain's blue-blooded furniture maker, designed a walnut writing desk inspired by Finsbury Circus. The inlaid, circular desk, with its hidden compartments and various symbols referring to local history, has a dark green leather surface, intended to evoke the bowling green.

BARBICAN CONSERVATORY AND ARBORETUM ㉕
Silk Street, Barbican, EC2
Open Sun 12-4 pm (occasionally booked for private functions;
call 0207 638 6114 to check)
Admission free
Transport Barbican tube

*Inner City
tropical garden*

This arboretum is incongruously located in a two-storey glass atrium suspended above the Barbican Centre. As you approach the Barbican's brutalist tower blocks from the Silk Street entrance, a luxuriant greenhouse is visible above the grey concrete flats. The lushness of the conservatory – which contains over 2000 species of trees and plants, as well as tropical finches, quails, and exotic fish - makes a startling contrast to the surrounding glass, steel, and raw concrete of the Barbican Estate.

The principal obstacle to visiting this hidden garden in the sky is the limited opening times. When it was inaugurated in 1982, the conservatory was open to everyone; but feeble public response forced the Corporation of the City of London to whittle away visiting hours. It is now mainly used as an unusual setting for private parties, often hosted by corporate sponsors of the theatre and concert hall at the heart of the Barbican Centre. The conservatory itself is wrapped around the fly tower (where scenery is lowered onto the stage) of the Barbican's main theatre.

Low visitor response has bedevilled the Barbican since it opened. It forms part of the Barbican Estate, a hermetically sealed island within the city. Access is often discouraged by seemingly endless walkways and blank concrete walls. Even the entrances to the performance spaces are oddly inconspicuous. Follow the painted signage on the ground if you get lost.

However, the Barbican has enjoyed a renaissance in recent years. Originally constructed for workers in the Corporation, the retro design, central location and cohesive urban system of the estate meant that when London flooded with money in the 1980s, flats were snapped up by City workers. Today, they are some of the most desirable lodgings in London.

BROADGATE ICE SKATING RINK ㉖

12 Exchange Square, Broadgate Circus, EC2
0207 505 4068
www.broadgateinfo.net
Open Oct - April: Mon-Thurs noon-2:30pm, 3:30-5:30pm,
Fri noon-2:30pm, 3:30-6pm, 7-9pm, Sat-Sun 11am-1pm, 2-4pm, 5-7pm
Admission £6 adults, £4 children + £2 to hire skates
Transport Liverpool Street tube or rail

Skating
with stockbrokers

Despite its location in the beating heart of investment banking, this is London's cheapest outdoor ice skating rink. It's also the only ice rink open for six months of the year, from late October to April. Hemmed in by office blocks, the circular arena is not very big – around 22 square metres – and has none of the gimmickry or pageantry of its Christmas counterparts at Somerset House or Kew Gardens. Ringed by limestone steps and benches, it looks like a movie set dropped into the City. On weekdays, the ice rink tends to be empty except for a handful of teenage truants skidding around to an incongruous '80s soundtrack. Apart from the investment bankers who stare longingly at the skaters from their glass towers, few people seem to know it is here.

The rest of the year, Broadgate Circus ice rink is converted into an outdoor performance and exhibition space.

'BROOMBALL': A POST-MODERN SPIN ON ICE HOCKEY

Broadgate Circus livens up considerably on Monday and Tuesday evenings, however, when 'broomball' matches are held from 6-9pm. A kind of post-modern spin on ice hockey, substituting brooms for sticks and sneakers for skates, this six-a-side sport is strictly for rubber-jointed adrenaline junkies. Big in Canada for over a century, broomball probably originated in Iceland, where a bloodthirsty sport known as *knattleikr* has been played since the 10th century. Apparently, casualties were commonplace, and games involving whole villages could last two weeks.

THE CORNHILL DEVILS

According to an inscription in the churchyard, St Peter upon Cornhill, on the corner of Cornhill and Gracechurch Streets, is the earliest Christian site in Britain, founded in 187. However, the church is most famous for the three devilish gargoyles perched on the Victorian office block next door. During its construction, the architect attempted to steal a foot-wide strip of church land; but the eagle-eyed vicar kicked up such a stink that the architect had to redraw the plans. In a fit of pique, he set these gruesome devils on the roof, which continue to curse the congregation as they enter. One spits, another sticks its fingers up like a rebellious teenager, while the devil closest to the street apparently bears a striking resemblance to the bothersome reverend. The devils are visible silhouetted against the sky if you stand on the north side of the building.

CITY LIVERY COMPANIES

Various locations, various opening times
www.cityoflondon.gov.uk/Corporation/LGNL_Services/Leisure_and_culture/Local_
history_and_heritage/Livery/

***Descendants
of the guilds***

ondon has 108 (and counting) Livery Companies; these are trade associations based exclusively in the City that were originally developed from guilds (hence Guildhall), which regulated their trades, controlling wages and labour conditions – a kind of proto-union. Medieval in origin, most are known as "The Worshipful Company of ...". Many of them represent obsolete trades, such as Bowyers (longbow makers) and Girdlers (sword belt and dress belt makers). However, numbers are rising as modern trades become incorporated – recent additions include The Worshipful Company of Management Consultants and The Worshipful Company of Security Professionals.

Nowadays, most Companies are primarily charitable organisations, but they still retain an aura of medieval pomp and circumstance; they have a strict order of precedence, and the first 12 are known as the Great Twelve. Around 40 have meeting halls, and many of these are open to the public on open days or by arrangement. Choice halls include the 1835 Goldsmiths' Hall, laid out in marble (www.thegoldsmiths.co.uk/hall), the riverside Fishmongers' Hall (www.fishhall.co.uk/tours.htm), which contains the dagger that Sir William Walworth, the Lord Mayor of London – and a fishmonger – used to end the Peasants' Revolt by stabbing the rebel Wat Tyler to death in front of King Richard II in 1381. The Apothecaries' Hall (www.apothecaries.co.uk) is the oldest halls, built in the 17th century – but tours are limited to ten or more. This is the difficulty with visits; each hall has a different entry policy, and arrangements are best made in advance with the offices. The spectacular Drapers' Hall (www.thedraperscompany.co.uk), for example, admits no tours between the end of July and mid-September. Persistence is worthwhile, however; very few Londoners ever see inside the halls.

DOGGETTS COAT AND BADGE

The City Livery are involved in charities, schools and investment, but they also operate one or two oddities. The world's longest continually running sporting event, Doggetts Coat and Badge, is organised by the Fishmongers' Company; this is a 4 mile rowing race on the Thames which has been run since 1714 against the tide between London Bridge and Chelsea Bridge. Irish comic actor Thomas Doggett gave money to endow the race between young watermen – the prize is a red coat with a silver badge on one arm. There is a pub of the same name south of Blackfriars Bridge – best avoided.

MARYLEBONE
TO SHEPHERD'S BUSH

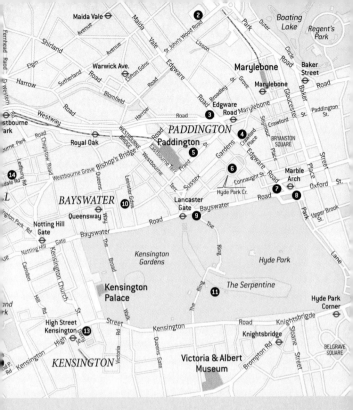

KENSAL GREEN CATACOMBS ❶

Kensal Green Cemetery, Harrow Road, W10
07904 495012
www.kensalgreen.co.uk
Open First and third Sundays of each month; meet 2pm on the steps
of the Anglican Chapel in the centre of the grounds
Admission £5, conc. £4
Transport Kensal Green tube

> *A glimpse
> of the Victorian
> cult of death*

The first of the 'Magnificent Seven' ring of garden cemeteries that sprang up around London in the mid-19th century (see Nunhead Cemetery p.321), Kensal Green is also the largest and most opulent. Inspired by Père-Lachaise Cemetery in Paris, the developers tried to import European funerary practices such as mausoleums. Beneath the Anglican Chapel at the heart of the cemetery, they also created catacombs. The Friends of Kensal Green, a conservation charity, offer regular tours of the cemetery, and twice a month lead visitors on a descent into the tombs.

The catacombs are everything you might expect – damp, cold and dark. The brick avenues are lined with coffins stacked on shelves, mostly in plain view, sometimes behind glass, or iron grilles – mourners liked to be able to commune with the dead. The caskets are often highly decorated, or at least the outer ones are. Each coffin is triple shelled; a wooden casket inside a lead one (made by a plumber), encased in an outer shell, often covered in scarlet velvet or ornate metalwork.

Most of the coffins are in a state of decay, covered in a powdery bloom where rot has set in. Others have the remains of mementoes – desiccated flowers, or in the case of the tomb of the Earls of Clare, a wooden coronet. Some of the coffins are outlandishly huge, as if giants were buried within; others are instantly recognisable as children. There is also a functioning catafalque – a hydraulic winch used to lower the coffins to the catacombs from the chapel above at a suitably funereal pace. Look out for a pair of glass domes containing immortelles – beautiful lifelike flowers made from the finest porcelain and copper. The catacombs are still functioning, and there is shelf space for sale if you're interested. Vacancies are marked with a grubby sign: "Available".

Kensal Green Cemetery opened in 1833. It became intensely fashionable after the Duke of Sussex was buried there in 1843, as people wanted to be interred beside royalty. Other "notables" include the graves of the Brunels, inventor Charles Babbage, and Charles Blondin, who crossed Niagara Falls on a tightrope. The fifth Duke of Portland is also buried there. Known as the Burrowing Duke, he built 15 miles of gaslit tunnels at his estate in Nottinghamshire to avoid human contact. If his staff ever made eye contact with him, they were dismissed or sent for punishment on a purpose-built roller-skating rink.

150th Anniversary
1848   Dr. W G GRACE   1998

MARYLEBONE CRICKET CLUB MUSEUM ❷

Lord's, St John's Wood Road NW8
0207 616 8595
www.lords.org
Open Tours 10am, 12pm & 2pm daily, except match days
Admission Museum: £3, concessions £1 Tours: £12,
children £6, seniors and students £7
Transport St John's Wood tube

The world's
oldest sporting
museum

lthough it began as a "gentleman's game" played exclusively by aristocrats, early cricket fans were all chronic gamblers. In the 19th century, the wicket was prepared before a match by inviting sheep to graze on the grass. There is a waiting list of 18 years for membership of Marylebone Cricket Club (MCC). These are just a few of the surprising facts you'll learn if you "take a tour of Lords", probably the world's most famous cricket ground. It's certainly one of the oldest, founded on a former duck pond in 1814 by a wine merchant named Thomas Lord.

The guided tour starts in the MCC Memorial Gallery, the world's first sporting museum. Among the signed bats, smelly boots, and old photographs spanning 400 years of cricket history, are oddities such as the stuffed sparrow that was "bowled out" by Jehangir Khan in 1936.

Visitors also have a rare opportunity to sneak around the 19th century club rooms reserved for the 22,000 members of the MCC. On match days, at least 200 VIPs are crammed into the elegant Long Room, with its picture windows and paintings of celebrated cricketers. Players make their way to and from the field through the Long Room's double doors – either to rapturous ovation or deadly silence, depending on their performance. When the Queen cares to watch a match, she sits in the Committee Room, where the worldwide laws of cricket are still thrashed out. But the best seats are undoubtedly in the Media Centre, a sleek white capsule that hovers 15 metres above the ground.

"THE WORST BEHAVED CROWD OF THE SEASON"
The annual fixture between the pupils of Eton and Harrow is a tradition that has flourished since 1805. According to the tour guide, it's "the worst behaved crowd of the season."

THE "ASHES" OF THE FIRST HOME DEFEAT OF ENGLAND IN 1882
The prized exhibit of the museum is a small Victorian perfume jar, containing "The Ashes". The term was coined after England lost to Australia on home soil for the first time on 29 August 1882. The next day, *The Sporting Times* published an ironic obituary to English cricket, concluding that: "The body will be cremated and the ashes taken to Australia". When the English team set off to tour Australia weeks later, Captain Ivo Bligh vowed to return home with The Ashes. After Bligh's team beat Australia, his future wife, Florence Morphy, gave him this miniature urn as a token of his victory. When Bligh died in 1927, he bequeathed The Ashes to the MCC where they have been on display ever since.

EST 06 06 06

SUBWAY
GALLERY

A HOME FOR UNDERGROUND ART

SUBWAY GALLERY

3

Kiosk 1, Pedestrian Subway below Edgware Road/Harrow Road, W2;
07811 286503
www.subwaygallery.com
Open Mon-Sat 11am-7pm
Admission free
Transport Edgware Road tube

> *Underground art*

With its nasty neon lights and vague smell of pee, the pedestrian subway beneath the Marylebone flyover is not a place most people would choose to linger – although the disorientating layout of the tunnels may prevent you finding your way out. Far below the thundering traffic, one of the stainless steel kiosks that normally sell cigarettes and stale samosas has been transformed into an underground art space. The Subway Gallery was set up in 2006 by artist and curator Robert Gordon McHarg III, a gangly Canadian who delights in provoking passers-by with subversive art.

Monthly exhibitions in the tiny, brightly lit cubicle feature both emerging artists and McHarg's own work. One permanent fixture is a brilliantly lifelike waxwork replica of art collector Charles Saatchi, entitled HIM. McHarg dressed this dummy in 101 hilarious disguises: a London bobby, a cowboy, Mickey Mouse, and Saddam Hussein (a witty riff on the fact that the advertising supremo was born in Baghdad). The result became both a photographic exhibition and a book. Although McHarg pledged not to sell the original - "It is the one piece of art that Charles Saatchi won't buy," he quipped – he has since made a second waxwork that was put up for sale at the Trolley Gallery. Whether or not Saatchi has enough of a sense of humour to snap up his effigy remains to be seen.

Artworks often spill out onto the 'Black Wall', a disused section of the tunnel that has become an extension of the Subway Gallery. It's a welcome break from the daily commute.

Director Julien Temple chose this suitably grungy setting to shoot the Babyshambles' single *The Blinding*, with a spaced out Pete Doherty and gang pressed against the gallery windows and 'Charles Saatchi' getting down with the band.

McHarg must have something of an obsession with the London Underground. Back in 2001, he organised Art-Tube, a month-long show set on a moving tube train on the Piccadilly Line. 120 advertising panels were hijacked by 42 artists, poets, and designers. He persuaded heavyweights like Damien Hirst, Juergen Teller, Gavin Turk, Yoko Ono, and even Vivienne Westwood to take part.

THE HANDLEBAR CLUB ④

Members meet at 8pm on the first Friday of the month
at the *Windsor Castle* pub, Crawford Place, W1
www.handlebarclub.co.uk
Transport Edgware Road tube

Wax factor

Scratch the surface, and London is full of odd members' clubs such as the Veteran-Cycle Club, the Time Travel Club, or the newly reformed Eccentric Club. Perhaps the oddest of them all is the Handlebar Club of Great Britain. It was founded in 1947 by Jimmy Edwards, a popular post-war comedian, who once sang: "Every girl loves a fella with a bush upon his mush!"

The Handlebar Club originally had ten members; today, it has around 100 acolytes from all over the world. The club's mission was and remains "to bring together moustache wearers socially for sport and general conviviality". The criterion for membership is simple: prospective members must have "a hirsute appendage of the upper lip, with graspable extremities". Beards are banned. The other essential qualification is "to be able to drink plenty of beer" at the club's monthly get-togethers at the *Windsor Castle* pub, just off Edgware Road. Naturally, the pub landlord, Michael Tierney, is a club member with impressive "lip foliage".

About a dozen members usually show up at these monthly gatherings and they are unmistakable. Most dressed in "member's regalia" – maroon silk ties emblazoned with a white moustache and matching club sweaters – and all have redoubtable chops. Bushy, twirly, waxed or curled, their moustaches are eminently graspable. These self-confessed "facial hair fanatics" don't appear to do much other than "furry fraternising", which involves frequently raising their pint glasses with the toast: "To the last whisker!" Apparently, members do occasionally engage in charitable stunts such as finding out how many moustaches fit into a Mini. However, they do at least pay lip service to the Handlebar Club's Constitution, a copy of which is available to prospective members. For instance, anyone who lets their sideburns merge with their moustache is fined.

Even before Hitler and the Village People, moustaches had long been reviled as an unfashionable accoutrement. So these brave souls who risk gawping and mocking sniggers from passers-by deserve a little respect for their hirsute pluck.

WORLD BEARD AND MOUSTACHE CHAMPIONSHIPS

Every two years, members enter the World Beard and Moustache Championships, where contestants battle it out in categories that include Dali, imperial, Hungarian, musketeer and freestyle.

As well as moustache memorabilia, the *Windsor Castle* is crammed with royal knick-knacks. Even the ceiling is covered in souvenir china.

ALEXANDER FLEMING LABORATORY MUSEUM ❺

St Mary's Hospital, Praed Street, W2
0207 886 6528
www.medicalmuseums.org/Alexander-Fleming-Laboratory-Museum/
Open 10am-1pm Mon-Thurs, or by appointment Mon-Thurs 2-5pm,
Fri 10am-5pm
Admission £2, children, senior citizens and students £1
Transport Paddington tube/rail

The discovery of "mould juice"

A blue plaque outside St Mary's hospital alerts passers-by that Alexander Fleming (1881-1955) discovered penicillin in the second-storey room above it. Few visitors venture up to the tiny museum, accessible via a dingy entrance on Norfolk Place.

When Fleming was born, antibiotics did not exist. Minor infections often proved fatal and a quarter of all hospital patients died of gangrene after surgery. When Fleming enrolled as a medical student at St Mary's in 1900, he dreamed of becoming a surgeon; but - luckily for the rest of us - he was given a temporary position in the Inoculation Department, where he remained until his death.

The poky laboratory where Fleming worked between 1919 and 1933 (when it was converted into a bedroom for students of midwifery) has been painstakingly recreated. The wooden counter is cluttered with vials and test tubes containing mysterious fluids, tattered leather-bound medical tomes, a couple of antique microscopes and countless glass culture dishes. One day in 1922, Fleming was hunched over his bacteria cultures as usual, despite suffering from a nasty cold. A drop of snot landed on his Petri dish, which led to his discovery of the antiseptic properties of mucus, saliva and tears. In September 1928, Fleming made another chance discovery that changed the course of medical history. When one of his cultures was contaminated with mould from a lab downstairs, Fleming hit on the healing properties of fungus – and effectively invented penicillin. "It couldn't have happened anywhere but this musty, dusty lab, as the mould would not have grown in a more hygienic environment," says curator Kevin Brown.

"MOULD JUICE" THAT TASTES LIKE STILTON...
Fleming's assistant, Stuart Craddock, ate some of this "mould juice" to prove that it was not poisonous. Craddock claimed that it tasted like Stilton, prompting a flurry of sensational headlines about mouldy cheese being a miracle cure for disease.

The mouldy Petri dish in the museum is actually a replica – the original is in the British Library along with several of Fleming's notebooks.

Alexander Fleming's grave in St Paul's Cathedral is decorated with the Scottish thistle and the fleur de lys, symbol of St Mary.

HORSEMAN'S SUNDAY ❻

St John's Hyde Park, Hyde Park Crescent, W2
0207 262 1732
http://stjohns-hydepark.com/
Open at noon on the penultimate Sunday of September
Transport Marble Arch, Paddington tube

Eccentric equestrian blessing

A t noon on the penultimate Sunday of September, Connaught Village celebrates a bizarre ritual dating back to 1968, when the nearby stables were threatened with closure. Outside St John's church, a Gothic pile on leafy Hyde Park Crescent, locals tuck into free tandoori chicken while children covered in face paint crunch through carpets of autumn leaves. It feels like a village fete, complete with a tombola, home-baked cakes, and a jazz band tinkling away. But as the Sunday service draws to a close, the Vicar appears on horseback in an emerald green cape and Napoleonic hat, followed by an orderly procession of about 100 horses. There are squat Shetland ponies with pint-sized riders, sleek stallions, posh blondes in skin-tight jodhpurs. There's even a Harrods carriage, its poker-stiff passengers kitted out in the store's distinctive green livery. An impatient stallion lets out a torrent of urine, frightening the toddlers and titillating the teenagers. The Reverend Stephen Mason gives "thanks to all the animals that give us pleasure in our homes and in the world." He even quotes John Wayne: "Courage is when you're scared to death and still get into the saddle."

ROYAL FRIVOLITIES ON ROTTEN ROW

After moving his court from Whitehall to Kensington Palace, King William III discovered that the route back to St James's palace through Hyde Park was thick with 'footpads', or muggers. So in 1690 he installed 300 oil lamps - the first artificially lit highway in Britain – along the Route de Roi (Route of the King), soon corrupted by the British to a much less majestic name, Rotten Row. This was where 19th century kings and courtesans paraded in all their finery. There are still five miles of 'bridleways' in Hyde Park. Ross Nye Stables (8 Bathurst Mews; 0207 262 3791) and Hyde Park Stables (63 Bathurst Mews; 0207 723 2813; www.hydeparkstables.com) offer horseback jaunts along them.

LONDON'S MEWS

These cobbled cul-de-sacs, now coveted for their quaint cottages, housed London's many stables when the most common form of transport for ladies and gentlemen was the horse and carriage. In 1900, there were 300,000 working horses in London. These days, Jaguars and Bentleys are parked behind the colourful stable doors of London's exclusive mews. The fanciest surviving stables belong to the Queen. Tucked away in the Royal Mews behind Buckingham Palace, designed by John Nash, they house the Gold State Coach, covered in four tons' worth of bling. Queen Victoria refused to ride in it. Apparently, it gave her "distressing oscillations".

TYBURN CONVENT ❼

8-12 Hyde Park Place, W1
0207 723 7262
www.tyburnconvent.org.uk
Open daily with 40-minute guided tours at 10.30am, 3.30pm and
5.30pm
Admission free
Transport Marble Arch tube

> *Cloistered from the consumers of Oxford Street*

The grand townhouses of Bayswater Road overlook Hyde Park, but the residents of Nos 8-12 can only enjoy these green vistas from a distance. They are home to around two dozen cloistered Benedictine nuns, who maintain a constant 24-hour vigil in the ground-floor chapel. Though just moments away from the bustle of Oxford Street, the nuns only venture out for medical emergencies. Food is delivered – but they don't do takeaways.

The nuns spend most of their time in silence, but seven times a day they sing Mass – a beautifully ethereal music, echoing through the domed chapel. Worshippers can listen, but cannot see the nuns – the altar is screened by a metal grille.

Tyburn Convent was founded in 1901 to commemorate the 105 Roman Catholics hanged nearby on the Tyburn Tree gallows during the Reformation (1535 - 1681). The crypt contains a shrine to these Catholic martyrs, including gruesome relics of their bones, hair, and bloodstained clothing. There are three daily tours of the crypt. Over the altar is a replica of the infamous gallows, which stood just east of here, on what is now a traffic island at the junction of Bayswater Road and Edgware Road. A small, circular plaque in the paving stones marks the site where around 50,000 people were executed between 1196 and 1783. Hangings were so popular that execution days were declared public holidays. However, Mayfair's posh residents didn't like this barbaric spectator sport on their doorstep, and forced the authorities to move the gallows to Newgate (see page 87 St Sepulchre) in 1783.

THE SMALLEST HOUSE IN LONDON

Now part of Tyburn Convent, this "house" is just over 106 cm wide. The ground floor consists entirely of a corridor, while the first floor contains nothing but a cramped bathroom. Dating from 1805, it was probably erected to block a passageway leading to St George's graveyard - popular with body-snatchers at the time.

SIGHTS NEARBY

MARBLE ARCH SURVEILLANCE ROOMS ❽

Marble Arch was built by John Nash in 1828 as a monumental entrance to Buckingham Palace. To this day, only senior royals and their guards are permitted to pass through its central arch. No matter: since it was moved in 1851, Marble Arch has been marooned at the junctions of Oxford Street, Park Lane and Edgware Road, making access impossible to all but the foolhardiest pedestrians. Legend has it that there are three small rooms inside the arch, used for police surveillance until the 1950s.

HYDE PARK PET CEMETERY

9

Victoria Gate, Hyde Park, W2
Open By appointment only, during office hours. Call Hyde Park Police
on 0207 298 2000 one week in advance to book your visit
Admission free
Transport Lancaster Gate tube; buses 10, 70, 94

> *Bestial burial ground hidden in Hyde Park*

Mad dogs and Englishmen have always been inseparable. The members of the Victorian upper crust were so obsessed with their pets that they buried them in special cemeteries. Barely visible behind the railings of Hyde Park, on the corner of Bayswater Road and Victoria Gate, hundreds of miniature, mildewed gravestones stand testament to this morbid tradition.

This particular pet cemetery was founded in 1880 by George, Duke of Cambridge, who had flouted royal convention by marrying an actress, Louisa Fairbrother. When his distraught wife's favourite dog, Prince, was run over, the Duke - who doubled as Chief Ranger of Hyde Park - asked the gate-keeper, Mr. Windbridge, to give the poor creature a proper burial in the back garden of his lodge.

By 1915, the graves in Mr. Windbridge's garden were so tightly packed that the cemetery was closed. Over 300 animals are laid to rest here - dogs, cats, birds, and even a monkey. Drowned, poisoned, or run over, Flo, Carlo, and Yum Yum's miniature gravestones bear epitaphs that range from the touching to the maudlin: quotes from the Bible and Shakespearean couplets are sprinkled among personal tributes: "To the memory of my dear Emma - faithful and sole companion of my otherwise rootless and desolate life." Some posh dogs even had bespoke coffins. One lady who buried her Pomeranian in a locked casket allegedly wore the keys around her neck until she went to her own grave.

This bestial necropolis received one last canine resident - also named Prince – in 1967, when the Royal Marines were granted special permission to bury their 11-year-old mascot in the southern corner.

Today, the place George Orwell called "perhaps the most horrible spectacle in Britain" can only be viewed by prior appointment, with a week's notice.

SIGHTS NEARBY

THE FAKE HOUSES OF LEINSTER GARDENS

10

When London's first Tube line was extended westwards, inevitably some houses had to be demolished. The owners of 23/24 Leinster Gardens in Bayswater sold up, but local residents demanded that the façades of these five-storey terraces be rebuilt to keep up appearances. At first glance, the fake façades are indistinguishable from their neighbours, but look closer and you'll see that all 18 windows are blacked out with grey paint. Although there are no letter boxes, the address is predictably popular with conmen. In the 1930s, unsuspecting guests turned up to a charity ball at 23 Leinster Gardens in full evening dress. They never got their money back.

THE SERPENTINE SOLARSHUTTLE ⑪

Serpentine Lake, Hyde Park, W2 • 0207 262 1330
www.solarshuttle.co.uk
Tickets One-way: £2.50 adult, £1 child, £6 family of four. Return: £4.50
adult, £1.50 child, £10 family. **Departures** Every hour noon–6pm from
the Princess of Wales Memorial Fountain and 12.30-5.30pm
from the Boathouse. Weekends only during the winter.

*Eco-friendly
Pleasure Cruise*

With its miserable weather, London is not an obvious choice for innovations in solar power. Yet among the 110 rowing boats and pedal boats that cruise the Serpentine in Hyde Park, the Solarshuttle glides silently across the lake, powered entirely by the sun. A streamlined vision of glass and stainless steel, the 14.5 metre Solarshuttle can carry up to 40 passengers and two crew members. The half-mile journey between the north and the south banks of the Serpentine Lake takes about half an hour, as the boat doesn't go much faster than five miles (8km) an hour. It's a wonderfully serene experience.

With its graceful design, the Solarshuttle feels more like a yacht than a miniature ferry. The wooden deck is lined with slatted steel benches which afford unbroken views of the park. All the architectural details emphasise light and transparency. Detachable glass panels protect passengers from the elements during the winter. Overhead, a curved canopy of 27 solar panels attached to a simple steel frame glints in the sunlight. Not much thicker than a credit card, these photovoltaic cells are embedded into Plexiglas tiles that are layered between a transparent membrane. The solar energy produced is stored in batteries that power two electric engines. When the boat is docked, any surplus electricity generated by the solar panels is fed back into the national power grid. The Solarshuttle took seven months and cost £237,000 to build – a worthwhile investment given that a diesel-powered boat of this size would produce 2.5 tons of carbon dioxide every year. Even on those overcast days so depressingly familiar to Londoners, there is apparently enough sunlight to keep the Solarshuttle cruising. If the weather gets really dire, the batteries provide enough reserve power to drive the shuttle for 20 miles in pitch darkness.

Solar Lab, the UK company behind the Solarshuttle, says their mission is to seduce people to embrace eco-friendly technology through exceptional design. Designer Christoph Behling also created one of the world's largest solar boats, the Hamburg Solarshuttle, which ferries passengers across the German city's harbour. As well as developing a larger solar-powered ferry for cruising the Thames and a solar-powered train for Battersea Park, Solar Lab is working on solar-powered golf carts, rickshaws, and even a mosque in Dubai.

CAB SHELTERS

Locations: Chelsea Embankment (near Albert Bridge) SW3 • Embankment Place, Charing Cross WC2 • Grosvenor Gardens, Victoria SW1; Hanover Square, Mayfair W1 • Kensington Park Road, Notting Hill W11 • Kensington Road (north side), South Kensington W8; Pont Street, Belgravia SW1 • Russell Square (west corner), Bloomsbury WC1 • St George's Square, Pimlico • Temple Place, Victoria Embankment WC2 • Thurloe Place, South Kensington SW7 • Clifton Gardens, Maida Vale W9 • Wellington Place, St John's Wood NW8.

Know-
ledgeable diners

The London Hackney Carriage Industry was first licensed by an act of Oliver Cromwell in June 1654, and Londoners can be justly proud of the city's characteristic black cabs, the direct descendants of the carriages. This is one of the few really pleasurable travel experiences in the city, where the congestion charge deters motorists and public transport is overcrowded, unreliable, and overpriced. The cabs have so much legroom that you can sit back almost horizontally and watch the city slide by.

London's cab drivers are equally impressive, as all of them are required to have 'the Knowledge'. This exam, introduced in 1865, means cabbies must remember every street within six miles of Charing Cross (the official centre of London). This formidable feat can take three years to achieve. If you keep your eyes peeled, you can see students of the Knowledge everywhere - people riding mopeds around the city with a clipboard and map on the handlebars are usually prospective cabbies learning routes before their exam, which involves a flawless rendition of a route between any two given points chosen at random by the examining board.

Naturally, the cabbies need feeding. Originally, cab drivers weren't allowed to leave their vehicles when parked, so in 1874 the Earl of Shaftsbury set up the Cabmen's Shelter Fund to construct and run shelters to provide cabbies with 'good and wholesome refreshments at moderate prices'. The result was a flourishing of green wooden sheds around the capital; because the shelters stand directly on a public highway, they could be no bigger than a horse and cart – even so, they still manage to squeeze in a working kitchen and space for over ten men.

There were originally 61 of these shelters, but numbers have now dwindled to 13 as cabbies now have the freedom to get out of their cabs. These few remaining sheds, often in some of the poshest parts of London, are now listed buildings. Thankfully, they still thrive as a place for colleagues to meet as much as eat. Only cabbies are allowed to sit inside, but anyone can get a take-away – bacon roll, brown sauce, tea, four sugars, thanks love – through the serving hatch.

The philanthropists who set up the shelters were typically high-minded Victorians: gambling, drinking and swearing were strictly forbidden. The original intent in getting the cabmen into the shelters was to keep them out of the pubs.

THE ARAB HALL OF LEIGHTON HOUSE 🕐

12 Holland Park Road, W14
0207 371 2467
www.rbkc.gov.uk/subsites/museums/leightonhousemuseum.aspx
Open 11am-5.30pm daily; closed Tues.
Admission £3; concessions £1. Free guided tours 2.30pm Wed and Thurs.
Transport High Street Kensington or Holland Park tube.

Many of the Victorian mansions around Holland Park were built by artists who gravitated to this urbane neighbourhood towards the end of the 19th century. The "Holland Park circle" included Lord Frederic Leighton (1830-1896), President of the Royal Academy, whose red brick show home looks fairly unassuming from the outside, apart from its dome.

> *'It was a bit of Aladdin's palace, which some obliging genius might have set down in London and have forgotten.'*

Inside, Leighton House is designed to make a very big impression. Mary H. Krout, an American who visited Leighton House in 1899, remarked: "…it was like a bit of Aladdin's palace, which some obliging genius might have set down in London and have forgotten." The entrance hall is clad in brilliant peacock blue tiles, while a real stuffed peacock guards the grand staircase. To the left is the Arab Hall, decorated with rare Islamic tiles, inlaid mosaics, and Arabic inscriptions, with a black marble fountain as its centrepiece. The rest of the residence is decked out in equally opulent style. Flock wallpapers, oriental carpets, and ornate fireplaces create an orgy of patterns and textures, against which the pre-Raphaelite paintings by Leighton and his contemporaries look positively sedate. Among his extensive collection are works by Edward Burne-Jones, Albert Moore, and George Frederic Watts, who lived around the corner on Melbury Road.

Leighton's vast studio appears to be decorated with friezes filched from the Parthenon. This was the setting for Leighton's annual musical recitals; the tradition continues today with chamber music concerts organised by the Kensington and Chelsea Music Society, with a similar smattering of socialites in attendance. You may also find local aristos brushing up their social skills at seminars on Victorian etiquette held at Leighton House.

SIGHTS NEARBY

KENSINGTON ROOF GARDENS 🕐

High above the boutiques of Kensington High Street, on the 6th floor of Barker's department store 99 Derry Street, are 6,000 square metres of secret gardens that date from the 1930s. There's a Spanish garden, with fountains, palms, and vine-covered walkways, a Tudor garden, whose archways are strung with wisteria, and a miniature English woodland, with some forlorn goldfish in a murky pond and a pair of pink flamingos prancing under a willow tree. Owner Richard Branson has rather spoiled the romantic setting with some heavy-handed Virgin branding and a dodgy discotheque. Sadly, the view is obscured by high walls, and you can hear the hum of traffic beneath the twitter of birds.

MUSEUM OF BRANDS, PACKAGING AND ADVERTISING

⑭

Colville Mews, off Lonsdale Road, W11
0207 908 0880
www.museumofbrands.com
Open Tues – Sat 10am-6pm, Sun 11am-5pm
Admission £5.80, children £2, concessions £3.50
Transport Notting Hill Gate tube

An extraordinary history of the everyday

Tucked away down a quaint Notting Hill mews, where half the houses have been commandeered by fashion designer Alice Temperley, a visit to the Museum of Brands, Packaging and Advertising is like leafing through a picture book of Britain's social history for the last two centuries.

Collector par excellence Robert Opie has assembled a vast repertory of everyday objects, from Victoriana ('harness liquid' for carriages and 'wind pills' for sea sickness) through to the 1980s (Spacehoppers and *Smash Hits*). Toys, cosmetics, clothes, and cleaning products – it's all here, artfully arranged by decade or occasionally by theme. The material sheds light on the changing fashions and consuming passions of British society.

Once upon a time, banal products like shoe polish and cough syrup came in ornate glass jars and dainty decanters. Housekeepers stocked up on Vermin Killer – 'mice eat it readily and die on the spot!' But how times changed from the days when 'Servants' Friend' stove polish was in vogue to the invention of the servants' bane: the first vacuum cleaner.

Opie's impressive hoard includes souvenirs from the Great Exhibition of 1851. There are wireless radios and wind-up gramophones, saucy postcards and a whole room devoted to magazines. From the art deco glamour of the 1930s, it's a jarring leap to the ration cards and Union Jack logos of WWII, when people were exhorted to eat 'health salts' in lieu of fruit. The 1950s brings a kitschy optimism, all colourful formica and plastic kitchenware, pin-ups in bikinis, and convertible cars for beach holidays. The '60s are summed up by the arrival of portable radios and TVs and, of course, The Beatles. And what a decade the 1970s was: Queen Elizabeth's silver jubilee, Planet of the Apes, and platform shoes.

Graphic designers will delight in the section devoted to brands, which revisits the evolution of classic British products like Brillo pads, Cadbury's chocolate, and Colman's mustard. Temporary exhibitions are held in the little café, where period films are screened on TV. You can also buy scrapbooks organised by decade, a wonderful source of inspiration for designers and illustrators.

Opie himself is occasionally around at weekends to talk you through his collection, which is so rich that it merits several visits. The museum is a charity and relies on volunteers - one alternative to paying the admission fee.

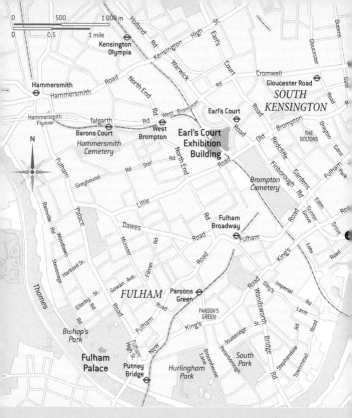

WESTMINSTER
TO HAMMERSMITH

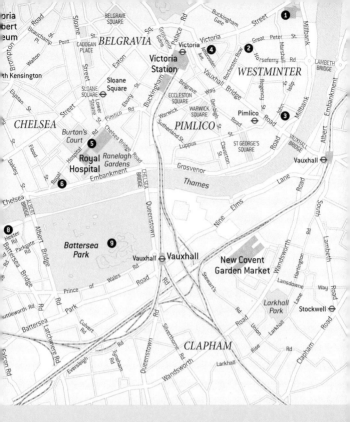

WESTMINSTER ABBEY UNDERCROFT ❶

Westminster Abbey, SW1
0207 654 4900
www.westminster-abbey.org
Open Times vary according to services
Admission £16.00; conc (under-16s, students and 60+) £7.00
family x 4 £24.00 **Transport** Westminster tube

> *Do the eyebrows of Edward III come from a plucked dog?*

If you can stomach paying a ten pound admission price to a church, if you can steel yourself to fight through the tour groups, and if you can ignore the relentless creepiness of the Abbey, then the Undercroft museum is really worth a visit. Almost all tourists only troop around the Abbey's tombs and monuments, giving the church the atmosphere of a fetish house for the Establishment. Worst of all is its co-opting of people deemed to have added to the lustre of England. The poet Shelley, despite being an avowed anti-Establishment artist and buried in Rome, is memorialised in Poets Corner, just across the transept from Viscount Castlereagh, (of whom Shelley once in a poem, "I met Murder on the way – He had a face like Castlereagh"). There is also an unseemly huddle of political statuary next to the northern door, inclusion here apparently constituting the acme of ambition for the great and the good sitting opposite in Parliament.

However, adjoining the church itself is the cloister, usually passed by and often empty. The Undercroft is off this, down a short flight of steps. It contains some of the oddest exhibits in London: a collection of royal funerary effigies. Until the Middle Ages, British monarchs were traditionally embalmed and left to lie in state for a set period of time. Eventually, the corpse was substituted by a wooden figure of the departed, fully dressed with clothes from the Great Wardrobe and displayed on top of the funeral carriage during the final journey. As the clothes were expected to fit the effigy perfectly, these likenesses are probably fairly accurate. All are surprisingly tiny, even fatboy Henry VIII. Edward III's face has a strange leer, a recreation of the stroke that he suffered in his final years; amusingly, the eyebrows supposedly came from a plucked dog. The collection also includes the effigies of Edward III, Henry VII, Elizabeth I, Charles II, William III, Mary II and Queen Anne. Later wax effigies include Nelson, William Pitt, and several soldiers known for years as the Ragged Regiment, due to their decrepit state.

Other related relics include the funeral saddle, helm and shield of Henry V, Mary II's coronation chair, and replicas of coronation regalia.

Westminster Abbey is a Royal Peculiar; that is, a church that falls directly under the jurisdiction of the British monarch, rather than a bishop's diocese. Given that, it is surprising that the Crown cannot do more to alleviate the gouging at the ticket office. Or perhaps not.

THE LONDON SCOTTISH REGIMENTAL MUSEUM

❷

95 Horseferry Road, SW1
0207 630 1639
www.londonscottishregt.org/museum.cfm
Open Wed, and Thurs, by appointment with the curator 11am-4pm Tues,
Admission free, but donations welcome
Transport Pimlico tube

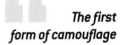

> *The first form of camouflage*

Behind the sombre façade of the Territorial Army headquarters is a soaring drill hall, whose red and blue balconies are decorated with memorabilia from the London Scottish regiment's colourful history. A volunteer corps set up by a group of influential Scots in London in 1859, its distinguished members have included Sir Alexander Fleming, travel writer Eric Newby, and movie star Basil Rathbone.

Access is by appointment, which means that visitors get an exhaustive tour from the zealous archivist – though he may reprimand you if your military history is sketchy. Some of the army acronyms might be rather arcane for the non-expert, but only the coldest of heart will be unmoved by the memorials to the hundreds of untrained soldiers who served and died in the South African War (1900-2) and the Great Wars.

Around the upper floor balconies are all manner of medals, machine guns, bagpipes, uniforms, and photographs of "old soldiers" going into battle in kilts and spats. There is even a scrap of Lieutenant-Colonel Lord Elcho's grey overcoat, which inspired him to invent the first form of camouflage. Fed up with soldiers from different clans bickering about tartans, Elcho decreed that the regiment should wear Hodden Grey, a coarse cloth typically worn in Scotland. This canny move also made the troops less of a target. On Tuesday evenings, between 7pm and 9pm, the magnificent hall is used for drill practice, which must be a stirring sight.

SIGHTS NEARBY

MILLBANK BUTTRESS AND TUNNELS

❸

Opposite Tate Britain is an innocuous-looking bollard bearing a tiny plaque that reads: "Near this site stood Millbank Prison, which was opened in 1816 and closed in 1880. This buttress stood at the head of the river steps from which, until 1867, prisoners sentenced to deportation embarked on their journey to Australia." These prisoners would be shuffled through a series of underground tunnels beneath the prison. A section of the tunnel survives in the cellars of the nearby *Morpeth Arms*, a pub built to serve the prison warders and now allegedly haunted by the ghost of a former inmate. Millbank, the first national penitentiary, was designed as a pentagonal "panopticon" by Jeremy Bentham (see page 25), whose revolutionary design did not live up to his ideals of social reform. Novelist Henry James called Millbank "a worse act of violence than any it was erected to punish". The Tate was built on this inauspicious site in 1897.

WESTMINSTER CATHEDRAL BELL TOWER ❹

Ambrosden Avenue, Victoria SW1
0207 798 9055
www.westminstercathedral.org.uk
Open April-Nov, daily 9.30am-12.30pm and 1-5pm
Dec-March, Thurs-Sun 9am-5pm. Vespers Mon–Fri at 5pm
Saturday 10.30am, Sunday 10.30 and 3.30
Admission £5, conc £2.50 **Transport** Victoria tube

> *Look out across London's skyline*

The Gothic spires of Westminster Abbey may be an all too familiar London landmark, but with its pseudo-Byzantine copper domes and terracotta bell tower striped with white Portland stone, Westminster Cathedral is also quite a sight. Yet apart from Catholics (including recent convert Tony Blair) who come to pray, few people seem to venture into the vast red-brick cathedral, camouflaged among the fine Victorian mansion blocks of the surrounding back streets.

Built between 1895 and 1903, the cathedral's interior was never in fact completed. Its rich marbles and mosaics shimmer in the shadowy gloom. In the northwest corner, concealed behind a gift shop, a lift whisks paying visitors up to the 7th floor of the 83-metre bell tower. Originally, one had to climb the 375 steps to the top. From viewing platforms on all four sides, you can look across London from this great height and marvel at how the ugly modern office blocks have dwarfed the landmarks of a lost empire. Look carefully and you will spot the Union Jack fluttering atop Buckingham Palace, the dome of St Paul's, and the spindly skeleton of Crystal Palace. The industrial bulk of the BT Tower, Canary Wharf, and Battersea Power Station make more of a statement. You can contrast today's skyline with blown-up photographs of the same views from 1912 and study architect John Francis Bentley's original plans for the cathedral.

Don't be alarmed if Big Edward, the 2.5 ton bell named after Edward the Confessor, suddenly tolls overhead. When the lift was installed in 1929, Big Edward had to be relocated above the belfry, which explains why the bell now sounds faintly muffled.

Most evenings, mass is sung by boys from Westminster Cathedral Choir School next door. Time your visit to take advantage of this free concert in one of London's most overlooked settings.

Originally known as Bulinga Fen, the marshland here was reclaimed by the same Benedictine monks who built Westminster Abbey. Its history is certainly varied: a market, a fairground, a maze, a bull-baiting ring and a children's prison have all stood on this site, before the Catholic Church bought the land in 1884.

In Alfred Hitchcock's 1940 thriller *Foreign Correspondent*, an assassin plunges to his death from Westminster Cathedral's bell tower as the Requiem Mass is chanted inside. Hitchcock's own Requiem Mass was held at Westminster Cathedral after his death in 1980.

THE ROYAL HOSPITAL, HOME OF THE CHELSEA PENSIONERS

⑤

Royal Hospital Road, Chelsea SW3
0207 881 5200
www.chelsea-pensioners.co.uk
Open daily 10am-noon, 2-4pm. Closed Sun Oct-March
Admission free
Transport Sloane Square tube

A retirement home designed by Christopher Wren

Renting a small flat on Chelsea's Royal Hospital Road would set you back at least £500 a week. For the price of their monthly pension, the lucky 300-odd army veterans who live at the Royal Hospital Chelsea get a nine foot square berth designed by Christopher Wren, three meals a day, access to a clubhouse, library, bowling green, croquet lawn, billiard rooms, and 66 acres of gardens beside the Thames. They also get to wear snazzy uniforms - scarlet jackets and tricorne hats for special occasions, smart navy blazers for everyday wear.

King Charles II founded the baroque, red-brick Royal Hospital in 1682 as a refuge for wounded war veterans. Back in the 17th century, when recruits joined the army at the age of 11 or 12, only one in ten pensioners were literate. These days, the charming old boys are happy to show visitors around the small museum, which tells the history of this miraculous time warp through paintings, historical artefacts, and over 2000 medals. There's even a model wooden berth, snug as a ship's cabin, recently equipped with plugs for modern appliances. For 150 years, they had no lights at all.

The Royal Hospital's residential halls are laid out around three immaculate quadrangles. At 10:30 on Sunday mornings, pensioners parade through Figure Court in their ceremonial finery. Only about a dozen have the energy or inclination these days. Listen carefully, and you might hear the master of ceremonies mumbling: "Shuffle about, boys!" There's also an infirmary, where inmates have en-suite bathrooms. The only drawback is that rooms overlook their last posting – the cemetery.

Meals are taken in the grand, wood-panelled Great Hall, lined with antique flags, royal portraits, and inscriptions detailing every British military exploit since its foundation. Inside the door is a large table on which the Duke of Wellington was laid in state in 1852. Today, it holds two five gallon 'black jacks', leather flagons that were once filled with ale. These days, residents have to make do with tea.

Chelsea pensioners must be over 65, "of good military character", and have no dependents. They must also be male, although there are tentative plans to admit women once en-suite bathrooms are installed throughout. When a pensioner applies for admission, they are invited to stay for four days to see whether the Royal Hospital suits them. Who would turn down the chance to live out their days in such magnificent surroundings?

CHELSEA PHYSIC GARDEN ❻

66 Royal Hospital Road SW3
0207 352 5646
www.chelseaphysicgarden.co.uk
Open April–Oct Wed noon-5pm, Sun noon-6pm
Admission £7, children and concessions £4
Transport Sloane Square or Victoria tube then 239 bus

Botanical gardens on the banks of the Thames

Horticulturalists and herbalists will delight in this enchanting walled garden containing almost 5000 plant species from all over the world. The collection was founded in 1673 by the Society of Apothecaries to study the medicinal properties of plants. In 1712, Dr. Hans Sloane, a wealthy physician, purchased the entire Manor of Chelsea. Ten years later, he leased some four acres of land to the apothecaries for £5 a year in perpetuity – a bargain even in back then. The deed of covenant is on display, stating the garden's purpose, that "apprentices and others may the better distinguish good and usefull plants from those that bear resemblance to them and yet are hurtfull." The location on the banks of the Thames created a warmer microclimate so that exotic plants could survive the biting British winter. Tropical plants are still cultivated in fetid greenhouses. The apothecaries' botanical experiments were influential in developing the American cotton industry and the tea trade in India. Given the 21st century trend for natural medicine, the Garden of World Medicine and Pharmaceutical Garden were way ahead of their time. Look out for the bizarre pond rock garden, partially built with Icelandic lava and stones from the Tower of London. The café is also notable for its home-made cakes.

DR HANS SLOANE: INVENTOR OF MILK CHOCOLATE

As well as giving his name to Sloane Square, Dr. Hans Sloane invented milk chocolate. After discovering locals drinking cocoa mixed with water in Jamaica, Sloane improved on the recipe by mixing it with milk. Back in England, his formula was sold as medicine until the Cadbury brothers cottoned on and began selling tins of Sloane's drinking chocolate.

SIGHTS NEARBY

CHEYNE WALK'S BLUE PLAQUES ❼

Boasting the most blue plaques in a single street, Cheyne Walk is one of London's most exclusive addresses. Recently, these genteel surroundings became an unlikely refuge for rock stars Mick Jagger, Keith Richards, Kylie Minogue, and Bob Geldof. The only house open to the public is the Victorian writer Thomas Carlyle's at number 24. Dickens, Tennyson and Browning were regular visitors at this literary sanctuary, preserved with all its original contents exactly as it was left in 1895. You can also visit Carlyle's specially sound-proofed study. (Open March Oct Wed, Thurs, Fri 2-5pm, Sat, Sun 11-5pm.)

COUPER
COLLECTION
www.coupercollection.org.uk

THE COUPER COLLECTION ❽

Riverside Walk, Hester Road, Battersea SW11
0207 738 1935
www.coupercollection.org.uk
Open Tues-Thurs 10am-4pm
Admission free
Transport Bus 19, 49, 239, 319, 345 or tube to Sloane Square
or South Kensington, then by foot or bus

*Floating
art gallery*

Moored between Battersea Bridge and Albert Bridge, a fleet of rusty barges hunkers down beside the gleaming new riverside apartment blocks. The boats may appear abandoned, but a small sign alerts visitors that this is the Couper Collection, an art gallery converted from the last surviving Thames barges, tethered on their original 18th century moorings. Accessible by a pontoon walkway of wooden bridges linking the barges, the Couper Collection is an intriguing exploration of life on the Thames, featuring installations by artist-in-residence Max Couper. Hidden from view inside the bellies of the steel barges, Couper's mysterious artworks consist of fictional charts, blurred navigational maps, and large-scale installations inspired by their watery surroundings.

There's also a Sky Garden barge, its rusty womb lined with giant flowerpots, and a permanent collection of impressive children's art in the Museum of First Art. Special events include educational and ecological workshops and the occasional live performance. Smaller vessels are home to plants and birdlife from the Thames, while two small opera barges make a dramatic setting for divas. Shrouded in mist or glinting in sunlight, this floating art gallery is one of London's most atmospheric venues.

Max Couper's collection of boats includes the last two barges built on the Thames, a pair of 1000-ton vessels for transporting wheat. London's barges, a vital source of the city's wealth as a shipping centre, were made redundant by the invention of the shipping container in the 1960s and '70s, when thousands of barges, hundreds of tugs, and dozens of moorings disappeared from the Thames. Shipping containers now transport about 90 per cent of the world's cargo, but container ships are too big to come up the Thames.

SIGHTS NEARBY

PUMP HOUSE GALLERY ❾

Battersea Park, SW11 • 0208 871 7572 • www.wandsworth.gov.uk/gallery
Open Wed, Thurs, Sun 11am-5pm, Fri, Sat 11am-4pm **Admission** free

Derelict for decades, the Pump House was built in 1861 to supply water to the lakes, waterfalls, and flowerbeds of the newly founded Battersea Park. Now this beautifully restored building has been converted into a four-storey gallery, all exposed brick walls and steel staircases, with enviable views of the surrounding lake. The contemporary art exhibitions are always edgy and often political.

FETTER LANE MORAVIAN BURIAL GROUND ⑩

381 King's Road, SW10
0208 8831833
www.moravian.org.uk
Open Times vary, contact church for details
Admission free
Transport Sloane Square tube then bus 11, 19, 22, 319

> *Humble remains of a religious settlement*

World's End sounds like a good location for a graveyard. Hidden from the fancy boutiques of King's Road by a high brick wall, the small burial ground adjoins the evangelical Moravian church. Established in 1742, the chapel itself looks like a secluded country cottage transplanted into the heart of Chelsea. But the back garden is actually a burial ground containing a handful of 18th century graves, marked only by flat, white stones. Traditionally, Moravians are buried separately in simple graves, men on one side of the graveyard and women on the other.

Originally from Bohemia and Moravia (now the Czech Republic), Moravians first came to Britain in the 1730s. The congregations created settlements with their own farms, businesses and schools. In 1750, their filthy rich leader, Count Zinzendorf, bought Lindsey House, a vast mansion in Chelsea built by Thomas More, as a refuge for Moravians fleeing persecution and a resting place for missionaries. After a lavish renovation, Lindsey House served as the international headquarters of the Moravian Church for two years. But the settlement never really took hold in London. After Zinzendorf's death in 1760, the Moravians sold off most of the land. Now privately owned, Lindsey House is only open to visitors on Open House weekend. Some of the Moravian religious murals are still intact. The Fetter Lane chapel was originally located near St Paul's, but was destroyed during the Blitz. The congregation was left without a permanent home until the 1960s when the congregation was re-established on King's Road at the northern edge of the burial ground, part of Thomas More's original estate.

Other Moravian churches in London are located in Harlesden, Stoke Newington, and Hornsey, whose predominantly Caribbean congregation have adapted the Moravian musical tradition of brass bands and trombone choirs to include steel pans and gospel singing at their Sunday service.

A FELINE SLOANE RANGER

During the Swinging Sixties, the Moravian graveyard became the playground of Christian, a pet lion belonging to John Rendall, an Australian antiques dealer who bought the cub over the counter at Harrods. (Fittingly, Rendall's furniture shop on Kings Road was called Sophistocat.) The obliging vicar allowed Christian to play football in the safe confines of the parish grounds. Christian was later taken to Africa and rehabilitated into the wild.

SOUTH BANK TO BRIXTON

GARDEN MUSEUM

❶

Lambeth Palace Road, SE1
0207 401 8865
www.gardenmuseum.org.uk
Open Tues- Sun 10.30am-5pm
1st January 2008). Voluntary admission charge £3.50,
concessions £2.50
Transport Westminster or Lambeth North tube

Admire a rare cucumber straightener

The Garden Museum is possibly London's best located museum, inside the former church of St Mary-at-Lambeth, which sits in the lee of Lambeth Palace, residence of the Archbishop of Canterbury since 1200. On the bank of the Thames right across from Whitehall and Westminster, it forms a triangle of the traditional seats of British power. Gardening is an enormous perversion for the British, so it is suitable that this is the first gardening museum in the world. Many of the visitors look like they should be scaring crows in fields. The museum was founded by John and Rosemary Nicholson, after tracing the tomb of the 17th century royal gardeners John Tradescant (father and son) to this churchyard.

Much of the vast collection remains in storage. The rest is split into three main categories: tools, ephemera and a library. The ephemera section is the best: there are prints, photographs, bills, and brochures. The tool collection also has its moments, notably a cucumber straightener and a collection of garden gnomes. The museum's beautiful, if small, grounds include a 17th century style knot garden. These geometric and highly formal compositions were typically lined with clipped low hedges. The churchyard contains some noteworthy graves, including the tyrannical Captain 'Breadfruit' Bligh of the mutiny on *The Bounty*. A plaque to the left of the church's front door commemorates Brian Turbeville, Gent., who bequeathed £100 to St Mary-at-Lambeth for the apprenticeship of two poor boys each year. The museum also hosts occasional concerts and lectures; check the website for details.

The museum hosts occasional jazz nights.
(seewww.museumgardenhistory.org/jazz for details).

Lambeth Palace contains some of the few surviving Tudor buildings in the capital, notably the red brick gatehouse built in 1495, as well as Lollard's Tower, visible from the outside.

LAMBETH PALACE GARDEN
Although the Lambeth Palace garden was split in two to create the neighbouring Archbishop's Park in 1901, it is still the second largest garden in London after that of Buckingham Palace. Lambeth Palace is open to the public for the annual Lambeth Parish Fete and on Open House weekends. Call 0207 898 1191 for opening times.

DUCK TOURS ❷

Departure point: Chicheley Street, SE1
Booking office: 55 York Road, SE1, approx 50 yards from the departure
point; 0207 928 3132; www.londonducktours.co.uk
Admission Adults £17.50; conc (ages 13-15, students and OAPs) £14.00
children (12 and under) £12.00; families (2 adults/2 children) £53.00
Transport Waterloo tube

Amphibious tours on the Thames

Not, alas, a tour of London either led by a duck or on the back of a duck – what a triumph that would be – Duck Tours offer a river tour in an amphibious vehicle called a DUKW, originally developed to take troops ashore for the D-Day landings.

The tour starts out by taking in the usual sights at street level: looping around via Parliament and Whitehall, up Piccadilly, down past Buckingham Palace, and along the Embankment via Westminster Abbey and the Tate. The Duck then crosses the Thames at Vauxhall Bridge and drives right into the river by the side of MI6 headquarters, before grunting and farting its way downstream to the London Eye and back. Returning to dry land, it whizzes passengers past Lambeth Palace and back to the departure point near Waterloo station.

If you can deal with the alarming prices, this is a great way to see the heart of London, especially for those have never been in an amphibious vehicle. The downside, of course, is driving around in a noisy old troop carrier painted a hideous yellow in full public view - very unhip.

But any visitor to London, or indeed any native, should get out onto the Thames as often as possible and feel the power of the "strong brown god", as TS Eliot alluded to the Thames in The *Four Quartets*. Any boat trip will do, really – but the Duck sits lowest in the water, thus enhancing the Thames' majesty and power. It is only from the river itself that one can get a sense of the city afloat and tethered to the river, rather than the river commanded by the city, which is the impression one gets from the bridges and banks.

FELIKS TOPOLSKI'S *MEMOIR OF THE CENTURY* ❸
150-152 Hungerford Viaduct Arches, Royal Festival Hall
Concert Hall Approach, SE1
Open Mon-Sat 5-8pm
Admission free
Transport Waterloo tube

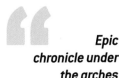

Epic chronicle under the arches

Feliks Topolski (1907-1989) was a Polish expressionist painter who arrived in London in 1935 and set up his studio in three cavernous railway arches tucked away behind the South Bank near Waterloo Station. The Memoir of the Century is a snaking mural painted on hardboard panels that depicts a mixture of the personal – Topolski's father looms out of one panel, and what appears to be an idealised portrait of his mother dominates another – and the political, as the artist chronicles what he viewed as the key events of the 20th century.

The sequence of murals covers 750 feet, and an equally ambitious range of subjects, from the Blitz to George Bernard Shaw, the Black Panthers to the British royal family. He seems to have met and drawn everybody who was anybody, from political giants like Mahatma Gandhi, Winston Churchill, and Martin Luther King, to leading actors Alec Guinness and Laurence Olivier. The panels rise twenty feet to the damp ceiling of the brick arches, a dungeon-like space whose weird angles and gloomy shadows are reflected in the work. As one admirer has scrawled in Topolski's gallery in graffiti: "You are creepy. You are a genius. You are rather magnificent."

What is engaging about the work is the feverish quality of the drawing. Topolski appears to be one of those artists who drew non-stop at high speed. As a result, some of the portraiture lapses in and out of caricature, but there is no denying the fluidity of Topolski's line and the power that emanates from the epic scale. His studio has been preserved in situ; what looks like a pile of junk in one corner are probably things used to paint the mural.

Topolski died in 1989, leaving his *Memoir of the Century* to the nation. Sadly, because of its damp and cold surroundings, the mural is now in a poor state of repair; parts of the unprotected panels have also been defaced at various points. Thankfully, the Lottery Fund recently allocated £1 million for its preservation.

Almost more impressive than the *Memoir* itself are the floor to ceiling copies of his fortnightly broadsheet *Topolski's Chronicle*. Printed on cheap brown paper, these visceral, often satirical sketches of contemporary events create an impressionistic diary of the highs and lows of the last century.

NATIONAL THEATRE BACKSTAGE TOURS ❹

South Bank, SE1
Open Tours several times a day, Mon-Sat. To book call
0207 452 3400
www.nationaltheatre.org.uk
Admission £5, £4 concessions, £13 family (2 adults & 2 under 18s)
Tours lasts 1hr 15mins. Max 30 people per tour
Transport Waterloo or Embankment tube

Behind the scenes at a national institution

Surprisingly for a nation with such a long and rich theatrical history, Britain's National Theatre only celebrated its 30th birthday in 2006. Designed by architect Denys Lasdun (who had never built a theatre before), the hulking concrete structure is loved and loathed in equal measure. Lasdun integrated the horizontal design with Waterloo Bridge, with one terrace actually built into the bridge to create the impression of an umbilical cord linking the West End theatres across the river with this modernist behemoth.

The National Theatre's three stages each host two shows in any given period, and always pull in big crowds. But apart from theatre students, few people take advantage of the backstage tours held several times a day. Animated guides whisk visitors behind the scenes, often battling it out with the sound and light technicians preparing for the evening's performances. Guides teach you about the history of this controversial institution, whose first artistic director was Laurence Olivier, and lead you through the warren of backstage corridors, workshops, and studios where some 900 staff members work their magic. You might catch a glimpse of period sets being painted, rubber vol-au-vents being created, or orchestras warming up: over 90% of music at the National Theatre is performed live.

The National also enjoys the luxury of an extensive in-house props department - from armoury to carpentry to costume to portrait painters. Set designers work from scale models, like architects.

Cutting edge back in 1976, some of the stage technology now seems archaic. In the Lyttleon Theatre, the traditional 'fly tower', used for moving sets, lighting, and microphones, is still operated by 75 'flymen', rather than controlled by computer. But the most extraordinary piece of stage equipment is buried deep beneath the Olivier Theatre. Four storeys high and 15 metres in diameter, the vast 'drum revolve' allows lavish sets to emerge from the bowels of the theatre at dramatic moments.

The design of Olivier Theatre was inspired by the ancient Greek theatre at Epidavros

Look for the original foundation stone on the ground floor near the cloakroom. It was laid by the Queen in 1951 at a site next to the Royal Festival Hall, but construction was delayed until 1969 following a series of funding problems.

Every evening at 6pm there is free live music in the foyer, usually jazz or often tango, which encourages impromptu dance sessions.

BFI MEDIATHEQUE

National Film Theatre, South Bank SE1
0207 928 3535
www.bfi.org.uk/mediatheque
Open Tue 1-8pm Wed-Sun 11am-8pm
Admission free
Transport Waterloo or Embankment tube

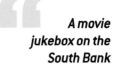

A movie jukebox on the South Bank

Since it re-launched to great fanfare in summer 2007, the re-branded South-bank Centre has lived up to the hype. But one of the most intriguing additions, the BFI Mediatheque, is overlooked by most visitors. Perhaps that's because it is hidden behind the former National Film Theatre's café and cinemas.

In a sleek, steel grey screening room designed by architect David Adjaye are 14 flat-screen viewing stations, where anyone can access hundreds of hours of footage from the British Film Institute's digital archive for free. The BFI's celluloid archives are huge: over 230,000 films and 675,000 television programmes, and counting. Until now, this material could only be seen on request or at special screenings. As the collection is slowly digitised, new material will be added to the Mediatheque every month.

From wartime propaganda films (*So Clever Are the German Spies in Their Disguises That Even Nuns Have to Have Their Passports Examined*, 1914) to early pornography (*Strip! Strip! Hooray!!!*, 1932) the material provides an eclectic overview of British history through footage spanning more than a century. The Essentially British strand ranges from Queen Victoria's Diamond Jubilee in 1897 to suffragettes rioting in Trafalgar Square in 1913, *Tea Making Tips* from 1941, to the 1960s Carnaby Street scene. London Calling showcases the capital's hidden charms and faded glories. Today's Kensington of Russian oligarchs and Arab billionaires bears little resemblance to the squalid slum it was in 1930. In *The London Nobody Knows,* James Mason guides viewers around the city's more esoteric sights in 1967. Many of them have vanished forever. The highlight for many British viewers will be another distant dream: the World Cup final in 1966. To use the Mediatheque, just show up and book a two-hour slot. You can stay longer if there is no queue – and there usually isn't. BFI will have to relocate from the South Bank in 2013, when trams start clattering across Waterloo Bridge. So go while you can.

SIGHTS NEARBY

POETRY LIBRARY

0207 921 0943; www.poetrylibrary.org.uk
Open Tues-Sun 11am-8pm. **Admission** free.

Another underrated collection on the South Bank is the spruced up Poetry Library, the most comprehensive collection of modern poetry in Britain, with over 95,000 books, magazines, posters, and postcards. Audio recordings of poets reciting their work are especially rewarding. Level 5, Royal Festival Hall.

The Ferryman's Seat

The Ferryman's seat, located on previous buildings at this site, was constructed for the convenience of Bankside watermen, who operated ferrying services across the river. The seat's age is unknown, but it is thought to have ancient origins.

Historic Southwark

THE FERRYMAN'S SEAT ❼

Bear Gardens, Bankside, SE1
Transport: London Bridge or Southwark tube

> *A little seat with a long history*

Wedged into the wall of The Real Greek *souvlaki* joint, not far from Shakespeare's Globe Theatre, is a small chunk of flinty stone. According to a modern plaque above it, this is the last surviving example of the boatmen's seats that once lined the South Bank. Until 1750, London Bridge was the only means of crossing the Thames in central London; so "wherrymen" ferried passengers across in narrow water taxis, or "wherries". The boatmen waited on these rough stone benches until their vessels filled up with rowdy patrons spilling out of the nearby Rose and Globe theatres, the bear-baiting rings and brothels (evocatively known as "stews" because they doubled up as steam baths) that littered the unsavoury suburb of Southwark. The wherrymen must have been lean, as the seat is a tight squeeze for even the trimmest of 21st century buttocks. It can't have been a pleasant resting place: the area reeked of open sewers and the stench of the surrounding tanneries.

BEAR-BAITING: "A VERY RUDE AND NASTY PLEASURE"

This street is still called Bear Gardens after the Davies Amphitheatre, the last bear-baiting pit on Bankside. Banned in 1642, bear-baiting was a popular pastime in Tudor times, frequented by roughnecks and courtiers alike.

SIGHTS NEARBY

THE BLACK-FACED CLOCK ❽

Borough High Street, SE1. Opposite Borough tube.

Sleazy Southwark was home to many famous literary figures, including Geoffrey Chaucer, William Shakespeare and Charles Dickens. Dickens' immortalised the area in *Little Dorrit*, whose fictional father – like the novelist's own – is imprisoned in Marshalsea prison for failing to pay his debts. The last remaining wall of this infamous jail now forms the northern boundary of the churchyard of St George the Martyr, where Little Dorrit is married at the end of the novel. Inside the church, in the east window behind the altar, is a stained-glass memorial to Little Dorrit, kneeling at prayer.

St George's steeple has four clocks, but one of them – facing Bermondsey – is black and is not illuminated at night. Allegedly, this was because Bermondsey's Victorian parishioners refused to cough up their share of funds for the clock.

CROSSBONES GRAVEYARD ❾

Redcross Way, SE1
Transport Borough tube
Memorial service of sorts at 7pm, 23rd of each month:
meet at the gates

A burial ground for misfits

This tiny piece of wasteland, currently used by London Transport as a storage yard, contains the bodies of over 15,000 people; yet there is no evidence of their passing because it was unhallowed ground, first for prostitutes and then for paupers. In early local records, Crossbones was referred to as a graveyard for "Single Women" – the whores working in the nearby "stews" or brothels of the Liberty of the Clink. This was an area of Southwark, south of London Bridge and outside the jurisdiction of the sheriff of London, where Londoners could legally enjoy theatre, bear-baiting and whoring.

In 1161, the Bishop of Winchester was granted the power to licence prostitutes and brothels in the Liberty, which persisted for 500 years until Oliver Cromwell closed down the whole area. Clink prostitutes were known as Winchester Geese (one of many questionable euphemisms Londoners had for prostitutes, including trulls, buttered buns, squirrels, punchable nuns). They were refused burial in the local St Saviour's parish, as their sin meant they had to be buried in unhallowed ground - an irony given that they owed their profession to the fathers of the church. After the closure of the Liberty, Crossbones graveyard served for the poor, and was closed in 1853 as it was "completely overcharged with dead". The site today is unprepossessing. However, the gates (opposite the *Boot and Flogger*) are now a kind of impromptu memorial; they are covered with ribbons and other totems in sympathy with the dead, and a memorial service of sorts is also held at 7pm on the 23rd of each month – meet at the gates. There's a strong feeling that this site is hanging on by its fingernails: in 2002, Southwark Council refused London Transport's application to build multi-storey car parking on the site, but they'll be back.

> The *Boot and Flogger* is supposedly the only bar in the country not to require an alcohol licence, because of special dispensation from James I in 1611.

THE GEORGE INN COURTYARD

Little remains of the Liberty of the Clink; the rebuilt *Globe Theatre* is its best memorial. However, it's not the only courtyard theatre in the area. The *George Inn* just off Borough High Street would originally have offered plays; this pub was built on three sides around a courtyard, and its wide, double-tiered balconies were perfect for play watching. British theatre evolved from places like this, and their design influenced purpose-built venues such as the *Globe*, the *Rose* and the *Cockpit*.

THE OLD OPERATING THEATRE ⑩

9a St Thomas Street, SE1
0207 188 2679
Admission £4.95 Adult, £2.95 Child
Open Mon - Sat 10.30am – 5pm
Transport London Bridge tube

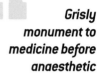

Grisly monument to medicine before anaesthetic

This little oddity was rediscovered by chance in 1957, during repairs in the eaves of St Thomas' Church in Southwark, on the original site of St Thomas' Hospital. This is the oldest surviving operating theatre in the country, and was used in the days before anaesthetics and antiseptic surgery. The garret also served to store the hospital apothecary's medicinal herbs, and the museum that stands there now displays a collection of terrifyingly primitive medical tools, including instruments for cupping, bleeding and trepanning, a hair-raising practice of perforating the skull to 'alleviate pain.'

The operating theatre was built in 1822, after the 1815 Apothecary's Act, which required apprentice apothecaries to watch operations at public hospitals. Prior to this, operations took place in the patient's bed right on the ward, which must have been a blood-curdling ordeal – all that blood and bellowing in such a confined space. The operating theatre was annexed to the women's surgical ward, so patients could be carried straight in via what is now the fire escape. Students crammed the viewing platforms to watch the operations, carried out without anaesthetic prior to 1847. Patients, who were typically from the poorer parts of London society submitted willingly, as this was the only way to get the best medical treatment which they otherwise could not afford. The wealthy underwent operations in the relative comfort and privacy of their home.

OPEN SURGERY

Surgeon John Flint South described the pandemonium on the sidelines of an operation here: *'Behind a second partition stood the pupils, packed like herrings in a barrel, but not so quiet, as those behind them were continually pressing on those before and were continually struggling to relieve themselves of it, and had not infrequently to be got out exhausted. There was also a continual calling out of "Heads, Heads" to those about the table whose heads interfered with the sightseers.'*

Florence Nightingale was indirectly responsible for the operating theatre's closure. In 1859, she set up her nursing school at St Thomas', but on her advice the hospital moved to a new site opposite the Houses of Parliament in 1862. But there is still a small Florence Nightingale Museum at St Thomas' Hospital. (www.florence-nightingale.co.uk)

LONDON'S LIVING ROOM ⓫

City Hall, The Queen's Walk, SE1
0207 983 4100
www.londonslivingroom.co.uk
Open Usually one weekend every month; check website for details
Limited access to other parts of City Hall Mon-Fri 8am-8pm
Admission free **Transport** Tower Bridge or London Bridge tube

A sneak peek of the Mayor's view

Though sometimes fondly referred to as 'the Mayor's testicle', Norman Foster's City Hall is a stunning building. Completed in 2002, the wonky glass sphere is a brilliant icon for transparent government. To endorse the notion of open politics, some restricted access areas of the Greater London Authority's HQ are opened up to the public on occasional weekends.

As you enter City Hall's hollowed-out reception area, look over the glass railing onto the exhibition space on the lower ground floor. The floor covering may at first glance seem to be merely a grubby green and grey carpet, but in fact it's the London Photomat, an aerial view of Greater London. Covering an area of 1,000 square miles, the 16 x 10 metre image is a collage of 200,000 photos, taken from four planes flying at an altitude of 5,500 feet over London, which were then printed onto the floor tiles. The result is so detailed that it is possible to pinpoint individual houses as well as major landmarks. The project took three years to complete, but you can now walk all over London in just minutes.

The heart of City Hall is a sweeping spiral ramp, half a kilometre long, leading all the way up to the ninth floor. It is like an asymmetrical version of New York's Guggenheim museum, but instead of galleries you look in at open-plan offices and out at sweeping views of London. The purple and grey Assembly Chamber on the second floor, with seating for 250 members of the public to watch London's government in action, creates the slightly disturbing impression that you are floating on the Thames. The Mayor's office is on the 8th floor. Above it is London's Living Room, a spectacular setting for political fundraisers, parties, and premieres with a 360° panorama of the London skyline. The minimalist design lets the view dominate. From the wraparound balcony, you can look down on the boats bobbing along beneath Tower Bridge and feel on top of the world. It's especially dramatic after dark as the city lights twinkle on.

> The basement café looks out onto The Scoop, a sunken amphitheatre of grey limestone where outdoor screenings and concerts are staged during the summer.

> Once a fortnight, London's Living Room is used by selected charities free of charge for fundraising events.

> Cunningly designed to consume 25% less energy than the average office building, City Hall is a great advertisement for eco-architecture. Heat generated by computers and lights is recycled and the building is cooled using water extracted from the water table beneath London.

THE CINEMA MUSEUM ⓬

The Master's House, 2 Dugard Way, SE11
0207 840 2200
www.cinemamuseum.org.uk
Open by appointment
Admission free
Transport Kennington tube

*Stars in
your eyes ...*

Hidden down a cul-de-sac in Kennington is one of the world's most extensive collections of film-related images and artefacts. Fittingly, the Cinema Museum has found a temporary home in the former Lambeth workhouse where a 9-year-old boy named Charlie Chaplin and his half-brother Sydney were "processed" in 1896. The building was once divided into wings for men and women of "good" or "bad character". Today, the musty corridors and dormitories are crammed with mechanical projectors and Art Deco cinema signs, original lobby cards, piles of periodicals dating back to 1911, and around 17 million feet of film.

This extraordinary collection was amassed by Ronald Grant, an unassuming, youthful septuagenarian with an encyclopaedic knowledge of film history. Grant's lifelong passion for cinema began when he helped out at his local picture house in Aberdeen as a boy. Since then, Grant has accumulated over 1 million film-related images dating back to 1895, the year the Lumière brothers screened the first "actualités" in Paris. This vast anthology of production stills and portraits of movie stars keeps the Cinema Museum afloat: the images are hired out to the media. The archive is divided by subject matter, from abattoirs to ventriloquists. Leafing through the "P" drawer, Grant offers up pictorial material on practical jokes, pratfalls, prisons and private eyes.

But it's the artefacts that really bring the early days of cinema to life. There are silent film scores and song lyrics that were projected onto the screen so that audiences could sing along as the organist played during the interval. Before X-rated movies, there was Category H: "horrific". There's a 1917 ticket machine that issued metal tokens with various shapes depending on the price, so ushers could feel the difference in the dark. These nattily dressed ushers would use floral sprays "to disguise the smell of 1,000 wet raincoats and cigarettes on a Saturday night". Cinemas may have had fancy fittings and names like the Majestic or the Picture Palace, but audiences could be rowdy. One old notice warns patrons: "No shouting or whistling allowed – applaud with hands only. In the interests of public safety please do not spit."

The Cinema Museum is currently threatened with eviction, so go now.

The friends and supporters of the museum gather every fortnight in the small screening room (its battered seats salvaged from various cinemas) to watch some of Grant's rare gems.

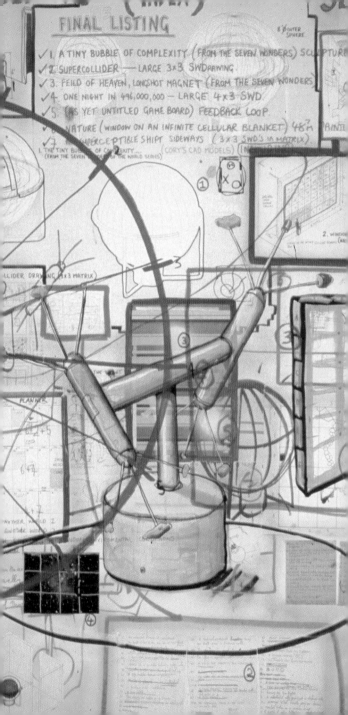

CUMING MUSEUM

Old Town Hall, 151 Walworth Road, SE17
0207 525 2345
www.southwark.gov.uk/cumingmuseum
Open Tues-Sat 10am-5pm
Admission free
Transport Elephant & Castle tube

⓭

> *The Tooth of King Alphonsus VI of Portugal, a Cat Skin, a Cow's Heart...*

The Cuming Museum hardly rates museum status – a room and a half filled with the highlights of the collection Richard Cuming. The collection is esoteric to say the least, covering archaeology, British & foreign social history, decorative art, geology, textiles, natural history, prints, coins, ceramics, Ancient Egyptian, and Etruscan objects. So much for the academic side; the meat is in the eccentricities. These include the Tooth of King Alphonsus VI of Portugal, a Cat Skin, a Cow's Heart, a Fish, a Milk Grinder from an elephant named Roger who lived in Surrey Zoological Gardens and a Dentist's cap, heavily embroidered with teeth. All of this stuff was bought in London; Cuming never travelled abroad.

Cuming was a rich man, with time and money to spend on what to him was a great and serious collection. Some of the stuff is good – the Egyptian objects were among the first to be brought to England, and are therefore of reputable provenance – but there is a definite atmosphere of the Olde Curiosity Shop about the collection. Contemporary press described it as a 'British Museum in miniature', but the personality of the collection is too singular and eccentric to stand comparison today. However, there are a mere 700 objects on display of what was once a collection of 100,000. Much of the remainder is loaned out to other museums. Other highlights include a collection of 'Billys and Charleys', forged medieval votive objects made in the 19th century that Cuming bought even though he knew they were fake. There is also the skull that was reputedly the last object touched by Richard Cuming before he died.

SOUTHWARK MUSEUM

In the same building, the Museum of Southwark explores the history of the surrounding borough. Southwark was London's first suburb – it was pillaged by William the Conqueror before he entered the city proper in 1066 – and has always had a reputation as a desperate, gamey place. It lay outside the walls of London, was poor and less closely governed, and also the home of the city's theatres and brothels. As a result, there is a certain tradition of showmanship, which may have inspired Cuming's collection. attracted new immigrants.

CHUMLEIGH GARDENS (14)

Burgess Park, off Albany Road, Camberwell, SE5. Park: 0207 525 1054
Café: 0207 525 1070
www.southwark.gov.uk/directory_record/1965/chumleigh_gardens
Open Mon-Fri 8am-5pm, 10am-5pm Sat & Sun. Café closes 4pm in winter
Admission free
Transport Elephant & Castle tube then bus
P3, 12, 42, 63, 68, 171, or 343

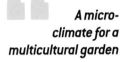

A micro-climate for a multicultural garden

Burgess Park is a rather non-descript expanse of stubby lawns off the urban wasteland of Camberwell's Walworth Road. But tucked away behind an L-shaped cluster of ivy-covered almshouses is a pretty 'multicultural garden', a tribute to the area's ethnic minorities.

The little walled garden surrounded by hedges provides a micro-climate that allows a variety of aromatic herbs, flowering plants and fruit trees from the Orient, Africa and the Caribbean, Australia and the Mediterranean to survive. The centrepiece is the Islamic Garden, built around a raised pond sheathed in blue tiles with a jelly palm tree sprouting out of the middle. It's a serene, unpretentious little place with a real sense of community – a perfect spot to settle in with the Sunday papers while your kids make a beeline for the poisonous plants. Looking onto the garden is a marvellously kitsch café, with citrus coloured walls, clashing tablecloths printed with fruit and flowers, plastic bouquets and garlands of star-shaped fairy lights. In her patterned headscarf and red specs, the equally colourful Gill Manly dishes up all-day English breakfasts, home-made banana bread, and delicious ice cream. Manly is also a formidable singer; locals in the know come to her live jazz sessions in the garden at 1pm every Sunday (British weather permitting).

> Chumleigh Gardens is also home to Art in the Park workshops, so you may stumble upon sculptors working in the grounds. Look for a permanent artwork in the pavement just outside the gardens: a circle of footprints of different sizes weaving through the inscription: 'I was a child, we were parents and grandparents, alive in the year 2000.'

SIGHTS NEARBY

HENRY MOORE'S TWO PIECE RECLINING FIGURE NO.3 (15)
Brandon's Estate, Cooks Road, SE11

Only die-hard Henry Moore fans need venture into Kennington's Brandon Estate, a heartland of hoodies. Built in the late 1950s, this grim, grey housing project is visible for miles thanks to its six 18-storey tower blocks. Stranded on a hillock of grass at its centre is a sculpture by Henry Moore, donated to the residents of Brandon Estate in 1961. Its bronze contours have since turned gangrenous green and there is some half-hearted graffiti on the concrete base. But there's a peculiar magic to this lonely figure marooned in such an incongruous and slightly sinister setting, especially at dusk when the lights in the tower blocks flicker on.

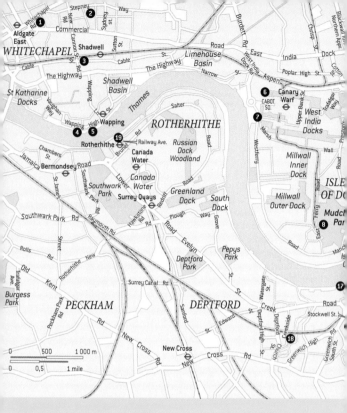

WHITECHAPEL
TO WOOLWICH

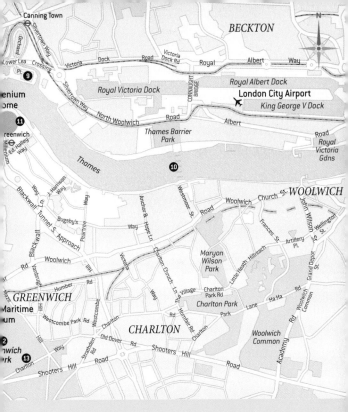

WHITECHAPEL BELL FOUNDRY ❶

32-34 Whitechapel Road, E1 • 0207 247 2599
www.whitechapelbellfoundry.co.uk
Open Shop and museum Mon-Fri 9am-4.15pm. Tours on selected Saturdays at
10am and 2pm (no late admission, no under 14s) – visitors should aim to arrive
15 minutes before tours begin. Tours must be booked in advance; expect a wait
Admission £10 **Transport** Whitechapel or Aldgate East tube

Oldest
manufacturers
in Britain

The Whitechapel Bell Foundry (Britain's oldest manufacturing company, in continuous business since 1570) has been at this site, the old *Artichoke* coaching inn, since 1738. The front rooms still feel like an old pub, with the company offices in the best room. It's impossible to take visitors around when the Foundry is in action, given the health and safety issues surrounding red-hot metal, so tours are limited to selected Saturdays. Visitors see the Foundry exactly as it was left by the workers on Friday evening. Tours are usually led by the Master Founder, so a detailed guide to the mysteries of bell-making is guaranteed. However, if you can't get a place on the tour immediately, the Foundry also offers a small museum of campanology and casting, as well as a shop where bells of all sizes can be ordered and bought. There is also plenty of evidence of the factory in operation. When the Foundry casts big bells once a month (the rest of the time it makes handbells and musical bells), the alarming smell of hot metal spreads through the building. On hot summer days, the workers sometimes open the shutters at the side of the building on Plumbers Row, so you can peek inside. The Foundry Yard, littered with heavy bells, is also visible through the glass door at the back of the shop. In 1858, the Whitechapel Bell Foundry cast its largest and most famous bell, Big Ben, weighing in at 13½ tons. Visitors to the museum step through a full-size cross-section of Big Ben that frames the main entrance.

"WHAT ABOUT THE WARRANTY?"

There is also a copy of the Liberty Bell, cast for the American colonies in 1751, and now famously cracked. In 1976, the year of the US Bicentennial, demonstrators from the Procrastinators Society of America marched outside the Foundry with placards proclaiming "WHAT ABOUT THE WARRANTY?". The Foundry told the protestors that it would be happy to replace the bell as long as it was returned in the original packaging.

SIGHTS NEARBY

RELICS OF THE ELEPHANT MAN ❷

Newark Street • 0207 377 7608 • **Open** Mon-Fri 10am-4.30pm • **Admission** free
The Foundry is just down the road from the Royal London Hospital, the final home of Joseph Merrick, the Elephant Man, who died there in 1890. The hospital has a small museum with a display on Merrick, as well as a forensic medicine section which includes original material on Jack the Ripper, Dr Crippen and the Christie murders. The Ripper murders were local, and still attract a surprisingly large number of ghouls to Whitechapel.

SIGHTS NEARBY

CABLE STREET MURAL ❸
Cable Street, E1, north of St George-in-the-East cemetery
Transport Shadwell DLR or tube

Instantly reminiscent of the social paintings of the great Mexican artist Diego Rivera, the Cable Street Mural commemorates the 'Battle of Cable Street' in 1936, when Oswald Mosley, dressed spiffily in a black military jacket, grey riding breeches, jackboots, black peaked hat and a red arm band, led the British Union of Fascists (BUF) on a march into the East End, at that time the centre of London Jewish life. Having secured the protection of the police, the BUF felt safe; however, large numbers of anti-fascists, including Jewish, Irish, socialist, and communist groups, came out in protest. It was more a matter of barricades and name-calling than actual fighting. The BUF were turned back. Some argue that this protest encouraged anti-Semitism in the area; the so-called Pogrom of Mile End, in which Jews and their properties were attacked far more violently, took place a week afterwards.

However, the mural is a treat. Started in 1976, it is the work of a number of local artists, who finally finished it in 1993, after a long running battle against vandalism and graffiti. The picture is wildly full of movement, and gives a strong sense of the almost tidal surges of large-scale street demonstrations. A propeller whirling in the top right of the picture is echoed in other eddies and vortices in the mural: a man throwing leaflets into the wind, men surging around barricades, horses turning in confined spaces. Comically, a figure who appears to be Hitler is borne aloft away from the action, wearing only his underpants. It's not an especially nuanced or subtle piece of art, but its energy makes it leap off the wall.

GRAFFITI TOURS
London's image as a visually staid and grey city is changing. Part of this can be attributed to a rise in street art – Banksy is the most visible graffiti artist to make the leap from street to gallery. Tours of the better quality stuff can be organised via http://shellshock.bulldoghome.com. On a slightly grander level, the capital has also seen a flourishing of house-end murals, like this one.

OTHER MURALS AROUND TOWN
Cable Street is probably the most political of all London's murals, although Nuclear Dawn on Brixton's Coldharbour Lane, which shows Death sowing the world with bombs, is a close contender. Brixton is fertile for murals – check the giant children painted on the back of the Academy music venue (Stockwell Park Road), the market mural in the railway station, and the slightly wistful river mural (corner of Strathleven and Glenelg Roads). Other good mural sites are outside Stockwell tube, where a portrait of French Resistance heroine Violette Szabo dominates the deep shaft ventilator. In Soho, look out for peculiar trees on the corner of Poland Street and Noel Street, and portraits of famous residents on the corner of Carnaby and Broadwick streets.

EXECUTION DOCK ④
Wapping Old Stairs (off Wapping High Street), E1
Transport Shadwell DLR, then 15 minute walk

Where timbers were shivered

London's connection with piracy is hardly surprising, given the city's history as one of the world's greatest ports. Pirate life seems to have been pretty desperate, despite all the fighting and drinking; pirate death seems to have been even worse: either killed in action, by picturesque diseases (Vomito Negro? Flux? The Itch? Yellow Jack?), or dispatched at Execution Dock.

Policing the sea was left to the Admiralty, and for 400 years it executed pirates on the foreshore of the Thames at Wapping, at a site far enough offshore as to be near the low-tide mark. Typically, prisoners were publicly executed en masse after being paraded from the Marshalsea Prison across London Bridge and past the Tower of London.

The hanging was unusual in that the rope was too short for the drop to break necks, so the condemned would "dance" as they strangled. Their bodies were left in place until three tides had washed over them. The more notorious corpses were then tarred and hung in cages along the Thames estuary to encourage other sailors to behave themselves. Captain Kidd, inspiration for *Treasure Island*, stepped off here, and George Davis and William Watts were the final two hanged for piracy at the docks on December 16, 1830.

The actual site is disputed, as the gallows are long gone; three pubs on Wapping High Street claim it as an attraction. *The Prospect of Whitby*, London's oldest riverside pub and formerly known as the *Devil's Tavern* is one, the *Captain Kidd* another, but the likeliest location is behind the *Town of Ramsgate*. Go down the alley at the side, descend Wapping Old Steps and you are on the river bed (obviously wait until the tide is out). Walking on the foreshore is well worth it; the river is constantly turning up weird debris, although to actually dig you need a special licence from the Port of London Authority.

MUDLARKING
Sounds like a filthy habit, but mudlarking is actually the word used for beachcombing along the Thames – named after a bird, apparently. Access to the river is surprisingly easy (especially from the south bank), either through ancient water-steps such as Pelican Stairs or down modern steps from the Embankment. The highlight of the mudlark's year is the annual opening of the beach in front of the Tower of London in conjunction with National Archaeology Week.

THAMES RIVER POLICE MUSEUM ❺

Wapping Police Station, 98 Wapping High Street, E1W 2NE
0207 275 4421
www.thamespolicemuseum.org.uk
Open To arrange a visit, send a written request to the police station,
enclosing stamped s.a.e.
Admission free **Transport** Wapping DLR

> *The world's first police force*

London is home to the world's first police force. Established in 1798, the Thames River Police were recruited by the West India Merchants and Planters Committees to protect their cargo from river pirates. Magistrate Patrick Colquhoun had worked out that half a million pounds' worth of freight was being filched each year. The original force had about fifty members: watermen, who rowed the boats; surveyors, who checked cargo; and lumpers, who supervised the offloading of vessels. Armed with cutlasses, pistols and truncheons, they had to monitor the 33,000 workers on the Thames, a third of whom - according to Colquhoun's calculations - were felons. In its first year of operation, the river police saved £122,000 worth of cargo.

The force was absorbed into London's Metropolitan Police in 1839. Now known as the Marine Support Unit, high-speed launches have replaced the rowing galleys and officers are more concerned with counter-terrorism than brigands. But the 78-strong force still operates from the original police station on Wapping High Street. The workshop where boats were repaired was converted into a museum in 1974. Visitors are treated to an expert commentary by curator Robert Jeffries, a retired marine policeman and City of London guide.

Motorised launches were introduced after the 1878 Princess Alice disaster, in which 640 day-trippers died after two ships collided. The Thames is now one of the cleanest rivers in Europe, but back then most of the passengers were killed by swallowing raw sewage. The ship's tattered ensign is on display in the museum, a gift from the captain's son, who joined the river police soon afterwards.

There is an impressive collection of handcuffs, uniforms, telescopes and rattles, used before whistles to sound the alarm. The most remarkable objects are the 18th century handwritten ledgers, detailing everyday crimes and punishments. The first page of a tattered inspector's pocketbook from 1894 details the discovery of a baby's severed head in the Thames. Most of the policemen's misdemeanours involve drinking on duty. Some thirty pubs lined the riverbank in Wapping, including the *Turk's Head*, where those condemned at nearby Execution Dock (see 245) enjoyed their last pint.

THE ORIGINS OF POLICE STATIONS

"Police stations" derives from the police craft "on station" (anchored) at various points in the Thames. The phrase "on the beat" comes from the beating of the oars in river police boats.

ST PETER'S BARGE ❻

West India Quay, Off Hertsmere Rd E14
0207 093-1212
www.stpetersbarge.org
Open Services on Wed 12:15 and 1:15, Sun 6pm. Occasionally open
at other times **Admission** free **Transport** Canary Wharf tube,
West India Quay or Canary Wharf DLR

> *London's only floating church*

Nowhere in London symbolises the power of money and the glorification of greed better than the gleaming towers of Canary Wharf. It is also one of the few places in the city where the local population looks so homogenous. When the stock exchange closing bell rings, some 70.000 identikit bankers are unleashed into the dockside shopping malls and bars to burn their hard-earned cash.

Amid all this conspicuous consumption, one lone institution tries to seduce these harried office workers to worship at an altar other than wealth. "We are here for the salvation of the thousands of new Dockland residents who are materially wealthy but spiritually bankrupt," declares the website of St Peter's Barge, London's only floating church. Moored on West India Quay opposite the Museum of Docklands, this former freight barge was bought by a group of committed Christian traders in the Netherlands in 2003. It was refitted and sailed across the North Sea to its present location, a quaint throwback in relentlessly modern, urban surroundings.

As the number of commuters to Canary Wharf mushroomed after its redevelopment in 1991, Christian groups realised there was an opportunity to create new converts. From its origins as a Bible study group in a wharf-side wine bar, the growing congregation moved to a pub, then to a multi-faith prayer-room, until it anchored here in 2003.

Although the church espouses the Evangelical faith, it takes a fairly low-key approach to proselytising – perhaps because it only holds 110 people. It is also self-consciously modern: the Barge is laid out like a café, with small tables and free coffee, and they even have their own blog and hold a quiz night. There's a half-hour lunchtime service every Wednesday and Thursday and an evening service at 6pm on Sundays.

HOW CANARY WHARF GOT ITS NAME

Until the mid 1960s, Canary Wharf was the hub of one of the world's largest and busiest ports. On the lower floor of the Jubilee Place Shopping Mall, a series of mosaics by artist Emma Biggs illustrates the exotic imports once stored in the area's warehouses. The products – beaver hats and python skins, carpets and coffee, feathers and ropes, textiles and tortoiseshells, spirits and sea shells – reflect the changing fashions of London's trade winds. Canary Wharf was named after the juicy tomatoes and fruit shipped from the Canary Islands.

TRAFFIC LIGHT TREE ❼

Heron Quays Roundabout, E14
Transport Canary Wharf tube or Heron Quays DLR

> *Modern art to madden motorists*

As you exit Canary Wharf tube, the shiny high-rise office blocks crowned with the neon logos of investment banks create a disorienting impression of a very different London – a futuristic economic powerhouse, quite unlike the rest of the rough-and-ready city seeped in history.

Walk down Heron Quay towards the Isle of Dogs and you might spot a distant glow of lights, flashing green, red and amber among the grey steel and polished glass. In the middle of an otherwise nondescript roundabout, at the junction of Heron Quay Bank, Marsh Wall and Westferry Road, stands a 26-foot tangle of 75 traffic lights that flash on and off at random. Installed in 1998, French artist Pierre Vivant´s Traffic Light Tree replaced one of three plane trees on the roundabout that was being choked to death by the constant flow of traffic. Vivant's sculpture is shaped like a tree, its branches a blur of blinking lights. According to the artist, "the changing pattern of the lights reflects the never ending rhythm of the surrounding domestic, financial and commercial activities." It may cause alarm in drivers, but for pedestrians who take the time to stop and stare, its rhythmic play of light has a strangely soothing effect amid the restless activity that surrounds it.

The Isle of Dogs was open countryside until 1800. In the 17ᵗʰ century, several hundred Chinese sailors married local women, creating London´s first Chinatown in the area bordered by Limehouse, Pennyfields, and West India Dock Road. With its opium dens and brothels, the neighbourhood soon became a no-go zone for salubrious Londoners. In the 1920s, local residents closed down the access roads to the Isle of Dogs in protest at their slum dwellings, and declared independence from the rest of London.

SIGHTS NEARBY

MUDCHUTE FARM ❽

Amid 31 acres of parkland on what was once a derelict plot beside Millwall docks, is London's largest urban farm. As well as horse riding lessons, kids can interact with dozens of farm animals and a more exotic family of llamas. The café does fantastic English breakfasts and homemade lemonade. Open daily 9.30am-4.30pm. www.mudchute.org. Mudchute or Island Gardens DLR.

LONGPLAYER ❾

Trinity Buoy Wharf, 64 Orchard Place, E14
www.longplayer.org / www.trinitybuoywharf.com
Open 11am-4pm, first weekend of every month
Admission free
Transport DLR to East India Dock then 10min walk, or Bus 2??

> *Musical*
> *installation that*
> *lasts for a*
> *millennium*

Housed in London's only lighthouse, Longplayer is probably the most protracted celebration of the Millennium. Launched on January 1, 2000, this musical installation features a composition for Tibetan singing bowls and gongs, digitally remixed so that the same sequence of sounds will not be repeated for 1000 years. On December 31, 2999, Longplayer will return to its starting point - and begin all over again. That is, as long as the technology that powers it survives or evolves, or some very dedicated musicians volunteer to perform the score in perpetuity. Creator Jem Finer, a founding member of The Pogues, is exploring the possibility of building six two-armed turntables 6 to 12 feet in diameter, with automated mechanisms to raise and lower the arms. Even if Finer figures that out, he will have to build a device capable of cutting 12-foot records.

Listening to this mesmerising soundscape in a disused lighthouse, with views across the Thames to the docks and the Dome, is captivatingly creepy. Trinity Buoy Wharf was named for the wooden buoys made and stored here in the early 19th century. Built in 1864, Trinity Buoy lighthouse was used to develop lighting for Trinity House, an association founded in 1514 to safeguard shipping and seafarers. Its headquarters are still located in the City (www.trinityhouse.co.uk).

CONTAINER CITY (www.containercity.com)

Once famous for pushing the boundaries in maritime technology, Trinity Buoy Wharf is now a hub for creative experimentation. Container City consists of two stacks of recycled shipping containers, whose brightly coloured, corrugated walls and porthole windows conceal low-cost homes for a community of artists and designers. Most of them open their studios for Open House weekend. A few more containers have been sound-proofed and can be hired as music studios. The scarlet steamboat moored nearby has been converted into a photographic studio.

FAT BOY'S DINER

Open Mon - Fri 10am - 5pm; Sat 11am - 3pm. Tel 0207 987 4334
www.fatboysdiner.co.uk

Featured in various *Vogue* shoots, this red and chrome mobile diner appears to have landed on the quayside from another time and place. It has: Fat Boy's was built in New Jersey in 1941. Pull up a stool, pick some classics from the mini juke-box, and chow down on a Fatburger topped with Yellow Paint (mustard) and Brown Bad Breath (fried onions). As the menu promises: 'It's love at first bite.'

THAMES FLOOD BARRIER ⑩

The gates are occasionally closed for maintenance; call
0208 305 4188 to check opening times.
Transport Canning Town tube or train from
Charing Cross to Charlton

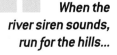

> **When the
> river siren sounds,
> run for the hills...**

About eight miles downstream from Tower Bridge is the Thames Flood Barrier, a row of ten movable gates across the river that protect London from flooding. The effect is that of ten metallic sails or fins moving upstream. On a sunny day, viewed from the river or the shore, they are a pleasingly modern feature in an otherwise run-down part of London. 520 metres wide, the flood barrier consists of a set of semi-cylindrical gates that rotate upward from the riverbed, closing the river to traffic. When closed, the four largest gates stand as high as a five-storey building.

The need for the flood barrier seems to escape most Londoners, who prefer not to think about the implications of its construction. But the barrier has been raised 90 times since 1982, and evidence suggests this frequency is rising. Global warming and rising sea levels are partly responsible for an annual rise of six centimetres in the Thames, while the movement of tectonic plates in the Mid Atlantic is gradually causing South East Britain to sink seaward. The wide mouth of the River Thames and its position at the foot of the North Sea also make the river vulnerable to surge tides. The construction of the Embankment has constrained the swollen river even more tightly – witness the height of the Thames during high tide at Blackfriars Bridge. So when the river siren sounds, run for the hills.

The Information and Learning Centre on the south bank contains a working model of the barrier and exhibits about its construction and the Thames.

Access to the barrier is a little awkward. It is best viewed as part of a walk along the Thames Path, which stretches 184 miles from the river's source in Gloucestershire. Pick up the trail by the Cutty Sark in Greenwich and walk downstream past the Millennium Dome to the barrier. Then press on to Woolwich, cross the river by ferry or foot tunnel, and catch a train back into central London from North Woolwich.

SLICE OF REALITY AND QUANTUM CLOUD ⓫

Thames Path, by the Millennium Dome
Admission free
Transport North Greenwich tube

*Radical
riverside
sculptures*

The cursed Millennium Dome may have been a failure in its initial function (a kind of politically devised big top for bad circus acts), and its current use as a concert venue still represents a phenomenal waste of money on top of the estimated £1 billion development costs. But there is no doubt that some of the best British design went into its construction.

In addition to the the Dome, the government also threw cash at artists to create municipal art in the surrounding area. Two of the most successful results are right by the river and are easily viewed from the Thames Path. (This stretch is best accessed from Greenwich proper; the short walk takes you through an abundance of decayed industrial architecture.)

Slice of Reality is by Richard Wilson, a sculptor who favours industrial materials. His most famous work is *20:50*, a whole room half-filled with sump oil; this sounds trifling, but the work is an astonishing experience, like being buried in a liquid black mirror. *Slice of Reality* is equally ambitious and transgressive: a 20-metre high cross-section of a 600 ton dredger set in the Thames riverbed. Seen at low tide, the sculpture looks as though it will keel over, being set on a dainty little plinth. The effect close up is unnerving – only 15% of the ship remains, yet the slice overwhelms. It serves admirably as a memorial to the maritime past of London.

The second sculpture, *Quantum Cloud*, is a 30-metre work by Anthony Gormley, probably the most high-profile creator of public art in Britain. At first sight, this giant work appears to be a cloud created by thousands of square, hollow sections of steel. Focus your eyes, and at the centre of the cloud the outline of a human form emerges. The river as a backdrop makes perfect sense; the sculpture appears to echo the whirling seabirds of the Thames and the static form is full of movement.

The Dome is worth seeing, partly as proof of political hubris, but mostly for the contemporary design. Conceived by Lord Richard Rogers, the Queen Mother of British architecture, the Dome is still the largest single-roofed structure in the world. The tube station that serves it, North Greenwich, with its blue-tiled and glazed interior and raking concrete columns was designed by Will Alsop, and merits a visit in its own right.

STARGAZING AT THE ROYAL OBSERVATORY ⑫

Royal Observatory, Blackheath Avenue, Greenwich Park, SE10
0208 312 6565
www.rmg.co.uk/royal-observatory
Open Observation events on selected evenings throughout the year
These events must be booked in advance and often sell out early
Admission £15, concessions £11
Transport Cutty Sark DLR or Greenwich rail

Secrets
of the stars

The Royal Observatory in Greenwich Park may have been designed for surveying the stars, but the views of London from this hilltop landmark are equally spectacular. The dazzling towers of Canary Wharf and the distant glow of the London Eye are most dramatic at night, but the park closes at dusk. To enjoy this view – and see the stars, too – book a place on one of the Royal Observatory's special 'Evenings with the Stars'.

After an illuminating zoom into the night sky overhead in the high-tech Planetarium, with live commentary from one of the resident astronomers, visitors climb up a tower crowned with a bulging dome. As E. Walter Maunder wrote in 1900: "This dome - which has been likened according to the school of aesthetics in which its critics have been severally trained, to the Taj at Agra, a collapsed balloon, or a mammoth Spanish onion - houses the largest refractor in England, the 'South-east Equatorial' of twenty-eight inches aperture."

This colossal feat of Victorian engineering is still the world's seventh largest telescope. Built by Sir Howard Grubb in 1893, it took eight years to complete and weighs 1.4 tons. The lens alone weighs 102 kg. The telescope is tilted parallel to the Earth's axis of rotation, so you can follow a star from east to west by simply rotating the mount. This isn't quite as clever as it seems: the mount doesn't actually fit inside the dome. Despite the addition of a GPS system, moving the telescope involves cumbersome manoeuvres of the dome's retractable shutters and crawling about on the floor. Early astronomers often had to lie flat on the floor to look through the lens. What you see depends on the time of year and the weather. The experience will be enjoyable even if it's overcast, as two enthusiastic astronomers, explain the mysteries of the solar system and stars with fantastical names, from Aspidiske to Zubenelgenubi.

LONGPLAYER: A 1,000-YEAR LONG PIECE OF MUSIC

When tours are not in progress, Jem Finer's *Longplayer* (see page 253) is played inside the dome. The music is designed to extend the temporal horizon, just as telescopes push back the spatial horizon.

MERIDIAN LINE LASER

As the official starting point for the new millennium, a bright green laser was turned on at the Royal Observatory in December 1999, illuminating the path of the Prime Meridian Line across the London sky. It is visible for 10 miles on a clear night.

PRINCESS CAROLINE'S SUNKEN BATH ⑬
Near the rose garden in Greenwich Park; entrance from Charlton Way
Transport Greenwich or Blackheath rail

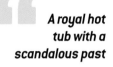

A royal hot tub with a scandalous past

I n 1795, Princess Caroline of Brunswick married her cousin "Prinny", the Prince Regent (later King George IV). It was not a happy marriage. Prinny, who had married Caroline for her fat fortune, was far more interested in his mistress, Maria Fitzherbert. So the philandering prince started spreading rumours about Caroline's sluttish and slovenly ways – apparently, she was hopelessly adulterous, never washed, rarely changed her underclothes, and had bad breath because of her fondness for raw garlic and onions.

After giving birth to a daughter, Caroline was promptly banished to Montague House in Greenwich, where she consoled herself with wild orgies and scandalous affairs. When Caroline finally tired of Britain and went into self-imposed exile in 1814, in a fit of pique Prinny had Montague House torn down. The site is now part of Greenwich Park. Between the Ranger's Lodge and the Rose Garden, however, a little piece of Caroline's pleasure palace survives: a sunken bath complete with a staircase. Used as a flowerbed for decades, the white-tiled plunge pool was unearthed in 1909. A small plaque commemorates the scorned princess, proving that although she may have been unfaithful at least she wasn't unhygienic.

THE GREENWICH GNOMES

Just inside Blackheath Gate are some public toilets. Hiding in the cisterns on the maintenance buildings behind them is a family of garden gnomes.

SIGHTS NEARBY

ANTIQUE ANCHORS ⑭
In the north-eastern corner of the Maritime Museum is a collection of antique anchors, complete with little plaques that recount their provenance. Look out for the anchor dating from 1805, the year of the Battle of Trafalgar.

A PRIVATE JOKE ⑮
Apart from its pink façade, E.M Sabo, a musty newsagent at Number 3 Stockwell Street, looks unremarkable. But take a closer look at the hand-written ads displayed in the window. Tucked among the real advertisements are several joke advertisements for a fried egg, a used trophy, a parachute "used once, unopened", and a blotchy, ink-stained ad for a "brand new fountain pen" – a snip at £8. (Thanks to The Greenwich Phantom for spotting this: www.thegreenwichphantom.co.uk.)

THE FAN MUSEUM

16

12 Crooms Hill, Greenwich SE10
0208 305 1441
www.thefanmuseum.org.uk
Open Tues-Sat 11am-5pm, Sun noon-5pm
Admission £4, conc £3. Free for children under 7
Free for OAPs and disabled on Tuesdays after 2pm
Transport Greenwich rail or DLR

Art in miniature

The Fan Museum in Greenwich is another of London's many specialist museums reflecting the obsessive, collecting side of the English. It claims to be the only museum in the world devoted to every aspect of fans and fan making (although a similar venture exists in Paris), and there may be good reason for this - the craft does seem limited. But the collection works as a set of miniatures and the building itself is worth visiting. Housed in a pair of listed Georgian buildings from 1721 that have been restored to their original state, the museum contains over 3,500 mostly antique fans from around the world. These date from the 11th century to the present day. However, the bulk of the collection is based around fans from the 18th and 19th centuries, when mass production of folding fans saw their use spread throughout society. Demand was such that the Fan Makers had their own livery company, which still exists, although with the dwindling of demand for fans, its membership now mainly derives from the heating and air-conditioning industry.

Fans may be practical objects, but the blank canvas of the 'leaf' meant that they became a highly decorative form of display. Fans often directly referred to contemporary events and allegiances, with Nelson's victories a particularly popular subject in mass-produced fans. They also served as a kind of primitive advertising hoarding. At the fancier end of the market, leading society artists painted fans for clients – the museum holds a fan painted by Walter Sickert. The functions of the fans on display thus vary wildly: ceremonial tools, fashion accessories, status symbols, political flags, or advertising giveaways.

At 2pm on the first Saturday of the month, the Fan Museum holds fan-making workshops. Classes cost £20 and last about 3 hours.

The museum also has an Orangery overlooking a secret Japanese garden, with a fan-shaped parterre. Afternoon tea is served on Tuesdays and Sundays from 3pm.

FAN LANGUAGE

The practical use of a fan is clear. However, at the apogee of their popularity at the turn of the 19th century, a whole language was involved in their use, much of which can be seen in contemporary paintings. A fan resting upon the lips, for example, means 'I don't trust you'; placed on the heart it declares, 'My love for you is breaking my heart;' hiding the sunlight implies that 'You are ugly;' and fanning with the left hand says, 'Don't flirt with that woman.' Go to the museum, buy a fan, and reinstate these practices in polite society.

GREENWICH FOOT TUNNEL

Cutty Sark Gardens, Greenwich / Island Gardens, Isle of Dogs
Open 24 hours
Admission free
Transport Island Gardens or Cutty Sark DRL

Tunnel under the Thames

The Greenwich Foot Tunnel, an underwater passageway linking Cutty Sark Gardens in Greenwich and Island Gardens on the Isle of Dogs, is one of the great engineering feats of 19th century London.

Lined with 200,000 glazed white tiles, which give it the unfortunate acoustics and ambience of a public toilet, the tunnel opened in 1902. Designed by Sir Alexander Binnie, it was commissioned to alleviate the overcrowded ferry service used by commuters who worked at the docks on the Isle of Dogs. Once barely populated, the marshy Isle of Dogs grew with the success of the British Empire. By the end of the 19th century, the population had risen to 21,000. International shipping poured into the new docks, which once stretched all the way from Tower Bridge to Barking, making London the largest port in the world. All of this is long gone. The Isle of Dogs maintains a reputation as one of the tougher parts of town, but 'The Docklands' is now synonymous with the executive housing that services the City of London to the west and Canary Wharf to the east.

The entrance shafts at both ends of the tunnel are topped by glazed cupolas. Lifts (not running at night) and spiral staircases allow pedestrians access to the tunnel, which is 370 metres long, with an internal diameter of about 3 metres. The tiled walls make the tunnel echo eerily, especially when you creep into it in the dead of night - the tunnel is a public highway and therefore by law is open 24 hours. At such times of low traffic, it feels like the loneliest, most desolate place in London, until the sound of approaching heels ring down the tunnel like bullets.

UNDERWATER ENGINEERING

Greenwich Tunnel is actually the third tunnel constructed under the Thames. The Thames Tunnel, designed by Brunel, (see page 269) opened in 1843. It came to be regarded as the haunt of prostitutes and 'tunnel thieves' who lurked under its arches and mugged passers-by. Greenwich Tunnel was duplicated about three miles downstream at Woolwich Crossing, which runs between Silvertown and Woolwich. There is little reason to visit this area, which remains emphatically ungentrified, unless a free boat ride across the river appeals. Unlike any of the other boats on the river, the ferry crossing here is free

---

CREEKSIDE CENTRE

⑱

14 Creekside, Deptford, SE8
0208 692 9922
www.creeksidecentre.org.uk
Open/Admission By prior arrangement only
Transport Deptford train station, Greenwich train/DLR station

*A muddy
refuge for boats
and birds*

The Creekside education centre looks as though it has washed up on the shores of the Thames along with the driftwood. Built right next to Ha'penny Hatch, on the edge of Deptford Creek, this showcase of sustainable riverside architecture was set up to raise awareness of the creek's unique environment. Deptford Creek is the tidal reach of the Ravensbourne, one of the Thames' tributaries, and among the last of them not yet tamed to make room for the city – the Fleet runs via a sewer under Farringdon Road, the Westbourne is piped over the platform at Sloane Square tube, and the Effra enters the Thames via a storm drain next to the headquarters of the British intelligence agency, MI6.

Deptford Creek is uncovered, and refreshed each day by the surge of the tide up the Thames; this, as well as its location in an abandoned industrial landscape, has produced a lively local wildlife habitat. Visitors to the centre are issued with waders; when the tide ebbs, the riverbed becomes a mile-long, firm path of black mud, embedded with the skeletons of old boats and docks. Expeditions are led up it by centre staff, pointing out both the wildlife and the history of the creek, which may include anything from Russian tsars to the mating cycle of eels. If you're visiting the centre, the best thing to do is to check the events diary on the website, as there are no regular outings. Volunteers are invited to join the frequent creek clean-ups, which are exhilarating – and very muddy – affairs.

There is a pleasing aura of decrepitude about the creek; this is deceptive, as the area throngs with artists working from an estimated 100 studios. Like much of the South Bank, Deptford has always attracted the gamier parts of the art world, as it is cheap and far from prying eyes. There is also a colony of houseboats, a far more piratical-looking fleet than the one at Chelsea. Remains lie everywhere and everywhere lies possibility.

The creek is home to one of the country's rarer birds, the Black Redstart. The industries and businesses along the creek provide this bird with an environmental paradise, as they nest in power stations, gas works, industrial plots, railway yards and old wharves.

CHRISTOPHER MARLOWE'S GRAVE

Playwright Christopher Marlowe, who wrote *Dr Faustus*, was stabbed in the face in a private house near Creekside, and is buried in an unmarked grave in nearby St Nicholas. The church is also worth visiting for the two glowering skulls that sit atop its gateposts.

THE BRUNEL MUSEUM

(19)

Railway Avenue, Rotherhithe SE16
0207 231 3840
www.brunel-museum.org.uk
Open 10am-5pm daily
Admission adults £2, concessions £1
Transport Rotherhithe tube

> *Floodlit tours through the Thames Tunnel*

Isambard Kingdom Brunel, builder of the Saltash Bridge, the Clifton Suspension Bridge, and the Great Western Railway, is a towering legend in the history of engineering. However, the Brunel Museum focuses on another Brunel - his father, Marc Isambard Brunel. Brunel père was born in Normandy, and initially seemed destined for priesthood, but became a naval cadet instead. In 1793, Brunel fled the French Revolution for the newly founded United States, where he became chief engineer of New York. He moved to Britain in 1799, hoping to exploit the possibilities of the Industrial Revolution. This museum is built around his most famous achievement, the Thames Tunnel.

Work started on the 406-metre tunnel in 1825. When it was finally completed 18 years later, it was hailed as the eighth wonder of the world. The ingenuity of its construction is considerable. The shaft was formed by building a brick tower, and then digging the earth out until the tower sank under its own weight to line the shaft. A tunnel shield was forced through the soft clay beneath the river to reduce the risk of collapse.

Originally designed for horse-drawn traffic, the development company ran out of money to build the requisite ramps. Access to the tunnel was only by a staircase in the shaft, limiting it to pedestrian use. After great initial success, public interest faded and the tunnel acquired a reputation as a hotbed of seedy activity. Subsequently, it was converted to rail and still carries the East London Line under the Thames.

The museum offers a fairly desultory collection of ephemera related to the tunnel and the Brunels. However, it regularly organises floodlit tours by tube train through the tunnel, so travellers can clearly see its columns and Doric capitals, apparently a structural must of any 19th century building work in London. The tours are suspended during engineering works, but will resume in 2010. See www.brunelenginehouse.org.uk/tours.asp for details.

Although Marc Brunel was knighted for his contribution to engineering in 1841, Brunel fils is the superstar. Little of his work is extant in London, but one of his iron bridges was recently discovered inside a modern brick road bridge over the Grand Union Canal near Paddington station.

Brunel father and son are buried together in Kensal Green Cemetery. The tomb is extremely unprepossessing, especially for two giants of Victorian engineering.

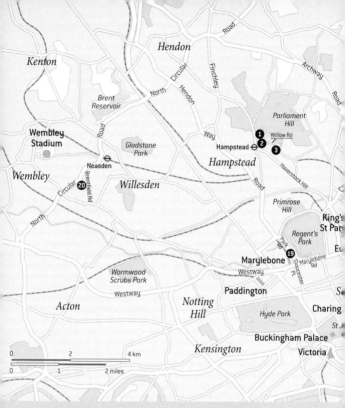

GREATER LONDON (NORTH)

HAMPSTEAD MUSEUM

Burgh House, New End Square, NW3
0207 431 0144
www.burghhouse.org.uk
Open Wed, Thurs, Fri, Sun noon-5pm
Admission free. **Transport** Hampstead tube

> *Ode to North London*

Built in 1703, Burgh House is one of the oldest houses in Hampstead Town, a leafy suburb in north London whose walled lanes and wonky cul-de-sacs are ripe for strolling.

Despite its exclusive character, this Georgian enclave still has the charm of a sleepy village whose steep slopes afford fine views across London. In its 17th century heyday, the spa at Hampstead Wells was fashionable for its fetid, iron-rich water, reportedly good for afflictions such as hysteria and neurosis, as prevalent today as they were then. Dr. William Gibbons, the spa physician, lived at Burgh House. His initials are carved into the wrought-iron gate although the house was named after Reverend Allatson Burgh, a wildly unpopular vicar who bought the house for £2,645 in 1822. During Burgh's sloppy tenure, the property fell into ruins. In the 1970s, it was finally restored and leased to the Burgh House Trust who set up a small museum here. Founder Christopher Wade, who still presides over this living memorial to his local community, is a rich source of history about the house and anecdotes about its diverse and colourful residents through the ages.

Upstairs, you can trace the history of Hampstead in the small, cluttered but intriguing museum, from the first silent film footage of London to Bauhaus furniture from the iconic Isokon flats. There are tributes to local luminaries John Constable, who painted the Heath before houses began to obscure the view, and John Keats, whose soppy odes were inspired by its wild landscapes.

Burgh House's basement Buttery is a favourite tea break for silver-haired visitors. Tables are set in the garden in summer, where you can glare at the lucky devils that live in council flats next door, the only affordable homes in this desirable neighbourhood.

THE FOUNTAIN OF HAMPSTEAD WELLS

Nearby, on Wells Passage, is the fountain from which Hampstead Wells' 'chalybeate' water was pumped. History survives in the local place names: the foul-tasting water was bottled at Flask Walk, and the nearest section of parkland is called the Vale of Health.

SIGHTS NEARBY

NEW END THEATRE

27 New End • 0207 794 0022

Ken Russell, Steven Berkoff, and Emma Thompson have all graced the stage of this cosy theatre that champions new writing. It was built in 1890 as the mortuary of New End Hospital across the road; an underground tunnel allowed corpses to be discreetly transported to the morgue.

2 WILLOW ROAD

❸

2 Willow Road, Hampstead NW3
0207 435 6166
www.nationaltrust.org.uk
Open Times vary, check website for details
Admission £4.90, children £2.50, family £12.30
Transport Hampstead tube or rail

> *Only the Eskimos and Zulus build anything but rectangular houses*

Erno Goldfinger is most famous as the architect of Trellick Tower, a 1960s high-rise council block in West London, as notorious for brutal crimes as its Brutalist design. Trellick Tower is now a listed building. But the first house the Transylvanian émigré ever built was this low-key, low-rise Hampstead home, where he lived with his family for almost fifty years. What makes this Modernist show-home unique is that everything is exactly as Goldfinger designed it in 1939 – and exactly as he left it on his death in 1987, from the prototype door handles on his desk to the baked beans in his wife Ursula's kitchen. The house is as fascinating for its ingenious, daring design as its insight into Goldfinger's life and work. The art collection is impressive, too: works by Bridget Riley, Max Ernst, and Marcel Duchamp hang alongside Ursula's surrealist paintings. In the 1930s, rural Hampstead had replaced Chelsea as the epicentre of a lively, left-wing arts scene. Lee Miller, Roland Penrose, and Henry Moore attended the Goldfinger's glamorous parties. Although the house is relatively small - at least by Hampstead standards - folding doors, hidden storage, and vast windows with unbroken views of Hampstead Heath create a sense of space and light. Passionate volunteers offer guided tours several times a day, starting with a video in the garage. A graceful spiral staircase leads to a lacquered scarlet landing. The house's Cubist colour palette - midnight blue, tomato red, mustard, terracotta – is oddly soothing. The furniture – designed by Goldfinger and associates like Ove Arup – still looks thoroughly modern. The house faced intense opposition when it was built. Goldfinger, who retorted that "only the Eskimos and Zulus build anything but rectangular houses", was forced to cover the concrete frame in brick cladding to blend in with its Georgian neighbours. One of the main objectors was the Tory Home Secretary, Henry Brooke. Ironically, it was his son, Peter Brooke, then Minister of the Environment, who took possession of the house on behalf of the National Trust: Goldfinger's children could not afford the whopping death duties.

NASTY NAMESAKE

By all accounts, the dashing Goldfinger was a difficult man, mitigated by his generosity and charisma. But the anti-Semitic Ian Fleming took such a dislike to Goldfinger that he named his infamous villain after him.

WEST RESERVOIR

❹

Green Lanes, Stoke Newington N4
Open 9am-5pm daily, 9am-9pm during the summer
Admission Free. Cost of watersports courses varies; check
www.hackney.gov.uk/west-reservoir.htm
Transport Manor House tube, or bus 141, 341 and 106

*Sailing
in the city*

It may seem like one of the world's wettest cities, but London has less rainfall than Madrid, Rome or Dallas. That doesn't stop every resident using an average 155 litres of water a day. Back in the 19th century, for most Londoners the only water supply was a communal standpipe that churned out a brackish trickle for a few hours a day. After several cholera outbreaks, in 1831-3 the East and West Reservoirs were built in Stoke Newington as a water reserve and purification plant. Stone from the recently demolished London Bridge was used to shore up the reservoirs' banks.

Surprisingly few locals know about this rural idyll in a nondescript residential area in the heart of Hackney. A muddy footpath surrounded by meadows circles the West Reservoir, where swans and seagulls swoop among colourful sailing boats. After a long campaign to save the reservoirs from property developers, a water sports and environmental education centre opened in the former pump station in 2001. You can take sailing, kayaking, and canoeing classes, marvel at the old hydraulic machinery, which apparently handled "a weight of water equivalent to that contained by 4,366 bathtubs or 3,492,800 glass fulls dropped from a height of seventeen metres up to six times each day." After your nautical exertions, tuck into a cheap and hearty English breakfast on the scenic waterside deck of the Reservoir Cafe.

THE NOT-SO-NEW RIVER

Stoke Newington has been instrumental in bringing clean water to London since the early 17th century, when the New River first ran through the area. Almost 400 years old, the New River is not technically a river at all. It is an artificial aqueduct constructed to transport water from springs in Hertfordshire to London, and still used to transport water today. Determined walkers can follow its course along a 45 km footpath from Clerkenwell to the countryside.

SIGHTS NEARBY

CASTLE CLIMBING CENTRE

❺

Open Mon-Fri 2pm-10pm, weekends 10pm-7pm • www.castle-climbing.co.uk
0208 211 7000.

As its name suggests, gritty Green Lanes was once a lush rural retreat. Very few houses stood nearby when the Stoke Newington Water Pumping Station was built in 1856. But the contractors opted to appease local objections by disguising the main building as a medieval fortress. Today, this flamboyant monument to Victorian engineering has been reinvented as one of the largest indoor climbing centres in Britain.

SUTTON HOUSE ❻
2 & 4 Homerton High Street, Hackney, E9
0208 986 2264
www.nationaltrust.org.uk
Open 12.30-4.30pm Thurs-Sun
Admission £2.80, child 70p, family £6.30
Transport Hackney Central or Hackney Down rail, bus

*The oldest
house in Hackney*

With its bleak council estates and countless fried chicken emporia, no amount of hikes in housing prices has made Homerton desirable. This is the dark heart of Hackney. In Tudor times, however, Homerton was so upmarket that dozens of aristocrats built country estates here. Even Thomas Sutton, supposedly the richest commoner in Britain, and founder of Charterhouse (see page 77), lived in Homerton. This National Trust property is mistakenly named after Sutton; in fact, he lived next door in a mansion that has since been demolished.

This mix-up is typical of Sutton House, whose mish-mash of architectural styles reflects its motley succession of residents since 1535. The original owner, Sir Ralph Sadler, Henry VIII's Secretary of State, had thirty acres of gardens and orchards attached to 'Bryk Place,' so called because it was the only brick building in what was then a half-timbered village. It was successively occupied by a sheriff, a silk merchant, a girl's school (coyly known as The Ladies' University of Female Arts), and a recreational club for men (euphemistically dubbed St John's Church Institute), until it was bought by the National Trust in 1938. Not much happened until the mid-1980s, when a bunch of punks squatted the derelict red-brick building, hosting gigs and gatherings of a decidedly downmarket nature.

Miraculously, many of the original Tudor features survived: oak-panelled rooms, carved fireplaces, a gorgeous secret courtyard, and an authentically rudimentary kitchen. The parlour is the most impressive room, lined entirely with 204 panels hand-carved over four hundred years ago. By another strange twist of fate (or artful crime), this panelling was stolen in the late 1980s, but later sold back to the National Trust.

The restoration of Sutton House by the National Trust in the early 1990s is cleverly designed to expose overlapping layers of history. The *trompe l'oeil* mural from the 17th century is considerably more accomplished than the wall paintings by the punks, but the contrast is refreshing. The experience is very interactive: visitors can lift a floorboard or open a panel to discover traces of the house's hidden past. You (or your offspring) can don fake beards and period costumes. There are regular exhibitions by local artists and concerts organised by the Sutton House Music Society, ranging from chamber music to African drumming.

RAGGED SCHOOL MUSEUM ❼

46-50 Copperfield Road, E3
0208 980 6405
www.raggedschoolmuseum.org.uk
Open Wed and Thurs 10am-5pm, first Sunday each month 2-5pm,
Victorian lesson at 2.15 & 3.30pm
Admission Free. Suggested donation of £2 for Victorian lesson
Transport Mile End tube or Limehouse DLR

> *A Victorian lesson in East End history*

Tower Hamlets is one of the poorest boroughs in London, but in Victorian times the East End suffered poverty on an incomparable scale. Families were crammed into one-room flats, and illiterate kids ran barefoot along the coal-blackened alleys. One third of all funerals in the area were for children under five. When Thomas Barnardo arrived in London in 1866 to train as a missionary, a cholera epidemic had swept through the East End. Barnardo set about founding the Ragged Schools to provide free education for London's poorest children. 21st century kids can dress up like Oliver Twist at the Ragged School Museum, a Dickensian throwback aptly located on Copperfield Road in Mile End.

From 1887 to 1908, tens of thousands of children were educated at this school, housed in a former warehouse beside Regents Canal. On the first Sunday of every month, a Victorian lesson is re-enacted by an actress in period costume in one of the original classrooms. Scratched desks with inkwells, slate writing boards, and dunce hats create an evocative setting for this local history lesson.

Downstairs is a small Museum of Tower Hamlets, which offers a potted history of local landmarks like the Bryant and May match factory, now converted into luxury flats. There are mementoes from the Blitz, including song sheets with jaunty titles like *In the Blackout Last Night*, designed to boost wartime morale. Visitors can learn about other well-meaning Victorian institutions like the Working Lads Institute, whose mission was to teach young workers to read and write, and The Factory Girls Club, run by 'refined Christian ladies' to teach girls 'feminine and domestic virtues' so they could become servants.

The promise of free meals led to overcrowding in the Ragged Schools, although school dinners were just as dire in those days: 'Breakfast was bread and cocoa. Dinner was lentil or pea soup and bread, varied occasionally by rice and prunes or haricot beans.' Threatened with demolition in the early 1980s, the building was converted into a museum after a campaign by local residents. Barnardo's is still one of the UK's biggest children's charities.

In the 16th century, Tower Hamlets, the sprawling borough that will host the 2012 Olympic Games, consisted of just a few scattered dwellings east of The Tower of London. Today, its drab council estates are overshadowed by the towers of Canary Wharf, gleaming on the horizon like the distant promise of wealth.

THE LONDON BUDDHIST CENTRE 8

51 Roman Road, Bethnal Green E2
0845 458 4716
www.lbc.org.uk
Admission Cost and time of classes varies, check website for details
Transport Bethnal Green tube

> *A Buddhist Village in Bethnal Green*

When a bunch of hippies persuaded the (now defunct) Greater London Council to let them convert a derelict Victorian fire station into a Buddhist centre back in the late 1970s, the locals were up in arms. These days, estate agents have dubbed the red brick building and its affiliated businesses "Bethnal Green's Buddhist Village." In fact, there isn't much evidence to alert passers-by to the fact that this fetching five-storey building is home to two Buddhist communities, a bookshop, library, and several meditation rooms. It is only when you turn the corner into Globe Road that you might spot the ornate metal lotus flower and wheel of life above the side entrance. But once you enter the overgrown courtyard, with its tinkling fountain and lotus murals, you'll leave the urban rat race behind. That is exactly what the London Buddhist Centre aspires to achieve: a type of mindfulness and meditation tailored to the realities of 21st century urban living. Thirty years after it opened in 1978, the London Buddhist Centre is undergoing extensive restoration to bring its rather shabby interiors into the New Age. When the building work is completed, the centre will have an illuminated 'stupa,' shiny new meditation rooms, and a revamped Breathing Space - a centre to help the victims of depression and addiction, pioneered by psychiatrist Dr Paramabandhu Groves, the Centre's director. "We want to give people the tools to manage their own mental health," explains Tim Segaller, manager of Breathing Space. The centre also provides workshops for carers and schools – just the thing for calming down unruly adolescents in Tower Hamlets. Although there is a preponderance of white middle class participants, the centre draws in a diverse mix of people of all ages and backgrounds who could use a little peace of mind. Anything designed to encourage "The Development of Loving Kindness" among go-getting, self-absorbed Londoners deserves a plug.

Lunchtime meditation classes (noon-1pm, Monday to Friday) are a bargain at just £1. "Some people never come back, others drop in regularly, but only a few go the whole hog and become full-blown Buddhists," says Segaller. If you do convert, you can sign up for a retreat in Suffolk

The Wild Cherry vegetarian café next door (241-245 Globe Road; 0208 980 6678) is a Buddhist cooperative run by women and does excellent all-day breakfasts on Saturdays.

W.C.s

CALVES

Rhubarb.
makes lovely crumble!
~ yummy ~

HACKNEY CITY FARM

❾

1a Goldsmiths Row, E2
0207 729 6381
www.hackneycityfarm.co.uk
Open Tues-Sun 10am–4.30pm
Admission free
Transport Bus 26, 48, 55

*My family
and other animals*

London may have more parks and green spaces than most metropolises, but the sheer size of the city can still make the countryside feel out of reach – particularly in a scruffy borough like Hackney. Wedged between the council estates on Hackney Road is a lovely refuge from the kebab shops and grotty pubs: a working farm run mainly by local volunteers.

Partly fuelled by solar heating and bio-diesel (using recycled cooking oil from the café and other local businesses), Hackney City Farm is a model of sustainability. As well as farming and gardening classes, the farm hosts all kinds of green living and craft workshops. The animals are the typical farmyard mix of sheep, goats, pigs, cows and poultry. Larry the donkey is a huge hit with kids. The best time to visit is at 4pm – the animals' dinner time.

If you don't have time to volunteer at the farm, you could adopt an animal. Sponsorship pays for a year of food and entitles you to four visits to your furry or feathered friend. If you can't afford to sponsor the whole beast, you can opt for just a rump or a snout. Back in the early 19th century, before it was taken over by West's Brewery, this site was occupied by farmers and market gardeners, who sold their produce to the City of London. These days, locals are more likely to pick up some antipasti and home-made gelati from the organic Italian café and deli.

CITY FARMS

There are fifteen city farms in London. The first, Kentish Town City Farm (www.ktcityfarm.org.uk), opened in 1972 and is still very popular today for the pony rides. Other notable farms are the city's largest, Mudchute (see page 251 - Traffic Light Tree) on the Isle of Dogs; Surrey Docks Farm (www.surreydocksfarm.org.uk), on the banks of the Thames at Rotherhithe, which has a pretty herb garden and resident blacksmith; Freightliners' Farm (www.freightlinersfarm.org.uk), where you can learn beekeeping; and Brooks Farm (www.walthamforest.gov.uk/brooks-farm-leyton.htm), whose furry inhabitants include a llama named Merlin.

SIGHTS NEARBY

CRICKET MATCHES AT LONDON FIELDS

❿

Cricket has been played at London Fields since 1802. On summer weekends, amateur matches start at 2pm. The plane trees around the pitch provide shade in the unlikely event that "it's" sunny, and the nearby *Pub on the Park* provides refreshments for the spectators.

CLOWNS' GALLERY AND MUSEUM ⓫

Holy Trinity Church, Beechwood Road, Dalston E8
0870 128 4336
www.clowns-international.co.uk
Open noon–5pm on the first Friday of every month
Admission free
Transport Bus 243, 38, 149, 236

Fool's paradise

The Holy Trinity has been London's Clowns' Church since 1959. Inside, two affable clowns (in civilian clothing) talk the curious through the small permanent display over a tinkling soundtrack of fairground tunes.

The prize exhibit is a stained-glass window depicting scenes from the life of Joseph Grimaldi (1778-1837), the godfather of all jesters. Among the clown stamps, cartoons and tributes are a few religious references to "The Holy Fools": a tapestry proclaiming "Here we are fools for Christ" and The Clown's Prayer (a slightly cloying ode to laughter). Another highlight is the collection of clown portraits painted on porcelain eggs. A tradition that originated in the 1950s, these eggs are faithful representations of the trademark make-up worn by each clown – a suitably humorous way of patenting their face-paint.

The bulk of the collection – which grew too big for the church – was despatched to a new Clown Museum in Wookey Hole, Somerset, in spring 2008. The remaining archive is hidden under the altar.

SLAPSTICK SERVICE

The church comes to life on the first Sunday in February, when the Reverend Rose Hudson-Wilkin oversees the annual clown service. Among the local congregation in their Sunday best, dozens of clowns in full "motley and slap" cause havoc in the pews – blowing bubbles, honking horns, wearing stilts, and singing along to "Send in the Clowns". Apparently, one popular hymn at the Holy Trinity goes like this: *"When we are tempted in our pride to dizzy heights of sin, beneath our feet, oh Lord, provide a ripe banana skin ..."*

THE ORIGINS OF THE MARIONETTE

Puppets were used in churches and passion plays in the Middle Ages to tell stories from the Bible to illiterate congregations – hence the name "marionette" (Little Mary).

Joseph Grimaldi, who made his debut at Sadler's Wells aged three, pioneered many modern clowning techniques, from visual pranks to the dreaded audience participation. A blue plaque marks Grimaldi's former home at 56 Exmouth Market, Clerkenwell. His grave is largely overlooked in the grubby little Joseph Grimaldi Park on the corner of Pentonville Road and Rodney Street, Islington. With a happy and sad mask dangling from the iron railings, it's a rather forlorn tribute to the fools' hero, but every June a lively festival is held here in Grimaldi's honour.

NEW RIVER WALK ⑫

Canonbury N1
0207 527 4953
Open 8am to dusk daily
Admission free
Transport Essex Road rail, Highbury & Islington tube

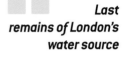

Last remains of London's water source

With its Georgian mansions built around leafy squares, Canonbury is one of the lushest and loveliest corners of London. Only developed as a residential area in the early 19th century, Canonbury retains the feel of an exclusive country retreat. Running through the vast - and vastly expensive - houses of Canonbury Grove is a little stream, hidden from view by weeping willows and luxuriant shrubbery. This sleepy waterway is one of the last remaining sections of Hugh Myddelton's New River, an aqueduct built in 1613 to bring drinking water from springs in Hertfordshire to a reservoir in Myddelton Square, near Sadler's Wells (see page 277 West Reservoir – The Not-so-New River).

Although the aqueduct still supplies 8% of London's water, most of the New River has been covered over by building development. Created in 1954, this waterside nature trail is maintained by local volunteers. Water is pumped upstream to preserve the effect of a moving river. Hungry herons and ponderous ducks drift along the mossy surface of the shallow waterway, which meanders for about a kilometre through fragrant gardens criss-crossed by wooden footbridges. Look for the New River Company's seal etched into the path.

SIGHTS NEARBY

THE ESTORICK COLLECTION ⑬

39a Canonbury Square N1 • 0207 704 9522 • www.estorickcollection.com
Open Wed–Sat 11am-6pm, Sun noon-5pm • **Admission** £3.50, Conc. £2.50, students and children free • **Transport** Highbury & Islington tube

Devoted entirely to 20th century Italian art, the Estorick Collection is named after Eric Estorick, an American collector with a brilliant moniker and a fondness for Futurist art. After moving to England after World War II, Estorick (1913-93) snapped up drawings by Picasso, Gris, Léger and Braque. But it was during his honeymoon in Switzerland and Italy in 1947 that Estorick discovered Futurism; enthralled, he bought practically the entire works of Mario Sironi. By 1960, Estorick had built up such an impressive collection of Italian art that he founded the Grosvenor Gallery, whose clients included Hollywood stars such as Lauren Bacall and Burt Lancaster.

Shortly before his death, Estorick left 80 artworks to a charitable trust. Spread over six galleries in a converted Georgian townhouse, the collection includes works by Amedeo Modigliani, Giorgio de Chirico and Zoran Music. The garden café is a blissful spot that serves proper cappuccino and, of course, pasta.

CANONBURY TOWER

(14)

Canonbury Place N1
0207 226 6256
www.canonbury.ac.uk
Open For public lectures or by appointment
Admission varies
Transport Highbury & Islington tube

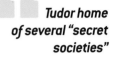

Tudor home of several "secret societies"

The oldest building in Islington, Canonbury Tower was built some time between 1509 and 1532. Its first resident, Prior William Bolton of St Bartholomew, enjoyed uninterrupted views of London rising above the surrounding farmland. Allegedly built on a ley line, the Tudor tower still commands views all the way to St Paul's Cathedral and Alexandra Palace, now enjoyed by the members of the Canonbury Masonic Research Centre (CMRC), who took up residence here in 1998. With its intimidating exterior and extraordinary history, the tower is a fitting home for this mysterious organisation, devoted to "the study of mystical and esoteric traditions, in particular Freemasonry".

It is only possible to visit Canonbury Tower by attending one of CMRC's lectures on Freemasonry and mysticism, but Carole McGilvery, the centre's chirpy manager, will gladly give visitors an illuminating tour of the building by prior arrangement. McGilvery has a wealth of tales about former residents such as Thomas Cromwell, who was gifted Canonbury Manor by Henry VIII in 1539 after masterminding the dissolution of the monasteries, only to be beheaded a year later. It was Sir John Spencer, the filthy rich Lord Mayor of London who occupied Canonbury Tower from 1570 to 1610, who commissioned the intricate wood panelling that covers the Spencer and Compton rooms on the second floor. Sir Francis Bacon, a prominent Freemason and potential author of Shakespeare's plays, lived here for nine years and allegedly planted the mulberry tree in the back garden.

Other distinguished residents include Ephraim Chambers, who compiled the first encyclopaedia in 1728 and writer and gambler Oliver Goldsmith, who hoped to evade his creditors in suburban Islington.

Washington Irving, author of *Rip Van Winkle*, was one of the residents. He promptly moved out after his landlady invited excitable fans to peer through his keyhole.

You can still see Bolton's Rebus (see page 105 St Bartholomew the Great) of a bolt (arrow) piercing a tun (barrel) at 6 Canonbury Place and 4 Alwyne Villas, once part of the extensive grounds of Canonbury House.

According to local legend, subterranean passages linked Canonbury Tower to the priory at Smithfield. However, the brick arches that led to this supposition were probably conduits that provided the priory's water supply.

LITTLE ANGEL THEATRE

⓯

14 Dagmar Passage, Islington N1
0207 226 1787
www.littleangeltheatre.com
Open times vary depending on performances and workshops
Admission varies
Transport Angel or Highbury tube

> *Theatre on a String*

Tucked away down an alley behind the bustling cafes and designer boutiques of Upper Street, the Little Angel Theatre has been staging puppet shows since 1961. Converted from an old temperance hall, this enchanting little theatre was purpose-built for puppets. Everything about the small, brick theatre with its bright blue door seems designed to delight children, who make up the biggest part of its audience. From re-workings of Shakespeare plays to operettas performed by marionettes, there are plenty of puppet shows to captivate adults as well. With pews for seats, the intimate stage is wonderfully atmospheric. The theatre is also home to a Puppet Academy, offering puppet-making classes for kids, and marionette workshops for adults.

FLOATING THEATRE

There is another, even more unusual venue in London devoted entirely to puppet theatre. With its bright red and yellow striped awning, the Puppet Theatre Barge stands out from the other colourful houseboats in Regent's Canal. Founded in 1982, this houseboat is now home to the Moving Theatre Company, an appropriate name given that the floating venue drifts to different locations along the River Thames during the summer, including Richmond and Kingston. From November to June, the barge is moored opposite 35-40 Blomfield Road in Little Venice, W9; 0207 249 6876; www.puppetbarge.com

---

SIGHTS NEARBY

GET STUFFED

⓰

105 Essex Road • 0207 226 1364 • www.thegetstuffed.co.uk

Taxidermy – a Greek word, which literally means 'the arrangement of skin' – is not as fashionable as it once was. Stuffed animals were popularised by the Victorians, driven by their obsession with classifying the natural world and desire to show off their exotic colonial spoils. This poky corner shop on Essex Road is packed to the gills with preserved animals contorted into all manner of positions - from a giant polar bear poised to pounce to a severed leopard head, fangs bared. Customers can bring their own (dead) specimens to be mounted, or choose from a macabre collection of skulls, skeletons, and insects, trophy heads, cased fish, or rugs with modelled heads. Not for the squeamish, but strangely compelling.

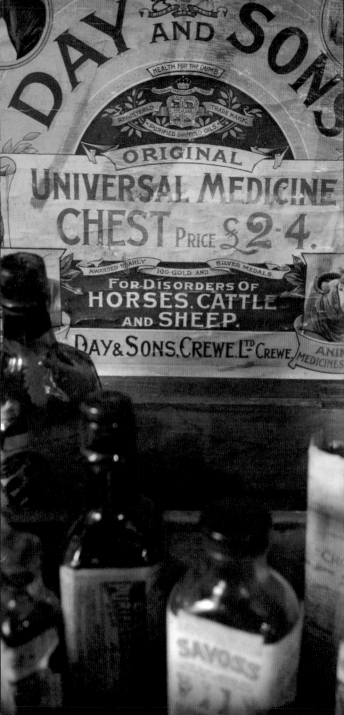

THE ICE WELLS OF THE CANAL MUSEUM ⑰

12/13 New Wharf Road, N1
0207 713 0836
www.canalmuseum.org.uk
Open 10am-4pm Tues-Sat
Admission Adults £3, concessions £2, children £1.50
Transport King's Cross tube/rail

> *The history of London's waterways*

Today, stolen bicycles and supermarket trolleys litter London's murky canals. But until the "great freeze" of 1963, barges cruised these waterways loaded with cargo of all kinds. London's network of canals was the cheapest means of transporting goods across long distances before the advent of railways. Regent's Canal was built in the early 19th century to link the Grand Junction Canal at Paddington with the Docklands. At first, canal boats were drawn by horses, but a steam chug was introduced in 1826. By the 1840s, there was talk of turning the canal into a railway, but luckily this never happened.

Converted from an old ice-house used to store ice imported from Norway, in the days before refrigeration, the London Canal Museum is an old-fashioned, offbeat little venue that tries to capture this forgotten history. Some details are slightly cheesy – a fake horse, clothed dummies - but you can nose around a reconstructed narrowboat decorated with traditional "roses and castles" patterns, and peer down into the impressive ice wells, where hundreds of tons of ice were stored.

From the canal-side terrace, spot the cranes and loading doors where barrels of Guinness were unloaded at the bottling factory on the other side of Battlebridge Basin, now transformed into trendy offices.

SIGHTS NEARBY

NARROWBOAT TOURS OF ISLINGTON TUNNEL ⑱

The Canal Museum organises occasional narrowboat tours of Islington Tunnel on Regent's Canal. When it first opened, this spooky tunnel, around ¾ of a mile long, could only be navigated by "legging": men lay in the boat and pushed against the slimy walls with their legs. Their hob-nailed boots would echo through the tunnel like the clapping of hands. A lantern at the prow lit this cumbersome operation.

Islington tunnel cost nearly £40,000 to build, using explosives, horses and hard labour. When the renowned engineer Thomas Telford inspected the results in 1818, he reported: "Materials and workmanship excellent, and its direction perfectly straight." The tunnel opened in 1820, when Regent's Canal was completed, facilitating the transport of goods to the city centre. Its architect, James Morgan, travelled on the leading barge of a grand procession from St Pancras all the way to the Thames. Accompanied by a band, they were met by cannon fire as they emerged from the tunnel.

RUDOLF STEINER HOUSE ⑲

35 Park Road, NW1
0207 723 4400
www.rsh.anth.org.uk
Open Mon-Fri 10am-6pm
Admission free to library and cafe, prices for lectures
and performances vary
Transport Baker Street tube

> *The only example of Expressionist architecture in London*

With its grey façade, first impressions of Rudolf Steiner House near Regent's Park are of an austere 1920s office block. Closer inspection reveals rounded door and window frames which hint more of a habitat for hobbits. Inside, you come face to face with the building's centrepiece: a curvaceous staircase painted in pastel shades. Its sculptural curves snake all the way up the heart of the building like an artery. The flowing forms and wonky shapes continue throughout the building, which is the only example of Expressionist architecture in London, inspired by nature and characterised by distorted shapes to create a sense of movement and metamorphosis. Surfaces are painted with lazure, a glazing technique using translucent plant pigments. One of the earliest proponents of Expressionism was the anthroposophical philosopher Rudolph Steiner, to whose teachings this building is dedicated. Designed by Montague Wheeler, Chairman of the British Anthroposophical Society from 1935-37, the house exudes a sense of calm and touchy-feely community. The small library is open to the public. As well as workshops and lectures on spiritual development, the specially designed theatre hosts performances of eurythmy. Derived from a Greek word meaning "harmonious rhythm", eurythmy attempts to interpret language and music through gesture and colour.

A biodynamic café was added when the building was refurbished in 2008. Steiner pioneered biodynamic agriculture long before organic farming became fashionable. The café's wooden beams echo the Goetheanum, the extraordinary Swiss headquarters of anthroposophy designed by Steiner in 1914. Originally built from wood, the Goetheanum burned down in 1922 and was rebuilt in poured concrete.

WHO WAS RUDOLF STEINER?

Rudolf Steiner (1861-1925) studied science and philosophy in Vienna. A scholar of Goethe and Nietzsche, Steiner developed the spiritual science of anthroposophy, or "wisdom of the human being". Exploring the alignment between science and nature, matter and spirit, the Anthroposophical Society was founded in 1913. The author of over 330 books, Steiner applied his holistic approach to everything from education to agriculture, medicine and architecture. Although prone to wearing flouncy bow ties, he was a less shadowy figure than fellow occultists such as Aleister Crowley. Today, his legacy lives on in the many Steiner schools worldwide.

BAPS SHRI SWAMINARAYAN MANDIR ㉑

105-119 Brentfield Road, Neasden NW10
0208 965 2651
www.mandir.org
Open Temple 9am - 6pm daily.
Admission free.
Transport Neasden tube.

The largest traditional Hindu temple outside India

Scarcely believable at first sight, this is the largest Hindu temple outside India. This spectacular edifice was opened in August 1995 by His Holiness Pramukh Swami Maharaj. It is but a stone's throw from the grim North Circular, the drab ring road circling London's northern suburbs. To build it, 5,000 tonnes of Indian and Italian marble and Bulgarian limestone were hand-carved into 26,300 pieces by 1,526 skilled craftsmen in India, then shipped to London and erected in less than three years. The finished building includes seven shikhars (or pinnacles), six domes, 193 pillars, and 55 different ceiling designs.

Deities and motifs representing the Hindu faith spring from the walls, ceilings and windows. The heart of the mandir, or temple, is its murtis, or sacred images of the deities, who are revered as living gods. In total, there are 11 shrines with 17 murtis, including Ganesh, Hanuman, and Swaminarayan – to whom the temple is dedicated. The deities are ritually served by dedicated sadhus (monks) who live in the temple. Before sunrise, the murtis are woken by the sadhus and the shrine doors opened for the first of five daily 'artis' (prayers). Feeding and bathing of the murtis continues throughout the day.

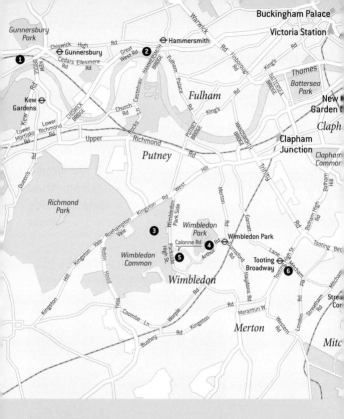

GREATER LONDON (SOUTH)

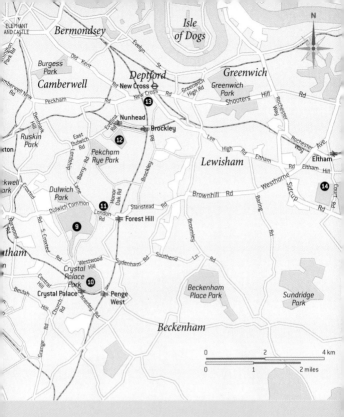

KEW BRIDGE STEAM MUSEUM ❶

Green Dragon Lane, Brentford TW8

0208 568 4757 • www.kbsm.org

Open 11am-5pm Tues-Sun. Closed Mon, except bank holidays. Last admission 4.15 pm. **Admission** Cornish Engine Steaming Weekends, adults £8, concessions £7, Rotative Engine Steaming Weekends, adults £7, concessions £6. Weekdays (engines not running), adults £5, conc £4. **Transport** Kew Bridge rail (South West trains from Waterloo, via Clapham Junction)

> *Vast feats of Victorian engineering*

The Steam Museum lies directly across the river from Kew Gardens. Housed in what was once the Kew Bridge Pumping House, it opened in 1838 as part of a system to provide West London with clean water. The Pumping House was largely driven by steam, and the museum's collection of pumping engines is the largest in the world.

As in most industrial museums, there is an obvious educational intent in the displays. The first part of the museum is explicitly worthy: visitors walk through exhibits detailing the history of London's water supply. Very dull for the most part, with the occasional exception. Part of the sewer display blankly talks about 'toshers', scavengers for flushed valuables, who worked the sewers in gangs of three to protect against rat attacks and death by gassing. When you pass through to the engine rooms, things become more interesting. The engines themselves, mostly 19th century, are flamboyant and functional at the same time. The Dancer's End engine (named for the Rothschild estate in Hertfordshire where it came from) is kitted out in bold red livery, the Waddon engine in chocolate brown.

The absolute star of the collection is the Grand Junction 90-inch Cornish steam engine. Built in 1846, its scale is overpowering. Housed in a separate part of the museum, it almost entirely fills the room and absolutely dominates the space. To stand beneath it is an overwhelming experience. Each stroke of the pump moved 2,142 litres of water; the beam alone weighs 52 tons. The engine is also deeply beautiful, and of all the exhibits highlights the Victorians' taste for the introduction of antique forms into technology. The engine is supported on fluted Doric columns, which are echoed in the shape of the cylinders and on the valve housing. The edifice is painted a very dark brown, like mahogany; this, along with the Greek influence, lends it the air of a temple – many English church interiors are filled with similar woodwork on tombs or organ lofts. This sense of greatness is magnified when the engines are in operation; their movement is hypnotically beautiful. It is essential, however, to check on the website for the operation schedule. Cornish Engine weekends are the best times to visit; not only is the Grand Junction working, but visitors can climb the Stand Pipe Tower. This landmark also helps to locate the museum from afar. Apparently based on a Florentine bell tower (another example of incorporating antique forms into industrial design), it offers views across most of London.

The museum also operates a pretty little steam railway that currently loops around the car park, but may soon be extended down the road to the Musical Museum, which contains a large collection of automatic instruments.

KELMSCOTT HOUSE

26 Upper Mall, Hammersmith, W6
0208 741 3735
www.williammorrissociety.org/house.shtml
Open Thurs and Sat 2-5pm
Admission free.
Transport Ravenscourt Park tube

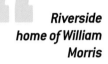

> *Riverside home of William Morris*

In truth, there isn't a huge amount to see at this tiny museum, the headquarters of the William Morris Society. The pleasure of the place is the house itself and its riverside location. Morris believed strongly that a beautiful house was a pinnacle of art, with a beautiful book the next highest order of creation. In Kelmscott House, where he spent the last years of his life and set up the Kelmscott Press, he melded these two loves. The house, which is stunning, sits on an upstream bend of the river where it starts to look like countryside. Across the path is *The Dove*, a beautiful little pub with a riverside terrace, as well as the smallest bar in England (4ft 2in. by 7ft 10in.). Find *The Dove*, which is more of a landmark, and you've found Kelmscott House. It is now privately owned, so only the basement and coach house are open for viewing. These house a collection of Morris drawings for his famous wallpapers, his printing press, and some beautiful furniture. There are also a number of photos of Morris (unlike a lot of late Victorian portrait subjects, he looks like a lot of fun). The coach house was used as a meeting place for Fabians and the other socialist-inclined groups Morris was involved with; Keir Hardie, George Bernard Shaw and Prince Kropotkin all gave lectures here. There is also a small shop, selling reproductions of Morris' prints and woodcuts.

Morris was an astounding man – he died 'having done more work than most ten men' – and these three rooms radiate some of the energy he threw into being a designer, artist, craftsman, writer and socialist, all of which has an instantly recognisable tone.

OTHER WILLIAM MORRIS LANDMARKS

The William Morris Gallery, (Lloyd Park, Forest Road, Walthamstow), in another of his impressive Georgian homes, has a far larger collection of prints, rugs, carpets, wallpapers, furniture, stained glass and painted tiles designed by Morris himself, as well as works by Edward Burne-Jones, Philip Webb, Dante Gabriel Rossetti, Ford Madox Brown. Left-wingers can admire the satchel in which Morris carried his socialist pamphlets. The pinnacle of Morris' aesthetic is the Red House in Bexleyheath, which Morris commissioned from his friend Philip Webb in 1859. Now run by the National Trust, the wonderful gardens and grounds make the perfect setting for a picnic. (Open 1 Mar to 21 Dec; Wed-Sun 11am-4.45pm. To book a guided tour, call 0208 304 9878.)

WIMBLEDON WINDMILL MUSEUM ❸

Windmill Road, Wimbledon Common, SW19
0208 947 2825
www.wimbledonwindmill.org.uk
Open end of March to end of Oct, Sat 2-5pm Sun and public holidays
11am-5pm
Admission adults £1, children and concessions 50p
Transport Wimbledon tube/train, Putney train or
East Putney tube, followed by 93 bus

The daily grind

W imbledon Common is famous for being home to the Wombles - furry creatures who recycled rubbish in the eponymous 1970s TV series. Like all London commons, Wimbledon was created as agricultural land for local residents. The last vestige of these origins is a windmill in the north-east corner of the heath.

Although there were several watermills on the River Wandle, the local community wanted to produce their own flour. So in 1817, Charles March was granted permission to build the windmill "upon this condition, that he shall erect, and keep up, a public Corn Mill, for the advantage and convenience of the neighbourhood". The millers also had to keep watch for duellers, who liked to clash swords on the common.

The mill was closed in 1864 when Earl Spencer decided to build himself a new mansion on the site and fence off Wimbledon Common as his private garden. Understandably, the locals protested. The Earl's plan was shelved by the Wimbledon and Putney Commons Act of 1871, which gave the common back to the people. The mill was converted into living quarters for six families. One of the residents was Lord Baden-Powell, founder of the Boy Scout movement.

Today, the windmill has been converted into a small museum. The entrance hall contains the Great Spur Wheel, which used to power it. There are countless models of windmills and interactive displays of working machinery. Kids can get to grips with grinding wheat, lifting sacks of flour, or changing windmill sails. A ladder leads up to the tower where you can see the machinery turning on windy days. The Windmill Museum also contains a small shop, which sells model windmills, honeycomb produced by bees on Wimbledon Common and, of course, Wombles.

SIGHTS NEARBY

ARTESIAN WELL ❹

In 1763, Earl Spencer built an artesian well in Arthur Road to provide water for his manor house nearby. A horse-driven mechanism pumped water up to the storage tank under the dome. The Earl decided to deepen the well in 1798, but it took over a year to strike more water – it gushed out with such force that the workmen almost drowned. The well soon dried up and in 1975 the domed tower was converted into a private home.

BUDDHAPADIPA TEMPLE

14 Calonne Road, SW19 • www.buddhapadipa.org ❺

The only Thai temple in Europe, this elegant edifice is decked in murals and surrounded by ornamental gardens. Tours on weekends between 9am and 6pm.

A VERY GLAMOROUS BINGO HALL ❻

50 Mitcham Road, Tooting, SW17
0208 672 5717
Open Mon - Sat 10:30am -11pm; Sun noon -11pm
Admission Members only; membership is free to anyone over 18
Transport Tooting Broadway tube

> *Chartres Cathedral meets Liberace*

N ow, alas, a bingo hall, this was the first cinema in the UK to be listed as Grade I - the most rigorous preservation order a building can get. From the outside, the tall, square building doesn't look all that special, give or take a few columns; on the inside, it looks like Chartres Cathedral if it had been designed by Liberace. Opened in 1931, this palace to entertainment was commissioned by Sidney Bernstein, an exiled white Russian who later founded Granada TV, and designed by Fyodor Fyodorovich Kommisarzhevsky, a Russian director and set designer briefly married to actress Peggy Ashcroft.

The heavily gilded foyer is lined with Gothic mirrors and fake leaded windows, punctuated by a pair of sweeping marble staircases. But all this is relatively restrained: the auditorium – inspired by its namesake, the Alhambra Palace in Granada - is where Kommisarzhevsky went bananas. Under a coffered ceiling are cathedral porches, heraldic symbols, and glass chandeliers, now partly obscured by the bingo lighting and screens. The decoration intensifies as you approach the stage. All around the auditorium are arches filled with murals of troubadours and wimpled damsels - but underneath all this medieval madness, the bingo fans play on, eyes fixed on the cards. The combination feels like a weird incarnation of a themed Vegas casino deep in South London.

In its day, the Granada was the only suburban cinema in London to have its own 20-piece orchestra. The glamorous usherettes wore gold silk blouses with blue slacks, pill box hats, blue cloaks over one shoulder, and white gloves, while the doormen wore a blue uniform with brass buttons, peaked caps, and gold epaulets. On its anniversary, the cinema would serve every customer a slice of cake – wheeled in from the baker next door, it weighed over a ton. Over 2,000 people were turned away on opening night, and over three million viewers came to the pictures here every year. However, the arrival of the television sent audience numbers into a tailspin, and the cinema closed in 1973. It was revived as a bingo hall in 1991.

You need to be a member to visit, though membership is free. Call the Granada for details.

Frank Sinatra, the Beatles, Little Richard, and the Rolling Stones all played to 3000 shrieking fans at the Granada, which doubled as a music hall. The original Wurlitzer organ is still here, but its chambers are buried beneath the stage.

BRIXTON WINDMILL

An open plot in Blenheim Gardens, SW12
Open during London Open House weekend
Transport Brixton tube, then any bus up Brixton Hill

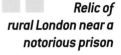

Relic of rural London near a notorious prison

Sitting in the shadow of Brixton Prison, one of the more dreadful London nicks, this flour mill was built in 1816 before the mid-19th century urbanisation along Brixton Hill. The windmill itself is strictly utilitarian; what is remarkable is that it exists in the middle of one of the most densely populated parts of the capital.

Originally the windmill sat in open fields with others; up to twelve sites nearby have been detected, with evidence of milling dating back to the Middle Ages. However, as the city grew around it, new housing shielded the mill from the strong winds needed for its operation. Brixton as farmland is hard to imagine, but there are comparatively modern agricultural references to the area – in the Sherlock Holmes story *The Blue Carbuncle*, Holmes tracks the criminal to a goose farm on Brixton Hill. In 1862, the owners moved their milling business to Mitcham. The windmill was used for storage until 1902, then fitted with a steam engine, after which it resumed milling until 1934. In its current incarnation it sits in a small park, a short distance from the high street in Brixton Hill. Visitors pick their way through residential side streets until after turning a corner, the windmill suddenly reveals itself. It is usually open during London Open House, and there is an annual festival organised by the Friends of Windmill Gardens (see http://www.brixtonwindmill.org/events.htm).

As London continues to spread across South East England – it now covers around 1,600 km ^{2} – it is hard to imagine that until relatively recently the city was dominated by the countryside. Evidence of the city's agricultural past is limited, having been concreted over at a time when the idea of putting preservation before progress was unthinkable. This relic is all the more incongruous for being situated in Brixton, one of the more notorious London suburbs thanks to a recent history of rioting, and its long standing as a magnet for immigrants.

Just over the wall squats Brixton Prison. The oldest correctional facility in the UK, it opened in 1820. One of the first prisons to introduce treadmills in 1821, it was first a women's prison, then a military prison, and now a remand centre with a terrible reputation.

Also worth checking out in the immediate vicinity is *The Windmill pub*, not for its looks (it has none), but rather for its gigs. The pub has a great tradition of alternative live music, often featuring bands on the verge of a breakthrough.

THE ROOKERY

8

Streatham Common South, SW16
Open 9am - 4.45pm
Admission free
Transport Streatham rail (20 min from London Bridge or Blackfriars)
To find the Rookery, turn right out of Streatham Station and keep walking until
you see Streatham Common. Walk to the top of the hill; the walls of the Rookery
are visible on the south side of the Common

Formal gardens in the suburban wilderness

It is unlikely that Streatham features in many guide books. Despite spawning a diversity of talents, including Rolling Stones' bassist Bill Wyman, supermodel Naomi Campbell, occultist Aleister Crowley (Streatham might very well turn you into a Satanist), and William Mildin, 14th Earl of Streatham and allegedly the model for Tarzan, it is an unlovely place. However, in the 18th century, Streatham was a rural haven close to the city, and thus the site of many large country houses.

The Rookery is an area of public gardens adjoining Streatham Common. First opened to the public in 1913, the gardens once belonged to a huge pile of a house that was demolished in the early 1900s.

It is an extremely formal garden, quite out of character with the rest of the Common. A series of walks, including a pergola supporting a vast wisteria, radiate from central beds. The segmentation of the garden provides ample possibilities for seclusion; this would be a good place for a really serious game of hide-and-seek. The garden slopes down a hill that offers extensive views - admittedly, these include the drab centre of Norbury. Other features include a garden with all-white blossoms (and even benches), modelled on Vita Sackville-West's grounds at Sissinghurst, a really good picnic area with fixed tables (very rare in London), and a little covered well in the middle of the garden.

Occasionally, Shakespeare plays are staged at the Rookery. There is also the Rookery Café nearby, a charming old café run by some very grumpy old women.

STREATHAM'S WELLS

This well is all that remains of Streatham's original mineral wells, which attracted huge crowds in the 17th and 18th centuries – it was common for coaches full of thirsty punters to queue for a mile along Streatham High Road. Presumably, Queen Victoria didn't have to wait in line when she came to drink her fill. The healing qualities of the waters were first discovered in 1659 when farm hands drank from the spring and experienced its 'purging effects'. This sounds precisely like a reason not to drink the waters, but they were said to cure all manner of ills including rheumatism, gout, jaundice, bilious attacks, and blindness.

SYDENHAM HILL WOODS ❾

Transport Train from Victoria to Sydenham Hill (15 min).

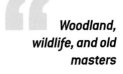

> *Woodland, wildlife, and old masters*

This is a great and worthwhile walk. Exit Sydenham Hill station via College Road, cross the road, and head up the broad path to the top of the hill, where the *Dulwich Wood House Inn* does good pub lunches. At the gate, turn left and walk 500 metres along Crescent Hill Road to the entrance to Sydenham Hill Woods. The left hand fork descends to the disused line of the High Level railway, built in 1865 to service the Crystal Palace (or Screaming Alice, in rhyming slang).

Follow the abandoned railway track for a kilometre – diversions in the adjoining woods include seasonal outdoor art installations and a ruined chapel. Eventually, a bench across the path invites you to climb a set of wooden steps leading up to the left. A metal fence separates the woods from a golf course with sweeping city views denied to non-members. Follow the path to an old footbridge, turn left through a metal gate, and descend Cox's Walk to Dulwich Common. Turn left and after a kilometre you will see the stone gates to Dulwich Park. There is a good café in the middle of the park, where you can take your ease. Press on to College Road, where you should stop at the Dulwich Picture Gallery.

You can either walk back up College Road to Sydenham Hill station or turn left up Gallery Road to the entrance of Belair Park, and walk through the park to West Dulwich Station on Thurlow Park Road.

DULWICH PICTURE GALLERY

Built by John Soane, Dulwich Picture Gallery was the first purpose-built gallery in the world. Its solid collection includes works by Poussin, Claude, Rubens, Murillo, Van Dyck, Rembrandt, Watteau and Gainsborough, originally assembled for the King of Poland in 1790 as an 'instant' national collection. When Poland was wiped off the map in 1795 after a series of disastrous wars, the King's collection became available and was eventually housed in Dulwich in 1811.

College Road is named after Dulwich College, one of the country's grander schools. The school motto, 'God's Gift,' largely reflects the attitude of its students. Oddly enough, it is the alma mater of Raymond Chandler, author of *The Maltese Falcon* and *Farewell, My Lovely*; but it is hard to imagine this as the birthplace of Sam Spade.

CRYSTAL PALACE DINOSAURS
Sydenham Hill, Crystal Palace Park, SE19
Open 9:30am to one hour before park closure at dusk
Transport Trains from London Bridge to Penge West
or from Victoria to Crystal Palace

> ## Life-size dinosaurs domesticated around a duck pond

One of the strangest pieces of Victoriana extant in London, these life-size concrete dinosaurs were built around a lake in Crystal Palace Park by the sculptor Benjamin Waterhouse Hawkins in 1853.

The dinosaurs sparked a huge controversy at the time. Designed to educate the British underclasses, their anticipation of Darwinism outraged the upper classes and the religious. The study of dinosaurs was in its infancy: the word 'dinosaur' was only coined in 1842 by Richard Owen, curator of the Hunterian Museum, who acted as an advisor to Hawkins.

What must then have seemed like a white-hot fusion between art and science now looks a bit silly – especially the idea that these animals could have been domesticated around a duck pond. The dinosaurs are lumpy and improbable; although in fairness to Hawkins, working with concrete must have been problematic.

Years later, and up until 2003, the dinosaurs were partially overgrown by the vegetation. Walking around the lake, concrete heads would loom suddenly out of darkness. The installation has since been fully restored, with the original colours re-applied as closely as possible and the addition of two new pterodactyls.

A DINNER PARTY IN THE STOMACH OF AN IGUANODON
The unveiling of the dinosaurs on December 31, 1853 was celebrated with a dinner party in the stomach of a half-built Iguanodon, with the toast: *'Saurians and Pterodactyls all! Dream ye ever, in your ancient festivities, of a race to come, dwelling above your tombs... dining on your ghosts'.*

Victorian London was in love with the idea of itself as a beacon of enlightenment. Crystal Palace Park on Sydenham Hill embodied this notion. It was purpose-built to re-house the Crystal Palace, centrepiece of the 1851 Great Exhibition in Hyde Park, which was conceived to demonstrate the industrial, military and economic superiority of Great Britain. Seven million gallons of water were pumped through the park every hour, including jets of water higher than Nelson's Column. The park was also where inventor John Logie Baird developed television, and the first British Football Association (FA) Cup was played in 1872. After the Crystal Palace burned down in 1936, the park's popularity dwindled, but it remains full of the ghosts of its glorious past.

THE HORNIMAN MUSEUM ⓫

100 London Road, Forest Hill SE23
0208 699 1872
www.horniman.ac.uk
Admission free, except for major temporary exhibitions
Open Daily 10.30am-5.30pm. Gardens open Mon-Sat 7.30am- sunset,
Sun 8am-sunset. **Transport** 5 min walk from Forest Hill rail
or 13 min from London Bridge

> *Stuffed animals and musical instruments*

The Horniman Museum is another creation of a Victorian philanthropist. Opened in 1901, it was commissioned to hold tea merchant Frederick John Horniman's collection of natural history, anthropology, and musical instruments. Like most Victorian collections, the assemblage looks impressively eccentric, due to its apparently random nature. However, there are some extraordinary objects here, well worth the journey into deepest Forest Hill.

The Horniman's most famous exhibit is probably its stuffed walrus. Taxidermists assembled this from the skin alone, without having any idea of what a walrus actually looked like. Not knowing that the walrus is deeply wrinkled, they stuffed it to the limit, so the finished item looks like a balloon with tusks, and is the size of a small car. Happily, the museum has never corrected this error.

The real jewels of the collection are in the ethnography collection, generally reckoned to be third in importance after the British Museum and the Pitt Rivers collection in Oxford. There is a large amount of fine African statuary - an estimated 22,000 objects, not all of them on display - including systematic collections from the Sua of Zaire and the Hadza of Tanzania.

Best of all is the musical gallery, which was completely renovated between 1999 and 2002. The room is lined with glass cabinets holding instruments from all over the world, and interactive tables allow you to play recordings of any of them. Refurbishment also included the opening of a small aquarium, and converted the entire museum to a more child-friendly format. Be warned; weekends see herds of haggard and hung-over South London parents with their kids, peering at the fish. Weekdays are probably the best for a serious visit.

Other things to look out for include a stuffed mermaid (the marriage of a dead monkey and a fish by a perverted taxidermist), a glass-walled beehive, and a disconcerting life-size statue of Kali, trampling some very serene heads. The museum café is probably best avoided, but the shop is full of quirky little presents.

THE ANALEMMATIC SUNDIAL

The museum is set in 16 acres of gardens with good views across London. The gardens contain an eclectic collection of ten sundials, including a butterfly, a stained glass window, and an analemmatic sundial, where you can tell the time using your own shadow. So make sure you visit on a sunny day.

NUNHEAD CEMETERY   ⑫

Linden Grove, SE 15
www.fonc.org.uk
Open April 1-Sept 30, 8am-7pm daily; Oct 1-March 31, 8am -one hour
before sunset daily. Tours start from the Linden Grove gates at
2.15pm on the last Sunday of every month
Transport Train to Nunhead from Blackfriars (15 minutes)
Bus 343 and P12

> *Gothic nature reserve*

Nunhead Cemetery was the second of the seven commercial cemeteries built in a ring around London in the middle of the 19th century to alleviate "overcrowding" in the graveyards of the City churches. Highgate Cemetery, burial site of Karl Marx - who lived a surprisingly bourgeois life in nearby Hampstead - is probably the most famous, but Nunhead, opened in 1840, is possibly the most attractive. Its formal avenues of lime trees still survive, but they enclose a jumble of fallen stone and wilderness. The cemetery covers 52 acres, rising to 60 metres above sea level, and thus offering extensive views over the City of London and St Paul's Cathedral between the trees.

In the early 1970s, the United Cemetery Company abandoned Nunhead because a lack of space meant it stopped making money: there was no room for new tenants. After an extensive restoration project the cemetery was reopened in 2001. Now almost completely overgrown, the place is effectively a wildlife reserve, where South Londoners can find songbirds, owls, woodpeckers and around 16 types of butterfly.

The cemetery is typically Victorian, obviously built by a city at the height of its economic power. Wealthy families commissioned mausoleums that are still magnificent today. Of course, like all Victorian developments, the cemetery was a model of efficiency – its circular drive meant that the turnover of services in the chapel could be kept brisk while remaining seemly. The chapel itself has a covered porch for the efficient disembarking of mourners in bad weather; it still stands above a crypt, like a setting from the novel *Dracula*. Large monuments, unsettled by root growth, loom out of the trees at strange angles; beseeching stone angels lie surrounded by flowers.

The Friends of Nunhead Cemetery (FONC) offer guided tours starting from the Linden Grove gates at 2.15pm on the last Sunday of every month. Monumental inscription recording is carried out on the third Sunday of each month. Volunteers are welcome and should meet at the FONC hut by the main entrance in Linden Grove at 11a.m.

Look for the Scottish Martyrs' obelisk on Dissenters Row, a memorial to five men transported to Australia in 1792 for advocating political reform. The Anglican Chapel designed by Thomas Little in 1843 was recently restored after arson in the 1970s.

THE GIANT SCRIBBLE

⓭

Ben Pimlott building
Goldsmiths College
University of London, New Cross, SE14
Transport New Cross rail (from Charing Cross)

*A scribble
on the skyline*

This purpose-built extension of the visual arts department at Goldsmiths College is largely unexceptional: a seven-storey building clad in metal with windows punched through to provide daylight and ventilation for the artists within. But architect Will Alsop has created a landmark in New Cross - one of the least lovely parts of the city - by draping the roof terrace with a giant metal scribble. British architects tend to be fiends for function over form, but the main purpose of this playful anomaly, highly visible on the South London skyline, seems to be to lift the spirits of travellers driving along the dreary A2. The super-sized scribble has 72 twists and weighs over 25 tonnes. If stretched out, it would be 534m long – over twice as tall as Canary Wharf tower. The fire escape on the south side, a jagged edge of self-supporting, prefabricated steel, is equally dramatic. The studios at the front of the building are glazed from floor to ceiling, so passers-by can spy on aspiring artists at work. At night, the building is illuminated by industrial lights, creating mysterious pools of light and shadow on the metallic surface.

RUBBISH & NASTY

The alma mater of high-flying British artists such as Damian Hirst, Gillian Wearing, and Anthony Gormley (see *Quantum Cloud*, page 257), Goldsmiths College prides itself on a certain edginess (probably a ploy to compensate for its drab location). The surrounding area is full of funky pubs; unfortunately, this tends to mean 'smelly' instead of 'cool'. But the brilliantly named, bright green Rubbish & Nasty (308 New Cross Rd, SE14) is a genuinely cool outlet for indie music and recycled clothes. Bands occasionally perform among the glad rags, but beware: the opening hours are erratic.

WILL ALSOP'S OTHER MODERN BUILDINGS

Modern architecture in London tends to be associated with either Richard Rogers or Norman Foster, so a day spent trailing Will Alsop's ingenious constructions would be one well-spent. Most notable are the playful Peckham Library (122 Peckham Hill Street), an upturned L-shape inspired by an open book, resting on seven wonky columns, and the off kilter Palestra office block, opposite Southwark tube station. Best of all is the Blizard Building at Queen Mary University (Turner Street, Whitechapel), wrapped in multicoloured glass and containing moulded pods modelled on giant molecules.

THE ART DECO INTERIORS
OF ELTHAM PALACE

⓮

Court Yard, SE9

0208 294 2548

Open Mon, Tue, Wed, Sun 10am–5pm. **Admission** £7.60 adults, £3.80 child
Transport Trains to Eltham leave from Charing Cross or London Bridge
From there, it is a half-mile walk
or a few stops on the 161 or 126 bus

*A
maximalist's
wet dream*

A little trouble to get here, but worth the effort, Eltham Palace is one of the most bizarre buildings in London. The original palace was given to King Edward II by Bishop Bek in 1305. King Edward IV added the Great Hall, the only part of the medieval structure still standing. In the 1530s, Henry VIII added royal lodgings and gardens, complete with a bowling green and archery range. It was the only royal palace large enough to contain all Henry VIII's 800 courtiers. The scattered Tudor remains suggest the palace must have been a venerable pile in its prime.

During the 18th and 19th centuries the palace fell into disrepair, but this merely heightened its attraction for the artists smitten by the Romantic notions so poular at the time. This was a period when wealthy aesthetes actually purpose-built ruins to flit around – lunacy, of course, but popular lunacy among the super-rich.

In 1933, the palace was leased by the extravagant socialites Sir Stephen and Lady Virginia Courtauld. The arrival of the Courtaulds (whose relatives founded the famous Courtauld Galleries) marked the palace's renaissance. They instantly ran into controversy by appointing architects Seely and Paget to design a new Art Deco residence incorporating the restored Great Hall. The homes of the English upper classes are too often blighted by an obsession with pseudo-heritage – inglenooks, Palladian bathrooms, half-timbered Tudor garages, and the like. To their credit, the Courtaulds chose a bold, modern design with lashings of English eccentricity.

The exterior of the house is not especially interesting, but the interiors are unexpectedly insane. Dripping with 1930s opulence, the place is a maximalist's wet dream - walls are dressed with exotic veneers and the sunken baths have onyx trimmings. The couple even built a miniature palace filled with jungle murals for their pet ring-tailed lemur, Mah-Jongg, whom they purchased from Harrods. Try to spot the Courtald's yacht moored in the mural of Venice that adorns the entrance hall. The house was also a showcase for the latest technological wizardy: a centralised vacuuming system, synchronised clocks, and concealed ceiling lights. A circular motif runs riot throughout - domed ceilings, round lights, and portholes. Virginia Courtauld's curved bedroom with a circular ceiling creates the impression of a classical temple. But the snazzy leather map of Eltham in her boudoir bears little resemblance to the Eltham of today, an unusually unlovely part of London.

UNUSUAL BARS, CAF

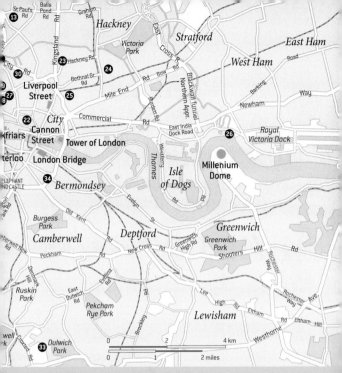

D RESTAURANTS

WEST END / SOHO / COVENT GARDEN

CELLARDOOR ❶
Zero Aldwych, WC2 • 0207 240 8848 • www.cellardoor.biz
This underground bar takes its postcode very literally. Formerly a gentlemen's public convenience (allegedly frequented by celebrity cruisers Oscar Wilde and John Gielgud), this louche drinking hole only holds sixty people, but that doesn't stop the management from staging live jazz and cabaret acts. And they serve snuff too.

CENTRE POINT SUSHI CAFE ❷
20-21 St Giles High Street, WC2 • 0207 836 9860
At the back of Centre Point Food Store - an Asian supermarket on the ground floor of this unlovely landmark - a staircase leads up to a secret Japanese canteen with leatherette booths and the obligatory sushi counter. Good value lunch boxes.

CORK AND BOTTLE ❸
44-46 Cranbourn Street, WC2 • 0207 734 7807 • www.corkandbottle.net
A hidden gem among the fast food joints and tourist traps of Leicester Square, this cosy basement bar has an exceptional wine list.

COURTHOUSE HOTEL BAR ❹
Courthouse Hotel Kempinski, 19-21 Great Marlborough Street, W1 • 0207 297 5555
The former Great Marlborough Street Magistrates' Court, where Mick Jagger, John Lennon and Johnny Rotten were all busted for drugs, has been converted into a clean-cut hotel. Some original features have been preserved: the prison cells are now private dining rooms (the urinals are used as ice-buckets).

MILROY'S OF SOHO ❺
3 Greek Street, W1 • 0207 743 9311 • www.milroys.co.uk
A Soho institution since 1965, Milroy's stocks over 700 whiskies. Around 300 of them are available by the glass in the tasting cellar, or you can book a tutorial with whisky connoisseurs, accompanied by British cheeses and expert commentary.

RAY'S JAZZ CAFE ❻
113-119 Charing Cross Road, WC2 • 0207 440 3205 • www.foyles.co.uk
On the first floor of Foyles bookshop, Ray's has one of the most extensive collections of jazz, blues and world music in London. At the pleasingly shabby café, there's free live jazz almost daily, usually at 2pm or 6pm. A much needed antidote to the identikit coffee chains infiltrating London at an alarming rate.

MARYLEBONE

CAFE T ❼
Asia House, 63 New Cavendish Street, W1 • 0207 307 5454 • www.asiahouse.org
This light-filled café in an Asian cultural centre doubles as a gallery. So you can admire the affordable art while feasting on pan-Asian dishes such as prawn and noodle soup or Goan chicken and coconut curry.

ATELIER DES CHEFS ❽

19 Wigmore Street, W1 • 0207 499 6580 • www.atelierdeschefs.co.uk

Make good use of your lunch break. Sign up for a half-hour cookery class at this French culinary school and you get to eat the results - perhaps roast cod with pumpkin mousseline and ginger foam.

INDIAN YMCA ❾

41 Fitzroy Square, W1 • 0207 387 0411 • www.indianymca.org

Dirt-cheap curries in old-school cafeteria surroundings, where impoverished students rub shoulders with Indian businessmen pining for a taste of home.

PAUL ROTHE & SONS ❿

35 Marylebone Lane, W1 • 0207 935 6783

This quaint café/deli dates back to 1900. Pick your favourite Formica table and tuck into Marmite on toast, home-made soup and a nice cup of tea. Walls are lined with neatly arranged jars of marmalade, chutney and other British treats to take home.

RIBA CAFE ⓫

66 Portland Place, W1 • 0207 631 0467 • www.riba.org

Looking for an elegant retreat from the scrum of Oxford Street? Besides a great book shop and exhibition space, the Royal Institute of British Architects has a fabulous café with marble columns and soaring ceilings. On sunny days, head for the patio screened by potted plants.

NORTH

CANDID CAFE ⓬

3 Torrens Street, EC1 • 0207 2789368 • www.candidarts.com

Tucked away in an alley behind Angel tube station is an arts centre with two cute cafés – one in the courtyard and one upstairs, which is like entering someone's living room. Curl up on the sofa with a slab of cake and a newspaper.

ESTORICK COLLECTION CAFE ⓭

39a Canonbury Square, N1 • 0207 704 9522 • www.estorickcollection.com

Italian snacks and real cappuccino in a peaceful garden setting. (see page 289 New River Walk)

THE GLASS BAR ⓮

190 Euston Rd, NW1 • 0207 387 4153 • www.theglassbar.org.uk

This tiny women-only bar in a lodge outside Euston station is technically a members' bar, but a quid on the door is all you pay to get in.

LORD'S MEDIA CENTRE ⓯

St John's Wood Road, NW8 • 0207 616 8500 • www.lords.org

All right, so you need a minimum of fifty people to arrange lunch, but this astonishing building at the spiritual home of cricket is worth it. You don't even need to be a cricket fan to be impressed. (see page 175 Marylebone Cricket Club Memorial Museum).

OSLO COURT ⑯

Charlbert Street, NW8 • 087 1332 7749

This isn't a Norwegian restaurant, it's a French fancy buried beneath an unpromising 1970s tower block. The interior is also trapped in time – a kitsch paean to peach and pink, with a set menu to match: lobster thermidor, veal Holstein, crepe suzette. Outstanding food in slightly surreal surroundings.

WELLCOME COLLECTION ⑰

183 Euston Road, NW1 • 0207 611 2222 • www.wellcomecollection.org

Sir Henry Wellcome, who made his fortune in pharmaceuticals, founded this wondrous medical museum where exhibits include a Victorian chastity belt and artificial eyes. Recover with a wedge of treacle tart in the colourful Peyton and Byrne café, which is always surprisingly quiet and has free Wi-Fi. (see page 21 Bleigiessen).

SOUTH-WEST

BONNINGTON CAFE ⑱

11 Vauxhall Grove, SW8 • www.bonningtoncafe.co.uk

Run by volunteers, this vegetarian cooperative started out as a squat. With a different cook every night - ring them to find out what's cooking (phone numbers on the website) - the cuisine and quality vary, but a three-course set dinner won't cost more than a tenner. Bring your own booze.

THE GALLERY ⑲

256a Brixton Hill, SW2 • 0208 671 8311

This looks like a fried chicken takeaway, but go through the secret door into the Portuguese restaurant at the back. It's designed like a cave, with weird murals and extreme tiling, but the food is great, especially the frango.

THE VINCENT ROOMS ⑳

Westminster Kingsway College, 76 Vincent Square, SW1 • 0207 802 8391
• www.thevincentrooms.com

This catering school has an award-winning restaurant with two dining rooms: haute cuisine in the Escoffier Room and a brasserie overlooking Vincent Square. Serious food at knock-down prices.

WIMBLEDON DOG TRACK ㉑

Plough Lane, SW17 • 087 0840 8905 • www.lovethedogs.co.uk

Eat at the last surviving greyhound racetracks in London. Scoff fish and chips trackside, or book a table in the 1950s dining room with picture windows of the track. There's a table betting service, and winnings are brought over to you.

THE CITY

THE PLACE BELOW ㉒

St Mary Le Bow Church, Cheapside, EC2 • 0207 329 0789 • www.theplacebelow.co.uk

As well as the peal of Bow Bells, Wren's church is worth a visit for the vegetarian restaurant in the vaulted crypt. The seasonal menu changes daily – but happily porridge with maple syrup is a breakfast staple.

EAST END

GEFFRYE MUSEUM CAFE ㉓

136 Kingsland Road, E2 • 0207 739 9893 • www.geffrye-museum.org.uk

Traditional British food in a museum of traditional British interiors. (see page 133 Geffrye Museum).

WILD CHERRY CAFE ㉔

241-245 Globe Road, E2 • 0208 980 6678

A Buddhist cooperative with a worthy menu. (see page 283 London Buddhist Centre).

ROOTMASTER ㉕

Ely's Yard, Dray Walk, E1 • www.root-master.co.uk

A vegan restaurant in a double-decker Routemaster bus, with an open-plan kitchen that dishes up tofu burgers, stir fries, and "bus baked bread". There are candlelit tables upstairs.

◀ FAT BOY'S DINER ㉖

Trinity Buoy Wharf, 64 Orchard Place, E14 • 0207 987 4334 • www.fatboysdiner.co.uk

Fabulous milkshakes, cheeseburgers and table-top jukeboxes in a 1940s mobile diner parked on the riverside. (see page 253 Longplayer).

CLERKENWELL/HOLBORN

THE CASTLE ㉗

Cowcross Street, EC1 • 0871 474 5558

It's not particularly attractive, but this is the only pub in England with a pawnbroker's licence. When King George IV ran out of cash at a cock-fighting ring nearby, he popped into the pub and pawned his pocket-watch in exchange for a handful of coins and a few pints. The king issued the innkeeper with a pawnbrokers' licence, which is still valid today.

THE CRYPT CAFE ㉘

St Etheldreda's Church, 14 Ely Place, EC1 • 0207 405 1061 • www.stetheldreda.com

The crypt of London's oldest Roman Catholic church is a lovely spot for a quiet, contemplative lunch. (see page 101 Relic of St Etheldreda).

DANS LE NOIR? 29

30-31 Clerkenwell Green, EC1 • www.danslenoir.com/london

Don't take a blind date to this French restaurant where guests dine in pitch darkness. The idea is that losing your sense of sight will enhance your sense of taste. Don't worry: all the crockery is unbreakable.

FISH CENTRAL 30

149-155 Central Street, EC1 • 0207 253 4970 • www.fishcentral.co.uk

In the middle of a council estate, this Cypriot-run institution is one of London's finest fish and chip shops.

OCTOBER GALLERY 31

24 Old Gloucester Street, WC1 • 0207 242 7367 • www.octobergallery.co.uk

Wooden tables, home-cooked food, and a glorious walled courtyard with red and black tiles for sunny afternoons make this bohemian café inside a gallery a real find. (see page 109 John Soane's Museum).

THE ORANGERY 32

Great Ormond Street Hospital, WC1 • 0207 405 9200

Architects SpaceLab transformed the unused rooftop of Great Ormond Street Hospital into a sexy, see-through pavilion – a far cry from the usual dreary and depressing hospital canteen.

SOUTH-EAST

DULWICH PICTURE GALLERY 33

Gallery Road, Dulwich, SE21 • 0208 299 8719 • www.dulwichpicturegallery.org.uk

Off the beaten track, London's first gallery is in a beautiful building with a well-run café. (see page 315 Sydenham Hill Woods).

MANZE'S 34

87 Tower Bridge Road, SE1 • 0207 407 2985 • www.manze.co.uk

Manze's pie and mash shops have provided cheap food for working men since 1902. Unfortunately, most of it has been stewed or jellied eels. Misty-eyed Cockneys may witter on about the joys of jellied eels, but you never see them actually eating the stuff. The rest of the menu is limited to beef pie and mashed potatoes, offered with gravy or liquor, a parsley sauce with a mystery ingredient. The real pleasure is the setting - a green and white tiled room that hasn't changed much in over a century.

SCOOTERWORKS 35

132 Lower Marsh, SE1; • 0207 620 1421 • www.scooterworks-uk.com

Lower Marsh is full of quirky independent shops, but this Vespa showroom-cum-coffee shop is a masterstroke. Among the scooters and spare parts is a 1957 Faema coffee machine that produces superb espressos. The soundtrack – from ska to Billie Holiday – is pretty special too.

ALPHABETICAL INDEX

ALPHABETICAL INDEX

ALPHABETICAL INDEX

THEMATIC INDEX

THEMATIC INDEX

THEMATIC INDEX

RELIGION/ESOTERICA

RIVERSIDE LONDON

SCIENCE/EDUCATION

THEMATIC INDEX

Photo credits:

Stéphanie Rivoal: Bevis Mark synagogue, BFI mediatheque, British Optical association museum, Bunhill Fields, Cab Shelters, Christchurch Greyfriars Garden, Dr Johnsons house, Feliks Topolski's Memoir of the Century, Fountain Court, Guildhall Yard, Horseman's Sunday, Leighton House, Little Angel theatre, London Library, London silver vaults, London Stone, Marx memorial library, National Theatre Backstage tours, Notre Dame de France, Queen Alexandra memorial, Ray's Jazz Café, St Dunstan-In-The-East, St. Bartholomew's the Greater, Thames Flood Barrier,The Foundling Museum, The Golden Boy of Pye Corner, The Horse Hospital, The Monument, The Old Operating Theatre, The Petrie Museum, Watts' Memorial.

Jorge Monedero: 2 Willow Road, Alexander Fleming Laboratory Museum, Ben Pimlott Building, British Dental Association Museum, Brixton Windmill, Broadgate Ice Skating Ring, Brunel Museum, Burgh House & Hampstead Museum, Cable Street Mural, Canal Museum/Ice Wells, Canonbury Tower, Crystal Palace Dinosaurs, Chumberleigh Gardens, Circus Space, City Livery Companies & Their Halls, Clerk's Well, Clown's Gallery & Museum, Couper Gallery, CreekSide Centre, Crossbones Graveyard, Dead House at Somerset House, Dead Man's Hole, Duck Tours, Fat Boy's Diner, Fetter Lane - Moravian Burial Ground, First Drinking Fountain, Fan Museum, Granada Cinema - Gala Bingo Hall, Gresham's Grasshopper, Hackney City Farm, HandleBar Moustache Club of Great Britain, Horniman Museum & Gardens, Hunterian Museum, Joe Orton's Library Books, Kelmscott House, Kensal Green Cementery Kew Bridge Museum, London Buddhist Center, London Scottish Regimantal Museum, London's Living Room, Longplayer, Marylebone Cricket Club Museum, Masonic Temple at The Andaz hotel, Materials Library, Mudchute Farm, New Gate Cells, New River Walk, Nunhead Cementery, Princess Caroline Sunken Bath, John Wesley's House, Ragged School Museum, Rudolph Steiner House, School For Life, ScooterWorks, Slice of Reality & Quantum Cloud, St Peter's Barge, Sutton House, Sydenham Hill Woods, Thames River Police Museum, The Cherry Tree at The Mitre, The Cinema Museum, The Coated Stone caryatids, The Excecution Dock, The Excecutioner's Bell, The mummy Of Jimmy Garlick, The relic of St Ethelreda, The Rookery, The Royal Hospital, The Serpentine Solar Shuttle, The Tent, Traffic Light Tree, Twinings Tea Museum, Tyburn Convent, Wellcome Collection, Werryman's Seat, West Reservoir, Whitechapel Bell Foundry, Windmill Museum in Wimbledon.

Shri Swaminarayan Mandir © Shri Swaminarayan Mandir

Bleigiessen © Bleigiessen

Auto icon of Jeremy Bentham © University College London

Museum of Brands, Packaging and Advertising © Museum of Brands, Packaging and Advertising

Camley Street Nature reserve © Anna Guzzo London Wild trust

Chelsea Physic Garden © Hans Slone

Cuming museum © Keith Tyson Studio Wall Drawing @cuming museum

Dennis severs house © James Brittain

Eltham palace © English Heritage Photo Library

Foundling museum staircase © Richard Bryant Arcaid

Garden Museum © Gavin Kingcome

Geffrye musem - Regency Room © Chris Ridley

Grant Museum © Fred Langford Edwards & UCL

St Paul Triforium © St Paul

Westminster undercroft Abbey Museum © Dean & Chapter of Westiminster

White Cubicle © Superm (Slava Mogutin and Brian Kenny) exhibition at White Cubicle

Acknowledgements
Our thanks to:

Gaby Agis, Carole Baxter, Frédéric Court, Adam Cumiskey, Nigel Dobinson, Alain Dodard, Benjamin & Maider Faes, Mattie Faint, Patrick Foulis, Ronald Grant, The Greenwich Phantom, Jaco Groot, Charlotte Henwood, John Hilton, Rose Jenkins, Ludovic Joubert, Xavier Lefranc, Islington Local History Centre, Robert Jeffries, Zoe Laughlin, Alex Parsons-Moore, Valérie Passmore, Clare Patey, David Phillips, Ellis Pike, Jeremy Redhouse, Michael van Rooyen, Muffin van Rooyen, avv. Renato Savoia, Chris Slade, Amélie Snyers, Angelos Talentzakis, Boz Temple-Morris, Christopher Wade, David Walter, Harriet Warden, Clem Webb, David White.

Cartography: Cyrille Suss
Design: Roland Deloi
Layout: Michel Nicolas
Proof-reading: Tom Clegg and Caroline Lawrence
Cover: Romaine Guérin

© JONGLEZ 2012
Registration of copyright June 2012 – Edition 02
ISBN: 978-2-9158-0728-8
Printed in France by Gibert-Clarey - 37 170 CHAMBRAY-LES-TOURS